39.9
FWH
6454

SUCCESSFUL
FLOWER
GARDENING

SUCCESSFUL FLOWER GARDENING

Created and Designed by
the Editorial Staff of Ortho Books

Project Editor
Barbara Ferguson Stremple

Author
Rick Bond

Encyclopedia Author
Allen Paterson

Major Photographer
Saxon Holt

Ortho Books

Publisher
Edward A. Evans

Editorial Director
Christine Jordan

Production Director
Ernie S. Tasaki

Managing Editors
Michael D. Smith
Sally W. Smith

System Manager
Linda M. Bouchard

National Sales Manager
J. D. Gillis

**National Accounts Manager—
 Book Trade**
Paul D. Wiedemann

Marketing Specialist
Dennis M. Castle

Distribution Specialist
Barbara F. Steadham

Operations Assistant
Georgiann Wright

Administrative Assistant
Francine Lorentz-Olson

Technical Consultant
J. A. Crozier, Jr., Ph.D.

Consultant
Steven Still

Illustrator
Cyndie Clark-Huegel

Copy Chief
Melinda E. Levine

Editorial Coordinator
Cass Dempsey

Copyeditor
Susan Lang

Proofreader
Keiko Ohnuma

Indexer
Elinor Lindheimer

Editorial Assistants
Deborah Bruner
Nancy McCune
John Parr

Composition by
Laurie A. Steele

Layout Editor
Deborah Cowder

Production by
Studio 165

Separated and Lithographed by
Ringier America, Inc.

Special Thanks to
Dick Turner
San Francisco, Calif.

Pamela Harper
Seaford, Va.

No portion of this book may be reproduced without written permission from the publisher.

We are not responsible for unsolicited manuscripts, photographs, or illustrations.

Every effort has been made at the time of publication to guarantee the accuracy of the names and addresses of information sources and suppliers, and in the technical data and recommendations contained. However, readers should check for their own assurance and must be responsible for selection and use of suppliers, supplies, materials, and chemical products.

Address all inquiries to:
Ortho Books
Chevron Chemical Company
Consumer Products Division
Box 5047
San Ramon, CA 94583

Copyright © 1990
Chevron Chemical Company
All rights reserved under international and Pan-American copyright conventions.

1 2 3 4 5 6 7 8 9
90 91 92 93 94 95

ISBN 0-89721-221-5
Library of Congress Catalog Card Number 90-80075

Chevron Chemical Company
6001 Bollinger Canyon Road, San Ramon, CA 94583

Front cover: *Tulipa batalinii*
Page 2: *Echinacea purpurea* 'Bright Star'
Back cover:
Top left: Tulips 'Oxford' (red), and 'Estella'
Top right: Rose 'Cherish'
Bottom left: *Convolvulus mauritanicus*
Bottom right: *Trillium grandiflorum*

Photographers
Photographs are listed by page numbers and positions (T = top, B = bottom, L = left, R = right, C = center)

Liz Ball: 197R

Charles O. Cresson: 209R

Thomas E. Eltzroth: 141L, 223L, 236R, 237L, 241R, 245L, 247R, 248L, 248R, 249R, 252L, 253L, 275L, 280R, 283R, 308R, 314L, 339L

Barbara Ferguson: 187L

Charles Morden Fitch: 209L, 290L

Saxon Holt: Front and back cover and all photographs to page 129; 137, 139L, 142L, 143L, 145L, 146L, 150R, 152L, 153L, 154R, 157L, 159L, 160, 164R, 165, 168L, 170L, 170C, 173L, 173R, 184L, 188L, 190R, 192L, 193L, 194, 195R, 198R, 203L, 207R, 210L, 211L, 214L, 215L, 216L, 221, 223R, 226R, 227R, 228C, 234L, 234C, 239L, 240R, 242R, 249L, 249C, 252R, 256L, 258L, 258R, 260L, 262R, 267L, 269L, 273L, 281L, 283L, 284L, 285R, 298L, 298R, 302L, 303R, 304R, 314R, 315L, 317R, 318R, 327R, 331R, 332L, 333R, 340L, 340R, 341R

Michael McKinley: 224

Allen P. Paterson: 136L, 136R, 139R, 141R, 143R, 144R, 145R, 149R, 150L 152R, 154L, 155R, 156L, 157R, 164L, 166R, 171R, 174, 175R, 177L, 179R, 182L, 183L, 184R, 191L, 191R, 192R, 195L, 198L, 200L, 200R, 204R, 205R, 206L, 211R, 216R, 217L, 218R, 219L, 219R, 220L, 222L, 222R, 225R, 226L, 229L, 232L, 232R, 236L, 254L, 256R, 257, 259R, 260R, 262L, 263L, 264L, 264R, 265L, 265R, 272L, 274R, 277R, 278R, 281L, 282R, 284R, 285L, 286L, 286R, 287R, 288L, 289L, 291L, 292L, 293L, 294R, 295R, 300L, 301, 306L, 309L, 309R, 310L, 312L, 313L, 313R, 321L, 323L, 325L, 327L, 328L, 329, 331L, 334L, 334R, 335R, 336L, 338C, 339R, 341L

Susan A. Roth: 148L, 151L, 151R, 156R, 176R, 185R, 186R

Steven M. Still: 134, 135L, 135R, 138L, 138R, 140L, 140R, 142R, 144L, 146R, 147L, 147R, 148R, 149L, 153R, 155L, 158, 159R, 161L, 161R, 162, 163L, 163R, 166L, 167L, 167R, 168R, 169L, 169R, 170R, 171L, 172, 175L, 176L, 177R, 178L, 178R, 179L, 180L, 180R, 181L, 181R, 182R, 183R, 185L, 186L, 187R, 188R, 189L, 189R, 190L, 193R, 196L, 196R, 197L, 199, 201, 202L, 202R, 203R, 204L, 205L, 206R, 207L, 208L, 208R, 210R, 212L, 212R, 213, 214R, 215R, 217R, 218L, 220R, 225L, 227L, 228L, 228R, 229R, 230L, 230R, 231, 233L, 233R, 234R, 235L, 235R, 237R, 238L, 238R, 239R, 240L, 241L, 242L, 243L, 243R, 244L, 244R, 245R, 246, 247L, 250L, 250R, 251L, 251R, 253R, 254L, 255L, 255R, 259L, 261L, 261R, 263R, 266L, 266C, 266R, 267R, 268L, 268R, 269R, 270L, 270R, 271L, 271R, 272R, 273R, 274L, 275R, 276L, 276C, 276R, 277L, 278L, 279, 280L, 282L, 287L, 288R, 289R, 290R, 291R, 292R, 293R, 294L, 295L, 296L, 296R, 297L, 297R, 299L, 299R, 300R, 302R, 303L, 304R, 305, 306R, 307, 308L, 310R, 311, 312R, 315R, 316L, 316R, 317L, 318L, 319L, 319R, 320L, 320R, 321R, 322L, 322R, 323R, 324, 325R, 326L, 326R, 328R, 330L, 330R, 332R, 333L, 335L, 336R, 337L, 337R, 338L, 338R

Contents

A DIVERSITY OF FLOWER GARDENS

*The best garden ideas are often hidden
in the backyards of other gardeners.
In this book, you are invited on a tour
of nine idea-filled flower gardens.*

Like any other artistic endeavor, gardening is a process of exploring new ideas and gathering experience. When planning and creating a garden, you can look for ideas in many places, but the best ideas are found in successful gardens. Unfortunately, finding wonderful horticultural examples to study can be difficult. Parks are usually designed on a scale too grand for the home landscape, and home gardens are often hidden behind fences.

To gain access to private gardens, many people join garden clubs. Several times during the year, club members throw open the gates and lead visitors through their gardens, explaining their ideas and sharing their successes. These horticultural versions of an open house spark the imagination and offer a marvelous opportunity to learn.

This book was created in the same spirit as a garden club tour. In the chapters that follow, you will explore eight private flower gardens and one not-so-private display garden. These chapters are filled with ideas—some that can be used directly in your garden and others that will need to be adapted to climatic conditions and requirements. For example, if you like an effect created by a combination of plants but cannot grow those plants in your area, create your own version by selecting species with similar colors and textures. Use the plant encyclopedia that follows the garden profiles to help you make your plant selections.

In addition to stimulating the imagination, you'll find that these chapters demonstrate how a garden expresses the personality of the individual who created it. Thus, by example, you can learn to make your garden an expression of your own tastes and interests.

The tour begins in a naturalistic, water-conserving garden of California native plants. The creator of this garden, Peggy Grier, is at heart a plant collector, and her landscape is designed to accommodate a diverse collection of flowering shrubs, perennials, and wildflowers.

In another naturalistic garden halfway across the country, Lorrie Otto restored patches of both the tallgrass prairie and the shortgrass prairie in her front yard. Otto's interest in conservation and love of prairie flowers has made her garden an inspiration to naturalistic gardeners throughout the Midwest.

For other gardeners, seeing the land as a canvas to be filled with color inspires a headlong rush of planting. Encouraged by the enthusiasm of a consulting nurseryman, Nancy Miller leaped into flower gardening and quickly turned her wild backyard into a garden filled with sophisticated combinations of perennials and roses.

Similarly, when presented with the grassy hill above her seaside home, Winifred Chris created a garden massed with brightly colored annuals and bulbs. Chris's flower selections reflect her sense of context; to her the bright reds and yellows she chooses belong in her sunny seaside garden.

In the garden of Winifred Chris, annual and perennial flowers are massed to create what Chris calls "an explosion of color."

A garden can also be viewed as an extension of the home, an outdoor living room. In Washington, D.C., Mike Zajic carefully designed and planted his garden to provide year-round beauty and comfort. In San Diego, Betty and Gerry Tietje were faced with an overgrown lot and little time for gardening, so they hired a landscape architect to help them. The low-maintenance flower garden he designed for them is ideal for entertaining.

All gardeners love plants, but nowhere is an appreciation of individual species so well demonstrated as in a rock garden. On the north shore of Massachusetts, Catherine Hull discovered the delicate beauty of alpine flowers and created a garden that frames and nurtures the jewel-like blossoms of her tiny plants.

Cutting gardens produce flowers to grace the home, and in Albuquerque, New Mexico, flowers from Marie Torrens's garden decorate her home throughout the summer. In winter, when the roses are leafless canes and the iris rhizomes lie dormant in the frozen ground, Torrens continues to decorate with flowers from her garden, creating wreaths and other arrangements with blossoms she dries.

And just outside Kansas City, Missouri, Doug and Cindy Gilberg run a perennial nursery complete with a demonstration garden to inspire and educate their customers. Here, combinations of texture and leaf shape are just as important as the color design.

Your approach to gardening may involve any or all of these themes. As you read, allow your imagination to explore the possibilities, translating the ideas of these gardeners into your own vision and bringing their successes to your own landscape.

A WESTERN GARDEN OF NATIVE FLORA

In this garden, plants native to California bloom in synchrony with their wild relatives, linking the garden to the landscape. With little added water and only occasional maintenance, these native plants put on a spectacular display of flowers.

In midwinter, when other gardeners in this coastal region of California are longing for the colors of spring, Bill and Peggy Grier are watching their garden burst into bloom. Manzanitas (Arctostaphylos *species*) *are festooned with tiny pink bells, cobalt and white clusters cover the wild-lilacs* (Ceanothus *species*), *and crimson, pink, and purplish flowers droop from the currants* (Ribes *species*). *Wildflowers paint the ground in sweeps of blue and white, warming to yellow and orange as spring approaches. The intricate flowers in the rock gardens glitter in the clear winter light. In the surrounding hills, these events are mirrored by wild plants; this is because the Griers' flower garden is made up entirely of California natives.*

Most plants native to California flower from midwinter to early spring, become dormant for the summer, and revive to produce new growth in December. This cycle is imposed by the weather patterns of the region: Most of the rainfall occurs between October and March, and the summers are hot and dry. Despite these annual dry spells, most of the gardeners here grow roses, petunias, and other traditional flowers that require regular waterings throughout the summer. Some years, though, the winter rains are sparse and local officials restrict water use during the summer. When this happens, many plants in traditional gardens perish, unable to survive without frequent irrigation.

Most California native plants can withstand these cycles of drought and still flower abundantly. In addition to needing very little water, they integrate the garden into the surrounding landscape and require minimal maintenance. Thus, to the Griers, it simply makes more sense to garden with California natives.

A Well-Designed Collector's Garden

This isn't the Griers' first garden of California natives. Their previous garden contained traditional flowers and shrubs that they replaced, bit by bit, with a collection of California native plants. Under these circumstances, it was difficult to create a strong overall design. After the couple decided to move to a new home, they chose to start a garden from scratch and selected the site for its native gardening potential. The lot they bought was completely wild except for a shelf graded to support the home and pool.

To design the garden, they hired Ron Lutsko, a landscape architect experienced in working with California natives. Together they created a naturalistic plan. Near the house they planted blocks of flowering shrubs to create an elegant, well-ordered effect. Farther from the house, the plantings are more free-flowing to mimic the patterns of nature. Spectacular views of the surrounding hills are framed by carefully placed trees and shrubs selected to blend with the species growing in the wild.

Pink winter currants
(Ribes sanguineum)
*bloom in bright contrast
to a background of
cobalt blue wild-lilacs*
(Ceanothus *species*).

Along the perimeter of the Grier garden, the naturally mounded dwarf coyotebrush (Baccharis pilularis 'Twin Peaks') mimics in miniature the surrounding hillsides. This ground cover needs no pruning or training.

Although the Griers wanted a strong design, they are plant collectors at heart. Lutsko's initial plans for a garden of thirty to forty species was too limited—they wanted three hundred to four hundred. To accommodate so many species Lutsko established a strong framework of flowering shrubs and added two large rock gardens to the design.

The Garden Framework

Two kinds of flowering shrubs, manzanita (*Arctostaphylos* species) and wild-lilac (*Ceanothus* species) are important backbone plants in this garden, establishing a sense of order and creating a backdrop for the rock gardens and other diverse plantings. Staples in the California landscape, these genera contain species ranging in height from low creepers to small trees. The Griers grouped these plants to create a transition from the natural patterns of the garden to the geometric forms of the paving, patio, pool, and home.

Manzanita and wild-lilac have lovely flowers. The small, bell-shaped flowers of manzanita may be white or white tinged with pink, and a few varieties have deep pink flowers. The puffy flower clusters and spikes of wild-lilac come in white and in all shades of blue.

Dwarf coyotebrush (*Baccharis pilularis* 'Twin Peaks'), another important shrub in the garden framework, is a lime green, mounding bush up to 2 feet tall. Although it doesn't have significant flowers, the rounded form of the plant mimics the shapes of the surrounding hills, linking the garden with the landscape. This, combined with the shrub's drought resistance and ability to prevent erosion, made it the ideal choice for the steep slopes on the Griers' property.

Plantings of wild-lilac, manzanita, and other flowering shrubs form a backdrop for the herbaceous flowers and provide wonderful colors on a grand scale. Pink-flowering currant (*Ribes sanguineum* var. *glutinosum*) brings the first strong color to late winter. Golden currant (*Ribes aureum*) blooms a little later in tones of yellow. Western redbud (*Cercis occidentalis*) planted along the back fence is interesting all year, but the spring display of cerise flowers followed by bright green new leaves is breathtaking. Specimens of bush-anemone (*Carpenteria californica*), fremontia (*Fremontodendron californicum*), wild mockorange (*Philadelphus lewisii*), and matilija-poppy (*Romneya coulteri*) contribute to the structure of the garden, and they also stand out when in bloom.

The lemon yellow flowers of fremontia (Fremontodendron californicum) open in early April through May.

An Outdoor Foyer

Although most of the garden is dry, the area on the east side of the home near the front door provides a microclimate similar to the shaded floor of a redwood forest; in this case, the house serves as the redwood trees. Redwood sorrel (*Oxalis oregana*), a delightful, noninvasive species, bears prominent pink flowers atop shamrock leaves. Wild-ginger (*Asarum caudatum*) carpets the ground with heart-shaped leaves and bears maroon flowers in the spring. Ferns and inside-out-flower (*Vancouveria hexandra* and *V. planipetala*), with its lush foliage and tiny white blooms, complete the woodland effect.

In May visiting friends often leave the Grier garden clasping paper-wrapped bouquets of Pacific coast irises (Iris species).

Wildlife in the Garden

One of the benefits of growing native plants is the wildlife they attract. A tremendous variety of birds visits the Griers' garden, so many that a local ornithologist conducts one of her bird-watching classes there each spring. Butterflies also flock to the garden. Western monarch butterflies stop in on their annual migration from the California coast to western Canada to feed on the creamy blossoms of milkweed (*Asclepias* species). California dutchman's-pipevine (*Aristolochia californica*), which climbs the rails of the bridge, hosts the beautiful pipevine swallowtail butterfly. The caterpillars feed on the foliage, but to the Griers the spectacle of the butterflies flitting around the bridge and ravine is worth the loss of a few leaves. California dutchman's-pipevine blooms in late winter, before the leaves emerge. Its pendulous flowers are cream with reddish purple veins and resemble small pipes with flared bowls.

❧ Easy Maintenance

To construct the garden, the Griers hired a landscaping crew, supervised by Ron Lutsko. Now that the garden is established, the Griers maintain it themselves, but they consult with Lutsko before making major changes in the garden.

Each spring, Bill Grier fertilizes the rock gardens and other beds, and covers the soil with a new layer of mulch. The mulch keeps most of the weeds out of the beds, but weeds do appear on the slopes among the wildflowers. Selectively removing these weeds without disturbing the wildflowers is Peggy Grier's most difficult task, accomplished with a sharp eye and a great deal of tiptoeing.

Summer is a quiet time in this garden; most of the plants are dormant, and with the relentless sun propelling the temperature into the 90s and 100s, the Griers aren't inspired to do much gardening anyway. Although many of the plants can get by without summer water, the Griers water the plants next to the house every 7 to 10 days throughout the dry season to keep them looking their best. The rock garden plants, which dry out quickly in the sandy soil, are watered with the same frequency. The rest of the plants go more than a month between waterings without wilting.

Fall is planting time in the Griers' garden. As they acquire new specimens, they place them among the older, established plants. This poses a problem: The newcomers need regular summer waterings for the first few seasons, but the established plants should not be watered so frequently. To avoid spoiling the existing growth with extra moisture, Bill uses a temporary drip irrigation system to water the new acquisitions. Once the new plants are established, he removes the tubing.

Top left: Sage
(Salvia sonomensis).
Top right: Island alumroot
(Heuchera maxima) *attracts hummingbirds and makes a good ground cover for naturalistic gardens.*

The flowers and berries of pink winter currant (Ribes sanguineum) *attract birds to the garden. In hot-summer areas, these shrubs thrive in the light shade of oak trees.*

Well-placed native shrubs don't need much pruning. The Griers have an eye for choosing plants that adapt well to their surroundings and serve the landscape purposes they desire. By choosing plants with naturally desirable mature forms, they eliminate the need for much pruning and training. To maintain the naturally elegant forms of the plants, they occasionally remove any dead or wayward branches.

Gardening With Natives

The challenge of growing natives is in obtaining the plants and the information on how to grow them. Few large-chain plant nurseries carry a good selection of natives; the gardener has to look to specialty nurseries and local horticultural societies. Similarly, nationally distributed gardening books have to emphasize plants that are widely available; therefore, only a few of the natives mentioned here warrant a place in the encyclopedia at the back of this book.

The Griers learned a great deal about native plants through their involvement with a local chapter of the California Native Plant Society. In addition to hosting field trips and lectures for its members, the Society has an annual plant sale at which a tremendous selection of unusual plants is offered. When Peggy and Bill Grier travel in California, they visit arboreta and botanical gardens to study the plants of the region. Closer to home, they take frequent walks—usually toting field guides to local flora—to discover new plants and enjoy familiar ones in their wild habitats. These activities provide an endless source of inspiration, information, and lovely new flowers for the garden.

Fertilizing the Garden

Growing flowers is one of the most intensive forms of gardening. For their spectacular displays, flowering plants must absorb large quantities of nutrients from the soil that must be replenished on a regular basis to keep the plants blooming at their best.

Before planting, blend a complete fertilizer (one that contains nitrogen, phosphorus, and potassium) into the top 6 to 8 inches of soil. The amount of fertilizer you apply depends on the analysis of the product (its concentrations of nitrogen, phosphorus, and potassium). To avoid harming the plants, be sure to apply the exact amount of fertilizer specified on the label.

Most fertilizers are very soluble; they are taken up quickly by the plant and bring about an almost immediate response. But this solubility has a drawback: The nitrogen is readily washed through the soil and past the roots. Most beginning gardeners think that fertilizing once or twice in a year will do the job.

Not so! To ensure that plants have a continuous supply of nutrients, you must add more fertilizer at three- to four-week intervals throughout the growing season. Sprinkle the fertilizer around the plants, work it into the surface of the soil if the

plants aren't too close together (gently, to avoid harming the roots), and water it in well.

In addition to fertilizer, you'll also need to add organic matter. This is extremely important, especially in sandy or

clay soil. Organic matter gives soil its structure, sticking the particles together into friable clumps. Because organic matter is continuously broken down by the microorganisms that live in the soil, you'll need to add more each year,

digging it into the top 6 inches before planting or replanting annuals or bulbs, or spreading it over the soil surface in beds of established plants (see Mulches, page 93). Organic matter comes in many forms,

such as peat moss, decomposed manure, ground bark, and homemade compost. The form to use is best determined by what's available at a reasonable cost.

You can hardly overdo it when adding organic matter to a new bed. At the very least, add enough so that the final mixture contains about one-third organic matter. For example, if you are working the soil to a depth of 6 inches, spread a layer of organic matter at least 2 inches thick over the ground before beginning to dig.

In some cases, a soil may require amendments other than fertilizer and organic matter. Nutrients in fertilizer may not be available to plants if the soil is too acid or too alkaline. In the dry Southwest, where soils tend to be too alkaline, gardeners add sulfur to make the soil more acid. In the eastern United States soils may be too acid; gardeners in these areas add lime. For more information on lime and sulfur, see Correcting Soil pH on page 107.

A PURE PRAIRIE GARDEN

*Many prairie species are grown in flower beds,
but in a naturalistic garden these plants take
on a special significance. In Milwaukee, Wisconsin,
an ardent environmentalist restored a
colorful patch of the prairie in her own front yard.*

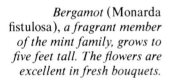 *Gardens of native plants differ dramatically from one region of the United States to another, a reflection of the rich diversity of vegetation on this continent. The second chapter, A Western Garden of Native Flora, offered a tour of a garden composed entirely of drought-tolerant plants native to California. In the Midwest, natural flower gardens are filled with prairie species, a thoroughly different community of plants. Despite the great differences in the plants they grow, native plant gardeners have a lot in common: a keen eye for the colors and patterns of nature, a love and respect for the environment, and a willingness to experiment. In this decade, prairie plants have become a popular alternative to traditional gardens in the Midwest, but 30 years ago, when Lorrie Otto started her prairie garden in Milwaukee, Wisconsin, she was a pioneer.*

When the Otto family moved into their home, the front yard was an acre and a half of lawn with a bed of yellow tulips and 64 spruce trees. It looked to Otto "like a Swiss chalet in Europe, surrounded by Christmas trees." Having grown up on a farm, Otto wanted her children to have "an interesting place to play," so she allowed blue and white asters (*Aster* species), vivid yellow goldenrods (*Solidago* species), and fragrant bergamot (*Monarda fistulosa*) to seed into the grass from a nearby vacant lot. Unfortunately, this first attempt at natural flower gardening was unceremoniously mowed down by the authorities of her Wisconsin community when a neighbor complained, thinking the plants were weeds. Otto explained to the contrite officials that her plants weren't weeds, but prairie wildflowers.

Bergamot (Monarda fistulosa), *a fragrant member of the mint family, grows to five feet tall. The flowers are excellent in fresh bouquets.*

The flowers grew back, but it wasn't until the first Earth Day observance in 1970 that Otto resolved to completely restore her yard to its natural state as a wildflower prairie. That was when she decided she didn't need a lawn: "I want my house to look as if it were just dropped down onto my property." This, it turned out, was easier said than done. In the 1970s there weren't any nurseries specializing in prairie plants, so she scouted the fence lines of nearby farms, obtaining purple and yellow coneflowers (*Echinacea purpurea* and *Ratibida pinnata*); false indigo (*Baptisia leucantha*), a stunning plant with waxy blue-green leaves and white flowers; and 6 of the 12 perennial sunflowers (*Helianthus* species) native to the state. Unlike today's gardeners, who can look to a number of books and articles for information on prairie gardening, Otto was on her own. Learning by trial and error, she set out young plants in holes dug in the grass, or she cleared small patches of turf to sow seed. As the sturdy perennials spread and seeded into the turf grass, her lawn slowly became a flower garden.

Despite these uncertain beginnings, Otto's garden of native wildflowers became a spectacular success. It now contains more than eighty wildflower and grass species, reflecting the diversity of the prairie. Once considered an eyesore, her garden now serves the community as a demonstration garden. From early May well into September, the garden is filled with flowers, providing an endless source of delight to Otto and inspiring her neighbors to plant their own natural landscapes of prairie flowers and grasses.

Yellow coneflower (Ratibida pinnata) *blooms profusely in the heat of midsummer. It is just one of the many plants that populate the tallgrass prairie.*

Top left: The foliage of big bluestem (Andropogon gerardii) *turns coppery red after the first frosts of autumn.*
Top right: Purple coneflower (Echinacea purpurea), *is also known as purple rudbeckia.*
Bottom: Yellow coneflower (Ratibida pinnata).

🌿 Prairie Colors, Spring to Frost

Prairie grasses are slow to emerge in the spring, and in May the garden is dominated by forbs—broad-leaved prairie plants—less than 2 feet tall. The pastel blue blossoms of pasqueflower (*Anemone patens*) appear early, fading into wispy white seedheads before the finely cut leaves emerge. Shooting-star (*Dodecatheon meadia*) tinges the prairie pink with its delicate, upswept petals. The purplish flowers of prairie-smoke (*Geum triflorum*) are quickly replaced by the wispy silver and pink seedheads for which the plant is named. Brilliant yellow blossoms top the hairy stalks of hoary-puccoon (*Lithospermum canescens*), a plant known for its tolerance of dry, inhospitable soils. Blue-eyed-grass (*Sisyrinchium campestre*), a tiny member of the iris family, bears deep blue starlike blooms above cool green clumps of foliage.

As the days continue to lengthen and the soil warms, bunches of Canada wild rye, Indian-grass, and other prairie grasses appear among the forbs. The grasses support the stems of the wildflowers and add another dimension to the garden. The wildflowers that bloom in summer are much taller than the spring-blooming plants; many blossoms are held 4 to 6 feet above the ground, and some reach a towering 10 feet tall. In late June, the pale purple coneflower (*Echinacea pallida*) blooms among blue spiderwort (*Tradescantia ohiensis*) and orange butterflyweed (*Asclepias tuberosa*)—a wonderful combination of textures and colors.

By midsummer, the garden is dominated by the rich golden hues of sunflowers (*Silphium* species), black-eyed-susan (*Rudbeckia hirta*), coreopsis (*Coreopsis tripteris*), and yellow coneflower (*Ratibida pinnata*). The downy sunflower (*Helianthus mollis*) thrives in the driest soils of Otto's garden and produces an abundant display of butter yellow flowers on soft, hairy stems. The western sunflower (*Helianthus occidentalis)* bears bright yellow daisylike flowers atop a nearly leafless stalk. The oxeye-sunflower (*Heliopsis helianthoides*) is not a true sunflower, but its yellow-orange flowers are remarkably similar to sunflowers and appear at the same time.

The flowers of *Silphium* species also resemble perennial sunflowers. This genus of classic prairie plants includes Otto's favorite prairie species, the cupplant (*S. perfoliatum*). The yellow flowers of the cupplant are borne atop tall square stems clasped by large pointed leaves. Rainwater collects in the cups formed by the leaf bases, providing a drink for hummingbirds and other pollinators. Another species of *Silphium,* the compassplant (*S. laciniatum*), is named for the way its fleshy, deeply divided leaves orient themselves north-south to avoid the harsh midday sun. It sends up a 4- to 7-foot flower stalk bearing up to a hundred large

Top left: Black-eyed-susan (Rudbeckia hirta) *is one of the easiest prairie wildflowers to grow, and it blooms through most of the summer.*
Top right: Cupplant (Silphium perfoliatum).

Left: The leaves of the cupplant (Silphium perfoliatum) *collect rainwater, providing a drink for hummingbirds and other pollinators. Right: Lavender spikes of prairie blazing-star* (Liatris pycnostachya) *emerge from a thicket of purple coneflower* (Echinacea purpurea), *pale purple coneflower* (Echinacea pallida), *and black-eyed-susan* (Rudbeckia hirta).

yellow flowers that open over a month-long period. Prairie-dock (*S. terebinthinaceum*) keeps its large, elephant-ear-shaped leaves close to the ground, but its slender stalk of yellow flowers reaches over 6 feet tall.

Otto patiently grew these slow-growing plants from seed. Ordinarily, the compassplant takes four to five years to mature and flower, but in Otto's clay soil it grew for eight years before the first blossoms appeared. Like most prairie plants, *Silphium* species is very deep rooted; the roots of the compassplant penetrate 14 to 18 feet into the ground, allowing it to survive dry spells without wilting.

Pink and purple flowers appear among the yellow blossoms throughout the summer. Joe-pye-weed (*Eupatorium maculatum*) is crowned with flat-topped clusters of pale purple flowers. Purple coneflower (*Echinacea purpurea*)—one of the best-known prairie plants—has pinkish purple petal-like rays that droop from the large, dark purple centers. It blooms later than the pale purple coneflower and has shorter, fatter rays that hang on into September.

In August, a more delicate group of flowers begins to bloom. Aster (*Aster* species), scarcely noticeable earlier in the summer, pops into view with white to blue flowers that have petals as delicate as eyelashes. The cool blues mix beautifully with the rich yellows of the late-blooming

Left: The leaves of the cupplant (Silphium perfoliatum) *collect rainwater, providing a drink for hummingbirds and other pollinators. Right: Lavender spikes of prairie blazing-star* (Liatris pycnostachya) *emerge from a thicket of purple coneflower* (Echinacea purpurea), *pale purple coneflower* (Echinacea pallida), *and black-eyed-susan* (Rudbeckia hirta).

yellow flowers that open over a month-long period. Prairie-dock (*S. terebinthinaceum*) keeps its large, elephant-ear-shaped leaves close to the ground, but its slender stalk of yellow flowers reaches over 6 feet tall.

Otto patiently grew these slow-growing plants from seed. Ordinarily, the compassplant takes four to five years to mature and flower, but in Otto's clay soil it grew for eight years before the first blossoms appeared. Like most prairie plants, *Silphium* species is very deep rooted; the roots of the compassplant penetrate 14 to 18 feet into the ground, allowing it to survive dry spells without wilting.

Pink and purple flowers appear among the yellow blossoms throughout the summer. Joe-pye-weed (*Eupatorium maculatum*) is crowned with flat-topped clusters of pale purple flowers. Purple coneflower (*Echinacea purpurea*)—one of the best-known prairie plants— has pinkish purple petal-like rays that droop from the large, dark purple centers. It blooms later than the pale purple coneflower and has shorter, fatter rays that hang on into September.

In August, a more delicate group of flowers begins to bloom. Aster (*Aster* species), scarcely noticeable earlier in the summer, pops into view with white to blue flowers that have petals as delicate as eyelashes. The cool blues mix beautifully with the rich yellows of the late-blooming

As the days continue to lengthen and the soil warms, bunches of Canada wild rye, Indian-grass, and other prairie grasses appear among the forbs. The grasses support the stems of the wildflowers and add another dimension to the garden. The wildflowers that bloom in summer are much taller than the spring-blooming plants; many blossoms are held 4 to 6 feet above the ground, and some reach a towering 10 feet tall. In late June, the pale purple coneflower (*Echinacea pallida*) blooms among blue spiderwort (*Tradescantia ohiensis*) and orange butterflyweed (*Asclepias tuberosa*)—a wonderful combination of textures and colors.

By midsummer, the garden is dominated by the rich golden hues of sunflowers (*Silphium* species), black-eyed-susan (*Rudbeckia hirta*), coreopsis (*Coreopsis tripteris*), and yellow coneflower (*Ratibida pinnata*). The downy sunflower (*Helianthus mollis*) thrives in the driest soils of Otto's garden and produces an abundant display of butter yellow flowers on soft, hairy stems. The western sunflower (*Helianthus occidentalis)* bears bright yellow daisylike flowers atop a nearly leafless stalk. The oxeye-sunflower (*Heliopsis helianthoides*) is not a true sunflower, but its yellow-orange flowers are remarkably similar to sunflowers and appear at the same time.

The flowers of *Silphium* species also resemble perennial sunflowers. This genus of classic prairie plants includes Otto's favorite prairie species, the cupplant (*S. perfoliatum*). The yellow flowers of the cupplant are borne atop tall square stems clasped by large pointed leaves. Rainwater collects in the cups formed by the leaf bases, providing a drink for hummingbirds and other pollinators. Another species of *Silphium,* the compassplant (*S. laciniatum*), is named for the way its fleshy, deeply divided leaves orient themselves north-south to avoid the harsh midday sun. It sends up a 4- to 7-foot flower stalk bearing up to a hundred large

Top left: Black-eyed-susan (Rudbeckia hirta) *is one of the easiest prairie wildflowers to grow, and it blooms through most of the summer.*
Top right: Cupplant (Silphium perfoliatum).

Prohibited from using the torch and shunning the internal combustion engine, Otto uses a Japanese rice harvesting knife to cut the spent flower stalks after the birds and members of the Natural Landscaping Club have taken the seeds. Even then, she only removes the plants that don't offer much winter interest. After the first snowfall, you'll find her in the garden, marveling at the clumps of snow caught in the candelabra-shaped branches of bergamot and delighting in the little white caps perched atop the dark round heads of the coneflowers.

Controlling Weeds

In addition to being unsightly, weeds compete with flowers for light, water, and nutrients. The first—and most important—step in preventing weeds is to remove them before they make seeds. Weeds are prodigious producers of seeds; a stalk of oatgrass may make 250 seeds, and the seed count on a pigweed plant can run into the millions. Most of the weeds in a garden come from seeds that formed there; only a small fraction come from outside. By removing weeds before they produce seeds, you'll be reducing future weed problems.

Removing Weeds
The methods you choose to weed your garden depend on whether the weeds are annuals or perennials and whether you wish to use an herbicide. Annual weeds can be removed by hoe or by hand. They can also be eliminated with a contact herbicide. These kill only the plant tissue that they touch, so thorough coverage is important.

Perennial weeds such as bermudagrass, plantain, and dandelion are tenacious pests that require more effort. You can effectively eradicate established perennial weeds by hand, but be sure to remove all the roots as well as the tops. Any roots or other underground parts left in the soil can resprout and take over the bed in a single season. The best time to dig out perennial weeds is in the early spring when the soil is moist and the weeds don't have much top growth. If you prefer to remove perennial weeds using chemicals, use systemic herbicides, which are absorbed by the leaves and then translocated throughout the plant. Glyphosate, a commonly used systemic, leaves no residue in the soil.

Staying Ahead
Once the weeds are gone, you can prevent new ones from growing by keeping the ground covered with plants and mulch so that the weeds don't have light. Flowers should be planted close together enough so that, when mature, they form a continuous canopy over the soil. Mulches are particularly effective in the battle against weeds—a 3-inch layer of mulch on the soil will keep most weed seeds from sprouting. (For more about mulches, see page 93.)

Despite these preventative measures, some weeds will persistently make their way into the garden. To stay ahead of them, you need to match their persistence by removing young weeds as soon as they appear. Weeds grow so quickly that, if left undisturbed, a few small ones can rapidly turn into a major project. When removing weeds around flowers, be careful not to disrupt the roots of the desirable plants. If a weed is very close to a flower, pinch or cut off the top of the weed at soil level. Try to get in the habit of picking a few weeds every time you walk through the garden. The sooner you attend to them, the easier they are to remove and the less chance they'll have of producing seeds—and the sooner you will have a weed-free garden.

SWIFT STROKES OF COLOR

*Using color as their guide and enchantment
as their goal, a gardener and a nurseryman
tame a wild hillside with a sophisticated
combination of perennials and flowering shrubs.*

In 1984 Nancy Miller asked Aerin Moore, a nurseryman and landscape contractor, to plant some flowers around her fish pond in the backyard. She was planning a tea for one of her granddaughters and wanted to liven up the patio area with a little bit of color. "Just a bit," Miller said. She had no intention of creating a flower garden.

Not that she didn't love flowers, but after battling the "horrible clay soil" of her 4-acre Northern California property, she'd contented herself with taming a small strip around the house with ground covers and low-maintenance shrubs and with a few raised beds of vegetables. On the slope above the fish pond, a tall privet hedge screened a croquet court and play area used by visiting grandchildren, but the rest of the property was an undulating hillside covered by a tangle of poison-oak and blackberry bushes, shaded by native coast live oaks.

When Moore arrived to discuss the patio planting, he and Miller immediately discovered remarkable similarities in their gardening tastes: Both loved English gardens of pink and blue-flowered perennials, classical architecture, and natural stonework. She was impressed by his horticultural knowledge and liked his ideas for the pond-side planting. Toward the end of their conversation, he revitalized her interest in flower gardening simply by glancing up the slope and saying, "Sometime I'd like to do something up there."

Roses (Rosa *species*) *are staple flowering shrubs in the garden. In the foreground 'Nearly Wild' blooms white and pink; in the back, 'Iceberg' is pure white; hot pink 'Betty Prior' blooms on the right.*

Left: Carpet-bugle (Ajuga reptans *'Burgundy Glow') covers the ground beneath the floribunda rose 'Nearly Wild',* coralbells (Heuchera sanguinea), *and cranesbill* (Geranium ibericum). *Right: In this woodland tableau, foxglove* (Digitalis *'Temple Bells') blooms with meadowrue* (Thalictrum aquilegifolium). *In the foreground is lamb's-ears* (Stachys byzantina).

Do something he did. Delighted by his work around the fish pond and inspired by his ideas for expanding the garden, Miller gave Moore what amounted, in the end, to carte blanche to fill the property with flowers. In the beginning, he and his crew started small, installing a few perennial borders around the play area, which they replaced with a new sod lawn. They added yards of mulch to loosen the clay soil, and they filled the borders with a wonderful composition of pink and blue perennials.

Few flowers are true-blue, but the speedwell *Veronica latifolia* 'Crater Lake Blue' comes close, forming dense tussocks covered with spikes of tiny flowers. Bethlehem-sage (*Pulmonaria saccharata* 'Mrs. Moon') is attractive in leaf and in bloom: The leaves are spotted with yellow, and the pink buds open into blue trumpets. Twinspur (*Diascia barberae*) has narrow, toothed leaves and bears dense spikes of rose-pink flowers. *Primula japonica,* from the candelabra class of primroses, (named for the erect, 2- to 3-foot stems of flowers) bears magenta and white blooms from May to July. The dark lilac-pink flowers of obedience plant (*Physostegia virginiana* 'Vivid') extend the blooming season with blossoms that appear in September. Another fall bloomer, sage (*Salvia guaranitica*), bears spikes of deep royal blue flowers.

To highlight the beds, Moore planted the fiery astilbe (*Astilbe* 'Fanal') and a deep-red abutilon (*Abutilon* 'Nabob'). Several roses and camellias add substance to the planting. 'Iceberg', a floribunda rose later planted throughout the garden as a unifying element, is pure white. 'Miss All American Beauty', an old garden rose, and *Camellia sasanqua* 'Shishi-Gashira' are magenta. The soft gray foliage of lamb's-ears (*Stachys byzantina* 'Silver Carpet') and lavender-cotton (*Santolina chamaecyparissus*) brighten the pastel tints and enhance the glow of the magentas.

A Japanese maple (Acer palmatum *'Burgundy Lace')
picks up the reds and pinks of nearby rhododendrons* (Rhododendron *'The Honorable Jean Marie de Montague' and 'Markeeta's Flame') and Kurume azaleas* (Rhododendron *'Coral Bells' and 'Ward's Ruby').*

No Sooner Said Than Done

Miller was particularly impressed by Moore's quick work. He seemed to anticipate her wishes. One day she mentioned that the privet hedge blocked her view of the lovely new flower beds; the next day it was gone. The path leading to the beds was too muddy; in a flash it was paved in gravel with steps made of oak branches. An ivy-filled border along the patio looked drab to her one morning; by that afternoon it contained an exquisite red-barked Japanese maple (*Acer palmatum* 'Sango-kaku') surrounded by clear blue creeping forget-me-not (*Omphalodes cappadocica*) and pink and white lenten-rose (*Helleborus orientalis*), ferns, and impatiens.

For the next three years, the garden swept up the slope, propelled by Miller's and Moore's enthusiasm. They looked at plants in his nursery, studied the pictures in books, and to Miller their conversations seemed to turn into flowers that spread across the hillside. "We never stopped to draw up any plans," she says. "If we had, it wouldn't have turned out like this."

Color Harmony

In the Miller garden, color is everything. Miller and Moore strived to create a relaxed feeling with a pleasing balance of color. They achieved this harmony by choosing flowers with blue-based colors, a palette containing crimson, pink, violet, blue, and blue-green. This scheme is based on a tried and true principle of color theory: If a color wheel is divided along an axis bisecting equally the red and green segments, with one side containing blue-based colors and the other side composed of colors based on yellow, flowers chosen exclusively from either side will harmonize.

For the first two years, they explored blue-based colors, experimenting with combinations composed mainly of pinks and blues. Clumps of Siberian and Japanese irises (*Iris sibirica* and *I. ensata*) fill a border backed by a mass of pink roses. 'Nearly Wild' unfurls its light pink flowers above the electric blue blossoms of the Siberian iris 'Blue Jay'. Like most of the roses in the garden, 'Nearly Wild' is a single—its flowers have a single row of petals. 'Betty Prior', another single rose, is darker pink. A lone blue spruce (*Picea pungens* 'Koster') adds a complementary

Top: Japanese iris (Iris ensata), left, and Siberian iris (Iris sibirica 'Blue Jay'), right, are combined with the pink shrub rose 'Carefree Beauty' in one of the first areas planted.
Bottom: In the same area, hot pink 'Betty Prior' and pink and white 'Nearly Wild' roses continue the theme. White rose 'Iceberg' dilutes the intense colors, softening the overall effect.

tone of gray-blue, but its pyramidal form and furry texture stand out dramatically against the rounded, leafy shrubs. In the background, the white markings on the pink flowers of weigela (*Weigela florida* 'Variegata') are accentuated by the clear white flowers of a nearby 'Iceberg' rose.

In another group of blue-based flowers, Miller and Moore achieved a serene balance of hues with flax-lily (*Dianella tasmanica*), a sword-leaved plant with loose clusters of pale blue flowers followed by bright blue berries; violet penstemon (*Penstemon* 'Sour Grapes'); and shell pink cranesbill (*Geranium sanguineum* var. *prostratum*). *Fuchsia thymifolia*, a species resistant to the devastating fuchsia mite, is covered with drooping pink flowers for most of the summer, and the twigs and leaves are attractively tinged with red.

As they planted their way up the hill, Miller began to explore the other side of the color wheel, the oranges and yellows. According to the traditional rules of color combination, blue-based colors should be separated from yellow-based colors to avoid clashes, but Miller learned to blend one group effectively into the other. She found that the soft,

*Foliage and flowers from the same blue-red palette: New Zealand–flax (*Phormium tenax *'Dazzler'*) and beard-tongue (*Penstemon *'Sour Grapes'*). Pale pink cranesbill (*Geranium sanguineum*) keeps the combination from overwhelming the eye.*

Top left: Speedwell
(Veronica latifolia).
*Top right: A canopy of oaks
moderates the environment of
the garden, allowing Miller
to successfully grow a great
variety of species.*
Bottom: In the foreground,
Geranium × cantabrigiense
'Biokovo'.

yellow-variegated foliage of *Carex morowii* 'Everbright', a grasslike
sedge, is compatible with lavender-pink foxglove (*Digitalis × merto-
nensis*) and purple Spanish lavender (*Lavandula stoechas*). *Geranium
× cantabrigiense* 'Biokovo', a soft pink cultivar of cranesbill, echoes the
pastel hues from farther down the slope. Blues are added to the scheme
with blue sage (*Salvia azurea* var. *grandiflora*) and speedwell (*Veronica
latifolia* 'Crater Lake Blue'). *Rosa* 'Mutabilis', a shrubby old garden
rose, ties these variously colored flowers together with its multicolored
blossoms. Its single flowers open peach, fade through several shades
of pink, and mature to magenta. The peach flowers tie in with nearby
orange and peach lilies (*Lilium* hybrids), the pinks touch on tints occurring throughout the garden, and the magenta blossoms contain enough
blue to link them with the blue sage and veronica.

Top: More pinks and blues: pink and white cultivars of hardy orchid (Bletilla striata) *mix well with lavender-pink cranesbill* (Geranium ibericum). *In the background are roses, including peach-flowering 'Just Joey', white-blooming 'Iceberg', and red-blossomed 'Fragrant Cloud'. Bottom left: Pink-flowered cranesbill* (Geranium ibericum). *Bottom right: Purple-flowered cranesbill* (Geranium endressii).

The top of the rise is crowned with roses: the brilliant coral pink 'Fragrant Cloud' and the peach 'Just Joey'. Miller's favorite, 'Voodoo', is a free-blooming, disease-resistant cultivar. The coral flowers have a touch of yellow at the base of the petals, making the blossoms appear to glow from within.

On the other side of the garden, they removed the periwinkle from the slope above the swimming pool and planted more brightly colored roses. The intense, coral pink blossoms of 'America', a large-flowered climber, are striking above the turquoise-blue water. 'Rocky', a shrub rose, has clear orange double flowers. Another climber, 'Fred Loades', has orange flowers, but with a single row of petals. The climber 'Joseph's Coat' bears yellow-orange double flowers. The luminous hues of these roses appear to surge across the garden toward the viewer, defining the garden boundaries and creating a sense of enclosure and security. This effect worked so well that Moore and Miller later planted a slope along the back fence with an assortment of large shrub roses bearing bright crimson, pink, and white flowers.

A View of the Garden

By the second year, the garden was beginning to grow very large, but there wasn't a good vantage point from which to take it all in. One day Moore called Miller to relate an idea he had about a lookout, built on a promontory, from which they could view the garden. Miller couldn't picture it, but gave him the go-ahead.

Moore's crew bulldozed the soil into a 10-foot mound. They shored up the sides of the mound with a dry stone wall and built a spiral stone staircase up one side to the flat, round top. In the spaces between the stones, they planted a Japanese maple (*Acer palmatum*) and a rockspray cotoneaster (*Cotoneaster microphyllus*). A couple of chairs and a small table completed the lookout, making it a perfect place for Miller and Moore to view their work and discuss ideas for the rest of the garden.

The top of the promontory offers a sweeping view of the upper portion of the garden.

Top left: Natural stonework provides plenty of nooks and crannies for species such as the tiny-flowered London-pride (Saxifraga umbrosa) and pink Geranium × cantabrigense 'Biokovo'. Top right: Coralbells (Heuchera 'June Bride'). Bottom: A bright pink azalea (Rhododendron phoenicea) borders a stretch of one of the stone paths that meander through the garden.

The remaining unplanted area was a flat, boggy patch of wild sedges. Miller and Moore's plan for this area included a gazebo and open expanse of lawn, excavated in the wettest spot to form a pool of koi and water lilies (*Nymphaea* species). But when the bulldozer arrived, they decided to add another pool. Now two irregularly shaped pools grace the center of the lawn, filled in summer with the blossoms of water lilies. *Iris laevigata* 'Alba' bears stately white flowers from partially sunken rhizomes. The blooms of cardinal-flower (*Lobelia cardinalis*) and the leaves of New Zealand-flax (*Phormium tenax* 'Dazzler') accent the pools with brilliant reds.

No Small Task

This garden is not in any way a typical neighborhood garden. Moore's crews worked full-time for nearly two years and part-time for

Top left: Yellow-archangel (Lamiastrum galeobdolon). *Top right: Flowering dogwood* (Cornus florida). *Bottom left: Garland flower* (Daphne cneorum). *Bottom right: Navelwort* (Omphalodes cappadocica).

another two. Seven oaks fell to admit more light, and the remaining oaks were thinned. Seventeen tons of flagstone were laid in place for the paths. The beds were terraced with dry stone retaining walls; by the end of the project, over 300 tons of stone had been set in the garden. Bulldozers were driven into the garden to grade the slopes and to carry the crane used to lower a pair of lion statues into place at the entrance to the uppermost lawn.

The plantings are rich with diversity; over nineteen hundred species and hybrids can be found in the garden. To bring water to all these plants, Miller and Moore installed an automatic irrigation system with over six hundred sprinkler heads. When it became apparent that their water allotment was insufficient, they built a 10,000-gallon redwood tank, connected to the sprinklers by a powerful pump. Water is added to the tank from a truck once or twice a week during the summer. To catch the water that runs off the slopes during winter storms, they dammed a small ravine.

Keeping It All Growing

Nancy Miller used to play golf three times a week, and traveled as much as possible, but now she'd rather be in her garden. She spends some of each day gardening, and she and her husband now take their vacation in February so they don't miss a minute of the garden's spring display.

Most of Miller's gardening efforts are devoted to maintaining and adjusting the extensive sprinkler system. "I love the plumbing," she says. "I love to adjust all the sprinklers." Her gardening toolbox contains pipe wrenches, fittings, sprinkler heads and risers, glue, and sealing tape. She feeds the plants once a month with liquid plant food dispensed by a hose-end sprayer. She employs a maintenance crew to care for the lawns, but entrusts the pruning, weeding, and grooming tasks to a gardener who helps her twice a week.

The heavy work—lifting, dividing, and moving plants—is accomplished by Moore and his landscaping crew. In fall, midwinter, and spring, they mulch the garden, spreading a total of 25 yards of mulch in the beds each year. They use an enriched, commercially prepared mulch, supplemented with compost from the garden.

Saffron yellow torch-lily (Kniphofia uvaria) *and beard-tongue* (Penstemon *'Huntington Pink') bloom beneath a young purple princess-flower* (Tibouchina urvilleana).

After years of intensive construction and planting, most of the garden is finished, but the design continues to evolve. Many perennials are easily moved, and Miller and Moore rearrange plants each winter to improve the design and experiment with new combinations. They use small flags to mark the herbaceous perennials they plan to move; without the flags, it would be difficult to find the plants in the winter when they have no leaves. In some cases, Miller and Moore have had to move plants that rapidly outgrew their spaces. The phenomenal growth of the new plants amazes Moore, and he attributes it to the generous mulchings.

Such a spectacular garden doesn't go unnoticed. Wildlife discovered the flowers first: At night Nancy Miller sees the glowing eyes of deer peering longingly at the succulent growth through the Cyclone fence. In summer, the garden is filled with the thrum of hummingbirds, attracted by abutilon, salvia, and penstemon. As word of the creation spread, the garden filled with another sound, the appreciative oohs and aahs of visiting members of local garden clubs, marveling at Miller and Moore's enchanting compositions of color.

The Flower Framework

A flower border at its peak is a medley of colors and textures that seems to be composed of nothing but leaves, blossoms, and stems. What often doesn't show is an underlying framework, a structure of sticks, wire, or string used to support the tall or floppy plants.

Tall plants with single stalks, such as delphinium, hollyhock, and gladiolus, can be braced by single bamboo or stiff wire stakes. The stake should be pushed into the ground about 1 inch from the base of the plant, preferably before it has grown to the point where it is starting to tip over. Attach the stem to the stake with plant ties, looping the ties in a figure eight around the stake and the stem and allowing room for the plant to move a bit.

Other plants, such as aster, chrysanthemum, coreopsis, heliopsis, and carnation, have a number of floppy stems; these need an entire framework to keep them upright.

Traditionally, twiggy prunings about 16 to 20 inches long from birch or cherry trees are stuck into the ground all around a clump of half-grown plants. The twigs are then bent over and intertwined to form a sturdy framework over the young plants. The shoots grow through the twigs, eventually covering them with foliage and flowers.

Heavy, sprawling plants like baby's-breath are best supported by wire hoops (available from garden centers) or by corseting. To construct a corset, push bamboo or stiff wire stakes into the ground in a circle around the plant while it is small. The number of stakes to use depends on the size of the plant; 3 to 5 is usually adequate. Once the stakes are in place, tie them together around the outside (not through the middle) with string, creating two or three tiers. The shoots will grow through and around the spaces between the stakes and string, hiding them from view.

ANNUAL COLOR
BY THE SEA

When it comes to garden dazzle, annual flowers steal the show. In this seacoast garden, beds of annuals, bulbs, and perennials create year-round displays of vivid colors.

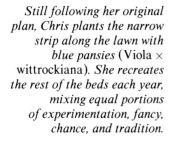

"This is the garden that wasn't supposed to be," says Winifred Chris of her spectacular backyard amphitheater of flower beds. "We built this house to spend time by the ocean—I didn't intend to do any gardening here." Despite her intentions, Chris couldn't resist the urge to plant. As soon as the house was finished, she was outside planting a bed of blue pansies to complement her new blue and white home by the sea near Monterey, California.

Now, 34 years later, that first flower bed is still planted with blue annuals—pansies in winter, petunias in summer—but the rest of the garden has become a multicolored quilt of flowers. Chris delights in flashy displays of mixed flowers created with combinations of annuals, perennials, bulbs, and succulents. Her garden is in bloom all year but peaks in the early spring, when the emerging bulbs produce a breathtaking display of color. Abhorring the constraints imposed by a garden plan, she designs as she goes along. "I do not plan ahead," she says. "The only way I know what to do is to have my fingers in the dirt."

Chris's approach to color is equally spontaneous, but she does have preferences. Blue flowers are her favorites "because blue belongs to the sea." Indeed, there are a great number of blue flowers in the garden, but what catches the eye are the brilliant reds and yellows, mixed with the blues in a riot of primary colors. Orange and apricot flowers also appear

Still following her original plan, Chris plants the narrow strip along the lawn with blue pansies (Viola × wittrockiana). *She recreates the rest of the beds each year, mixing equal portions of experimentation, fancy, chance, and tradition.*

Each bed is a mixed bouquet. Petunias (Petunia × hybrida)*, dahlias* (Dahlia *cultivars*)*, poppies* (Papaver *species*)*, marigolds* (Tagetes *species*)*, delphiniums* (Delphinium *cultivars*)*, and other bedding annuals blend in a rich patchwork of color.*

in the garden, especially in spring, when the beds are filled with tulips. Although these warm colors don't echo the expanses of ocean and sky, they glow in the bright sun reflected by the sand and water. The only colors Chris doesn't like to use are pink and lavender, subtle hues that she feels are out of place in the intense light of a seaside garden.

In summer, Chris's backyard bouquets contain blue and white petunias (*Petunia* hybrids), multiflora cultivars that produce great quantities of medium-sized flowers. Multiflora petunias are also resistant to gray mold (*Botrytis* species), a disease that disfigures the blossoms of susceptible plants in humid regions. Behind the petunias, the spectacular blue spires of Pacific hybrid delphiniums (*Delphinium elatum*) tower over the other flowers in the bed.

The middle of another bed is ruled by the regal red blossoms of dahlias (*Dahlia* hybrids). Near the dahlias, both yellow and red flowers of avens (*Geum quellyon*) are borne atop 2-foot spikes and bloom through the summer. French marigolds (*Tagetes patula*) and California poppies (*Eschscholzia californica*) merge in a cheery profusion of yellows and oranges. Powder blue Chinese forget-me-not (*Cynoglossum amabile*) flow in delicate rivulets among the warm-colored flowers.

In October, many of these summer-blooming flowers are still going strong, but Chris pulls them out and plants winter- and spring-blooming bulbs and annuals for the peak of her gardening year, a spring explosion of color. Royal blue English primroses (*Primula × polyantha* hybrids)

By March the daffodils
(Narcissus *species*) *have*
given way to—among
so many other things—
calendulas (Calendula
officinalis), *Persian*
buttercups (Ranunculus
asiaticus), *and baby-blue-*
eyes (Nemophila menziesii).
In the background is the
noble blue bulk of
pride-of-Madeira
(Echium fastuosum).

and the yellow, daisylike blossoms of calendula (*Calendula officinalis*)
bloom through the winter and into the spring. Snapdragons (*Antirrhi-*
num majus) accent the low masses of bloom with their upright spikes.
Toadflax (*Linaria maroccana*) and nemesia (*Nemesia strumosa*) echo
the shape of the snapdragon, a close relative, with interesting variations
in size and color. Stock (*Matthiola incana*) fills the cool moist air with
the fragrance of spice and honey.

A wooden frame encloses an old sandbox, and the sand is amended
annually with humus to create a well-drained bed for a spring show of
golden daffodils (*Narcissus* hybrids). The daffodils are followed by
bronze, orange, and yellow Persian buttercup (*Ranunculus asiaticus*).
Delicate baby-blue-eyes (*Nemophila menziesii*) and a scattering of
toadflax cover the bulbs.

In a shady spot on the north side of the garage, a mass of deep blue cineraria (*Senecio × hybridus*) thrives in front of a row of red camellias. The cineraria self-sows; Chris pulls any plants that don't bear the blue flowers she likes. In summer, when the sun reaches the front of the bed and burns some of the cineraria, Chris replaces those plants with purple and white petunias, which she says spark up the color of the remaining cineraria.

The uppermost tier of the garden is steeply sloping and difficult to care for. Here, against the background of a mature Monterey cypress tree (*Cupressus macrocarpa*), Chris planted low-maintenance, drought-tolerant shrubs and perennials. The most dramatic plants on the slope are pride-of-Madeira (*Echium fastuosum*). In spring, the thick whorls of gray-green leaves bear massive clusters of purplish blue, light blue, or

Top left: Cyclamineus hybrid daffodils (Narcissus *hybrids*).
Top right: Persian buttercups (Ranunculus asiaticus) *among baby-blue-eyes* (Nemophila menziesii).
Bottom: A stately Monterey cypress (Cupressus macrocarpa) *presides over Chris's amphitheater of spring flowers.*

Top left: Dependable pansies (Viola × wittrockiana). *Top right: Hen-and-chickens* (Echeveria × imbricata). *Below: Volunteer sweet-alyssum* (Lobularia maritima) *provides a bright white background for Chris's iceland poppies* (Papaver nudicaule).

lavender flowers. Dusty-miller (*Senecio cineraria*) and blue-gray ice plant (*Maleophora crocea*) bring out the gray tones of the pride-of-Madeira; Chris loves the silvery sheen of these plants on days when a thin fog races across the sun.

In the front yard, along the entryway to the home, a bed of pansies (*Viola × wittrockiana*) creates a serene pool of blue until late January, when scarlet and golden tulips burst from the soil. Chris plants early-, mid-, and late-season cultivars to produce an ever-changing display of flowers that blooms in waves of color from January into May.

Across the driveway, the blue perennial tussock bellflower (*Campanula carpatica*) and several succulents, including hen-and-chickens (*Echeveria × imbricata* and *Sempervivum tectorum*), nestle in the pockets of a dry stone wall. Chris also tucks a variety of annuals into the

soil-filled cracks of the wall each year and plants others in the narrow strip of soil at the base of the wall. Planting the wall can be a nuisance, she says, because "soil and water go up your sleeves," but the results are worth the trouble. Neighbors stop to admire the flower-studded stonework on their way up the street, and the wall has been photographed for a calendar company.

Nature also contributes to Chris's plantings; seedling violets (*Viola odorata*), sweet-alyssum (*Lobularia maritima*), basket-of-gold (*Aurinia saxatilis*), yellow lupine (*Lupinus densiflorus*), and other flowers pop up all over the property. Whenever possible, Chris allows these volunteers to grow where they appear. "Volunteers do better than anything else," she advises. "Leave them where they come." Although this advice may thwart the plans of other gardeners, for Chris it works.

Color With Annuals

Despite its 34 years of growth, Chris's garden is composed mainly of plants that are less than a year old. Most of her flowers are true annuals (flowering plants that live for a year or less) or perennials that she grows as annuals, planting them only for seasonal color. Annuals—the workhorses of the garden when it comes to flower production—are

Succulent stonecrop (Sedum *species*), *dusty-miller* (Senecio *species*), *and hens-and-chicks* (Sempervivum tectorum) *thrive in the soil-filled pockets of a dry stone wall.* Cineraria (Senecio × hybridus) *blooms in the deeper soil at the base of the wall.*

Papery red oriental poppy
(Papaver orientale),
yellow calendula
(Calendula officinalis), *and*
orange annual coreopsis
(Coreopsis tinctoria).

ideally suited to Chris's gardening style. By using annuals, she has the freedom to arrange the garden as she goes. When a plant passes its prime, she pulls it out and tucks in another. If a flower looks out of place, she simply digs it up and moves it.

Annuals are also well-suited to the mild, coastal climate. Seasons merge subtly here; winter weather alternates between warm and cool spells, and summer days may be warm and sunny or cool and foggy. Perennials and bulbs from other climates are fooled by the weather into blooming at odd times, making it impossible to orchestrate the flowering times of plants with short blooming seasons. Annuals, however, bloom dependably over a long season; Chris can count on the flowers to be there when she wants them.

Gardening by the Sea

To shield the house and garden from the salt-laden wind, Chris planted rows of shrubs that tolerate seaside conditions. Above a steep slope covered with ice plant and patches of sweet alyssum, Australian tea-trees (*Leptospermum laevigatum*) bear the brunt of the salty breezes without burning and produce a spring display of white flowers. Behind the tea-trees, a taller row of myoporum (*Myoporum laetum*) lifts the wind higher. The white and purple spring flowers of this glossy shrub are followed by reddish purple fruit. The back row, a tall line of yellow-flowered pittosporum (*Pittosporum eugenioides*), is the last line of defense. In spring, the sweet fragrance of the pittosporum flowers wafts into the windows of the home. To encourage the dense growth needed for wind protection, Chris shears the shrubs once a year.

Other parts of the garden are protected from the wind by strategic plantings of Monterey cypress, yellow-flowered Canary Island broom (*Cytisus canariensis*), and wild-lilac (*Ceanothus* 'Julia Phelps'), a floriferous shrub covered in spring with clusters of indigo blossoms.

'Julia Phelps' is one of the best-blooming cultivars of wild-lilac (Ceanothus species)*, a popular genus of western shrubs.*

Top: Red geraniums (Pelargonium domesticum 'Grand Slam'). Bottom: Garden petunias (Petunia × hybrida) are sure-fire performers— in pots (reds) and in the ground (purple/blues).

Container Color

Pots of flowers add to the festive atmosphere of Chris's garden. Pots and planters are placed anywhere and everywhere—on the patio, atop the garden walls, in the corners of the garden steps. Bright red geraniums (*Pelargonium domesticum* 'Grand Slam') bloom almost continuously in pots along the garden wall. After about three years of growth, when the plants begin to decline, Chris pulls them out and plants new ones in fresh soil. Bougainvillea (*Bougainvillea* species) lasts indefinitely in containers if pruned regularly; it is covered through the summer with showy red bracts that enclose the tiny flowers.

Tulips make impressive, if short-lived, container subjects. Chris extends the display with a technique called double planting, in which two layers of bulbs are placed in a pot. The top layer of bulbs blooms first. By the time the flowers of the top layer fade, the flowers from the bottom layer have emerged to bloom among the leaves of the first.

To create a double-planted pot of tulips, Chris fills a deep pot (at least 15 inches tall) with soil so that the distance from the surface of the soil to the rim of the pot is roughly equal to the length of two bulbs. She arranges the first row of bulbs on the soil so the sides are almost touching, and she adds more soil to cover all but the very tips of the bulbs. Then she places another layer of bulbs in the pot, positioning them between the tips of the first. To make the foliage more symmetrical, the bulbs in the top layer are oriented so the flat sides face the outside of the pot. The top layer of bulbs is then covered with soil. Transplants of the blue-flowered edging lobelia (*Lobelia erinus*) are the finishing touch; planted around the edge of the pot, they cascade over the rim, softening the lines of the container and framing the upright shoots of the tulips.

Double-planting tulip bulbs in a pot extends the period of bloom. A second wave of flowers begins to open just as the first blooms reach their peak.

In early spring, wildflowers begin to make islands of color in the empty field on the other side of the hedge. Chris interferes with the natural growth of the hillside as little as possible; she introduces the seeds of a few favorite wildflowers and allows the native plants to grow where they can.

A Wildflower Tradition

In a break in the myoporum hedge on the side of the garden, blue and white morning glory vines (*Ipomoea tricolor*) and white potato vine (*Solanum jasminoides*) cover an arbor leading to a field of wildflowers. Sixteen years ago, when she first planted the empty lot, Chris sowed a mix of 15 species of wildflowers developed for the Pacific Northwest. Many of these species became naturalized, and now she plants only the seeds of her favorites.

The glowing colors of Chris's backyard garden are found in this field, in the orange to carmine cups of California poppy (*Eschscholzia californica*), the red and yellow sunbursts of coreopsis (*Coreopsis tinctoria*), the soft yellows and whites of cape-marigold (*Dimorphotheca sinuata*), and the yellow warmth of basket-of-gold (*Aurinia saxatilis*). Bachelor's-button (*Centaurea cyanus*) and baby-blue-eyes (*Nemophila menziesii*) reflect the blues of the sky and sea. The lacy gray-green leaves and clustered white flowers of yarrow (*Achillea millefolium*) soften the texture of the field.

Family tradition coincides with the weather to dictate the wildflower planting schedule. In early November, Chris hires gardeners to prepare the field for planting. On Thanksgiving Day, she and her grandsons broadcast the seeds. A heavy sprinkling of water—by cloudburst or sprinkler—covers the seeds enough to hide them from the birds without burying them too deep for germination. Within a week or two, the ground is tinged with the delicate green of the new seedlings. Watered by the winter rains, the wildflowers bloom from late February into July, when summer drought dries them to a golden hue.

Unfortunately, with the wildflowers come the weeds. Perennial weeds and grasses have always been a problem in the field, and in some patches the weeds choke out the wildflowers. To give the wildflowers a better chance, Chris was advised by the seed supplier to treat the field with a systemic herbicide to kill the underground portions of the weeds and keep them from resprouting. She prefers, however, to let nature take its course, removing a few of the weeds by hand but letting most of them grow where they may.

Yellow and white cape-marigold (Dimorphotheca sinuata), *orange California poppy* (Eschscholzia californica), *and baby-blue-eyes* (Nemophila menziesii) *bloom reliably among the vigorous native grasses.*

In midsummer, the garden is at its peak. The flowers here—dahlia (Dahlia cultivars*), foxglove (Digitalis* species*), avens (Geum quellyon), cosmos (Cosmos bipinnatus), slipperflower (Calceolaria integrifolia), sweet-alyssum (Lobularia maritima), and marigold (Tagetes* species*)—are all described in the Encyclopedia of Flowers, beginning on page 131.*

Keeping It All in Bloom

When she started the garden, Chris hired Royal Manaka, a care-taker of the neighborhood trees and shrubs, to water her newly planted garden when she was away. As the garden expanded, so did Manaka's responsibilities. In addition to watering the entire garden by hand, he be-gan to help Chris produce the large numbers of annuals needed to keep the garden blooming throughout the year.

Chris and Manaka plant the garden in two seasonal cycles. Flowers for winter and spring bloom are planted in October; summer-blooming flowers are planted anytime from March to May. To make sure they have all the plants they need when they need them, Chris and Manaka plan ahead.

Chris purchases transplants in six-packs, or she buys seeds if trans-plants are not available. To give the transplants some time to grow be-fore they are placed in the beds, she buys them at least a month in advance and transfers them from the six-packs to 4-inch pots. When planting day rolls around, the transplants have sturdy roots and are already in bloom.

Rather than going to the trouble to start the seeds in advance, Chris and Manaka sow them directly in the beds, but they plant extras in flats of soil as insurance. The extra plants, which Manaka grows in a small lath house in the side yard, are used to fill in bare spots in the directly seeded areas, or they are tucked in wherever a dash of color or new color combination is inspired.

In the last few years, Chris's eyesight has blurred, limiting her ability to work in the garden. Manaka now does most of the gardening, but Chris still designs the beds, arranging the flowers according to her new view of the landscape, which she describes with an optimism characteristic of those who love to garden. "I see my garden exactly like a Monet painting," she says, "and you can't do better than the impressionists."

Grooming the Garden

Dead-heading, pinching, and disbudding are the lightest and easiest gardening tasks and, therefore, are often given little priority. But dead-heading (removing the spent blossoms) makes plants more attractive and prolongs the blooming season; pinching keeps plants from sprawling, reducing the need for stakes; and disbudding is a special technique that increases the size of flowers. For a spectacular flower garden, all three jobs should be done regularly.

Dead-Heading
Although the seedheads of some varieties, such as the stonecrop Sedum *'Autumn Joy', are as decorative as*

the flowers, some perennials look ragged and unkempt if the blooms are allowed to remain on the plant after they go to seed. Also, for most plants (particularly annuals), seed-making slows or stops the production of new flowers. Dead-heading maintains the fresh look of spring and prolongs the blooming season and is easy: Just break or cut off the faded flowers and discard them. Weekly dead-heading is sufficient for most plants. Some perennials that produce many flowers each day— for example, Shasta daisy (Chrysanthemum maximum), daylily (Hemerocallis hybrids), and coreopsis (Coreopsis lanceolata and other species)—require dead-heading almost every day to look their best.

Pinching
Pinching is a very light form of pruning; only the very tips of the shoots are removed. To pinch a plant

grasp the very tip of each shoot between your thumb and forefinger and break it off with a downward twist. When pinched, a plant responds by branching, becoming more compact and floriferous.

Plants that tend to sprawl should be pinched once in the spring. Repeated pinchings can destroy the form of a plant, turning it into a topiary blob of color. Garden mums (varieties of Chrysanthemum × morifolium*) are an exception— they elongate so rapidly without branching that they need to be pinched several times during the*

growing season to keep them full and bushy.

Disbudding
Disbudding is the selective removal of flower buds, which allows the remaining flowers to grow larger. Disbudding is usually practiced only by commercial growers of chrysanthemums, long-stemmed roses, and carnations. Gardeners who want to grow large flowers need to disbud if they expect their plants to produce the huge blossoms found in commercial flower shops.

To disbud a plant, pinch out the lateral (side) flower buds

as soon as they become large enough to grasp between your fingers. To avoid tearing the stem, twist the buds as you snap them downward or use your fingernails to cut them as you twist.

An Outdoor Living Room

Designed as a place to stroll, sit, and relax, this Washington, D.C., backyard is a floriferous retreat that includes stunning flowers, winding paths, a splashing waterfall, a redwood deck, and a koi-filled pool.

In front of Mike and Elisabeth Zajic's colonial brick home in Washington, D.C., is a simple yard of turf, boxwood, yew, plum, and native dogwood. Except in spring, when the dogwood and plum are clothed in white and pale pink flowers, the yard is strict green formality. No one would ever guess that on the other side of the house, opposite this understated yard, is an enormous garden of flowers bursting with color, fragrance, and the sound of falling water.

The Zajics's flower garden is an extension of their home, an addition of garden rooms where they entertain friends or relax after a day's work. It is full of surprises—paths wind into areas unseen from the house, leading past beds of flowering shrubs, bulbs, perennials, and annuals to a small pavilion or vine house dripping with the blossoms of wisteria or to the centerpiece of the garden: a pond filled with golden koi, surrounded by the bold foliage and richly colored flowers of aquatic plants. Next to the pool is a larger pavilion sheltering a table and comfortable chairs.

By late April, Darwin hybrid tulips (Tulipa 'Jewel of Spring' and 'Ivory Floradale') are in full bloom above the pool.

From this vantage point, the Zajics and their guests enjoy the dramatic beauty of blue irises (*Iris versicolor*) and yellow irises (*I. pseudacorus*), both of which grow from submerged rhizomes; blue pickerelrush (*Pontederia cordata*); yellow waterpoppies (*Hydrocleys nymphoides*); floating lilac-blue waterhyacinths (*Eichhornia crassipes*); and a collection of water lilies (*Nymphaea* hybrids). Overhanging dogwood and willow branches enclose the space, and the splashing waterfall obscures sounds from the neighborhood, completing the feeling of enclosure and serenity.

Year-Round Appeal

Winters in Washington are relatively mild; the first frost usually does not strike before Thanksgiving and on many winter days the temperature reaches into the 50s or higher. Summers are warm and humid but comfortable in the shade. Whenever the weather beckons, the Zajics go out to the garden to enjoy the flowers that bloom in succession from early February to late November.

A native dogwood (Cornus species), floating like snow above the pavilion, combined with the yellow-flecked foliage of aucuba (Aucuba japonica) and red-budded hybrid azaleas (Rhododendron species), adds a Japanese touch to the garden.

Top: Grape hyacinth
(Muscari armeniacum).
Bottom left: Narcissus
(Narcissus actea).
Bottom right: Darwin
hybrid tulip (Tulipa
'Ivory Floradale').

The blooming season begins with bulbs—thousands of them. Many bulb enthusiasts grow early-, mid-, and late-season cultivars to create a succession of bloom from late winter through the spring, but Mike Zajic concentrates on early-season cultivars to maximize the late-winter impact. He prefers a dramatic, early-season display because it occurs at a time when the eye is starved for color; early bulbs are the first flowers to break winter's stranglehold. "Mid- and late-season bulbs aren't as necessary," he says, "because they appear when the flowering shrubs are at their peak." In his shady garden, early bulbs also naturalize more readily than later cultivars because they have time to grow in the winter sun before the overhead canopy fills in with leaves.

Top: Thick patches of grape hyacinth (Muscari armeniacum) *provide a compelling reason to leave the lawn mower in the shed. The golden tulips are* Tulipa *'Golden Apeldoorn'.*
Bottom: The hammock beckons above witchhazel (Hamamelis *'Arnold's Promise') and beds of daffodils* (Narcissus *'Fortune') and tulips* (Tulipa *'White Emperor').*

Mike Zajic grows bulbs everywhere in the garden. The lawn mower sits idle for most of the spring because the grass is filled with crocus (*Crocus* species and Dutch hybrids), squill (*Scilla siberica*), snowdrop (*Galanthus* species), grape hyacinth (*Muscari armeniacum*), daffodil (*Narcissus* hybrids), tulip (*Tulipa* hybrids), and netted iris (*Iris reticulata*). Some flowers are even scattered across the paths.

In the beds, the same bulbs bloom among early-flowering shrubs such as quince (*Chaenomeles speciosa*), witchhazel (*Hamamelis* 'Arnold's Promise'), and weeping forsythia (*Forsythia suspensa*). Golden yellow tulips (*Tulipa* 'Golden Apeldoorn') are scattered among the blue spires of ajuga (*Ajuga pyramidalis* 'Metallica Crispa').

Ten rhododendron cultivars thrive in the garden; the earliest bloomer is a vivid purple-pink PJM hybrid. Later, trusses of deep pink flowers cover *Rhododendron* 'Roseum Elegans', an easy cultivar recommended for beginners. *R.* 'Rosebud', a low, spreading Gable hybrid azalea, has purple-pink double blossoms that unfurl like rosebuds. The Kurume hybrid *R.* 'Coral Bells' bears a profusion of light pink flowers with darker pink throats. *R.* 'Gumpo', a Satsuki hybrid with pink to white flowers, is the last rhododendron to bloom, flowering in June with the native white-flowered species *R. maximum*.

As the trees leaf out, the light becomes more subdued, but the garden continues to bloom. In April, the bulbs in the turf give way to wild violets (*Viola odorata*), which fill the air with sweet fragrance and dapple the ground with a mixture of bluish white and violet flowers. In the beds, bronzy new growth and dangling chains of pink flowers appear on andromeda (*Pieris japonica*); yellow-tipped white flowers arch over

*This evergreen Kurume azalea (*Rhododendron 'Coral Bells'*) blooms pink but other Kurume hybrids bloom in shades of red or purple.*

the delicate foliage of Dutchman's-breeches (*Dicentra cucullaria*); and white blossoms are borne above the bold, grayish leaves of bloodroot (*Sanguinaria canadensis*). Some years, Zajic extends the bulb season with the golden and apricot Darwin hybrid tulips, a midseason type. Forget-me-not (*Myosotis scorpioides*) fills the spaces among the bulbs with a carpet of exquisite blue flowers. As tulips fade, Zajic hides their foliage by interplanting regal stands of foxglove (*Digitalis purpurea*).

Throughout the summer, over forty different species of perennial flowers play out their parts in the shaded beds. Luxuriant masses of hostas fill the shadiest areas and produce thin spikes of trumpet-shaped blue or fragrant white flowers. Zajic edged a stretch of bark-covered woodland path with golden variegated hosta (*Hosta fortunei* 'Aureo-marginata'); in the evening the effect of the glowing leaves is magical. Also along the path, lilyturf (*Liriope spicata*) and variegated lilyturf (*L. muscari* 'Variegata') retain patches of periwinkle (*Vinca minor*) with grassy leaves and dense spikes of violet flowers. Rose-pink flowers of fringed bleedingheart (*Dicentra eximia*) and common bleedingheart (*D. spectabilis*) bloom against a background of ferns.

Farther down the path, a border is dominated by the mauve blossoms of garden phlox (*Phlox paniculata*) and golden black-eyed-susan (*Rudbeckia fulgida* 'Goldsturm'). In another area, lilies thrive in deep soil and filtered shade. Tall bearded irises grace the beds with their upright stalks and fantastic variety of colors and patterns; many make their way to vases in the Zajics' home as well.

Top left: Forget-me-not (Myosotis scorpioides) *thrives in the partial shade and ample moisture of a woodland garden—cascading down steps, filling in among bulbs, and carpeting the soil below shrubs.*
Top right: Early-flowering tulip (Tulipa *'Apricot Beauty'*).

Paths wind throughout the garden, leading over bridges and under arbors. The indispensable nursery area lies hidden behind the fence.

Vines add another dimension to the Zajics' garden. A bridge over the stream is overhung with billowy masses of fragrant white clematis (*Clematis paniculata*). *Clematis × jackmanii* covers one of the back fences with rich purple flowers. Mike Zajic planted goldflame honeysuckle (*Lonicera heckrottii*) on a prominent part of the fence where he could enjoy its summer-long display of coral pink and yellow flowers. Although beautiful, the flowers of goldflame honeysuckle have no fragrance; on the other side of the fence, he grows Hall's honeysuckle (*L. japonica* 'Halliana') to perfume the air. In the back corner of the garden is a smaller pavilion, a vine house covered with Chinese wisteria (*Wisteria sinensis*). Deep green English ivy (*Hedera helix*) rambles through the twining wisteria, contrasting with the light green wisteria foliage and giving substance to the structure in winter when the wisteria is leafless.

Behind the fence in the nursery area—Zajic's secret garden—impatiens, coleus, caladium, and ornamental cabbages await their turn in the flower beds. Zajic purchases six packs of these annuals in May (sometimes June) and transplants them into the ground in a nursery bed. Then, late in August, he cuts the faded perennials back and transplants the annuals into the beds. These flowers last, with dead-heading and weekly fertilizing, until frost, thus completing a long and spectacular season of bloom.

*Not far from the splashing waterfall, a fountain of flowers is created by bridal-wreath (*Spiraea × vanhouttei). *Later in the spring the vine house will drip with the blossoms of Chinese wisteria (*Wisteria sinensis*).

Designed to invite exploration, the entire garden cannot be viewed from a single vantage point. From this spot at the rear of the house, the garden extends a particularly enchanting invitation.

The Making of the Garden

Eleven years ago, when the Zajics moved into their home, the back-yard was an uninviting expanse, heavily shaded by deciduous trees in summer, cold and stark in the winter. The house had been rented for years, and none of the renters had been inclined to invest their time in the garden. When he purchased the house, Zajic developed his design by first listing the features he desired: pond, pavilion, vine house, nursery, lawn, and flower beds.

He let the lay of the land determine the best placements for these features. The property slopes away from the house to a point along the fence toward the back of the garden. Thus, the most natural place for the pool was at the bottom of the slope. Next to the pool, opposite the waterfall, he placed the pavilion. The lawn stretches into the garden from the rear of the home, creating an open space that invites exploration of the path looping through the trees into unseen areas of the garden. Borders fell naturally into place around the perimeter of the property, next to the turf or along the path. A large central island bed was defined by the turf, pool, and paths. The nursery and compost pile were placed in a back corner of the property, behind a wooden fence.

Breaks in the overhead canopy of native trees allow spotlights of sun to pan across the flowers in changing patterns of light and shade.

Zajic has no formal background in design, but he has visited the famous gardens of England and Scotland, and he is interested in Japanese gardens. The design of his garden reflects his love of mystery and surprise. He abhors straight lines; a curving stone wall separates the turf from the flower border, and even the planters are round.

To Zajic, the tall columnar trunks and high, curving branches of the tulip-poplars, hickories, cherry, locust, and oak trees made the garden feel from the very beginning like a cathedral. He wanted to preserve this feeling but needed more light to sustain turf and flowers. After careful consideration he had a few of the trees removed by an arborist, creating breaks in the canopy to illuminate patches of turf, bed, and border. Two trees were removed from the nursery area, admitting several hours of late morning and midday sunlight.

Zajic constructed the garden himself, digging the hole for the pond, pouring concrete, and carrying 20 tons of quarry stone wheelbarrow by wheelbarrow from the driveway where it was dumped. Working evenings and weekends, it took him three years to build the pond, waterfall, bridge, pavilion, vine house, toolshed, and fences. He planted the garden as he went along, improving privacy with large shrubs, adding body to the winter landscape with evergreens, and "frosting the cake" with flowers.

Maintenance

With the changing displays of color, the pond of fish and flowers, a lawn to mow, and leaves to rake, the garden might have turned into a full-time job. Actually, Zajic maintains it with surprisingly little effort. Most summer evenings he does a little gardening after work, pinching, dead-heading, and pulling an occasional weed. On weekends, a half-day cleanup keeps the garden in top shape.

Zajic minimizes his maintenance chores by choosing plants that care for themselves. Because the bulbs are naturalized, annual planting, lifting, and storing is unnecessary. He grows only a few roses because they

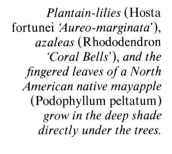

Plantain-lilies (Hosta fortunei *'Aureo-marginata'*), *azaleas* (Rhododendron *'Coral Bells'*), *and the fingered leaves of a North American native mayapple* (Podophyllum peltatum) *grow in the deep shade directly under the trees.*

require so much spraying. Black vine weevils chew the new leaves of
the rhododendrons, but Zajic protects the plants with a single spraying
in spring when the leaves appear.

Of all the plantings, the turf requires the most care, but Zajic keeps
that to a minimum by allowing a mixture of shade-tolerant grasses and
wildflowers to grow without the intervention of selective herbicides or
other weed killers. This meadowlike planting requires less fertilizer than
a grass-only lawn, so it grows slowly and doesn't need frequent mowing.
In the spring, the mowed area of the lawn is diminished by the sweeps of
bulbs, and when the violets are in bloom Zajic leaves his lawnmower idle
in the garage.

Nature meets most of the garden's need for water, supplying about
40 inches of rainfall each year. In times of drought, Zajic waters the
garden with hoses and sprinklers. He plans eventually to install an automatic irrigation system. He fertilizes the perennials and shrubs in the
spring, and gives the annuals a weekly dose to keep them blooming vigorously. During the summer, he composts garden debris in the nursery
area. In the fall, after the annuals have finished, he spreads a layer of
the compost (about an inch) over the flower beds.

*In the design of this garden,
privacy is a priority. With
a sunken area near the center
and tall shrubs around the
perimeter, Zajic created
a sense of seclusion
and enclosure in a suburban
backyard.*

Top left: Flowering dogwood
(Cornus florida).
Top right: Virginia bluebell
(Mertensia virginica).
Bottom left: Ostrich fern
(Matteuccia struthiopteris).
Bottom right: Hyacinth
(Hyacinthus orientalis).

In the first few years, Zajic was vigilant in removing weeds before they produced seeds (see Controlling Weeds, page 35). This persistence paid off; now weeds rarely appear in the garden. The occasional seed that finds its way into a bed is faced with formidable competition from the densely planted shrubs and flowers.

Although Zajic's garden is well-established, it still looks different each year. Zajic selects different annuals from year to year; his favorite display is an all-white composition of white caladium (*Caladium* × *hortulanum* 'Candidum'), impatiens, and pansies, accented with pink impatiens or coleus. As perennial plants and shrubs outgrow their places, he removes and divides or replaces them. Even the trees are replaced occasionally. Zajic loves the way the hanging branches of the willow tree swing in the breeze over the pond, but the space is too small for a full-size willow. Every four or five years, he cuts the willow down and replaces it with a two-year-old tree grown from a cutting in the nursery area.

Zajic's nursery area is an indispensable part of his garden and a key to his success. Ideally, every flower gardener should have a place for propagating plants, composting mulch, and holding annuals. With such a place, it's possible to create the changing displays that make the garden a spectacular place to visit in every season.

Choosing Bulbs for Your Garden

No matter where you live, you are sure to find bulbs that will naturalize—grow and bloom year after year without special care. Winter cold is one of the most critical factors that determines whether a bulb will naturalize, but summer heat, rainfall, and exposure to sun also play a part. Because winter cold is largely out of the control of the gardener, bulbs are classified according to their cold hardiness.

Hardy bulbs not only tolerate winter cold, they require it. True bulbs (composed of modified leaves) usually bloom in spring. Some of the most

bulbs must be exposed to a long period of cold weather in order to flower, they are not commonly grown in the warm southern areas of the United States. Some southern gardeners do grow them, treating them as annuals. However, purchasing new bulbs every year is very expensive.

Tender bulbs, which may be true bulbs or corms, tuberous roots, or rhizomes, won't withstand freezing temperatures for long and usually flower in summer. These include gladiolus, dahlia, canna, caladium, tuberous

To store tender bulbs, carefully dig them up after their leaves have been

store them at the same temperature as other bulbs. Plant the bulbs

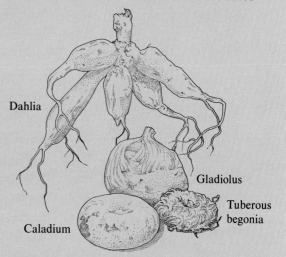

Dahlia

Gladiolus

Caladium

Tuberous begonia

nipped by the first frost. Shake off the soil clinging to the bulbs, and cut off the foliage to within 1 to 2 inches of the top of each bulb. Place the bulbs in a well-ventilated, shady place for a few days to allow them to dry. When they are dry, pack them in a net bag or other open container full of slightly moistened peat moss. Store them at 40° to 50° F. Check the bulbs every so often and moisten the peat moss if necessary—the bulbs should never dry out completely. Gladiolus and other corms should not be packed in peat; place them in cardboard boxes or paper bags and

back in the garden when the soil warms in spring.

Finding the right spot to store bulbs can be difficult; the basement may be too cold, the attic too warm. In marginally cold climates many tender bulbs will survive in the garden if covered by a thick layer of mulch. Using this technique, gardeners in the Washington, D.C., area grow dahlia, agapanthus, and canna without the effort of digging, storing, and replanting. The staff at a local garden center can help you decide which bulbs will thrive in your garden with little or no special care.

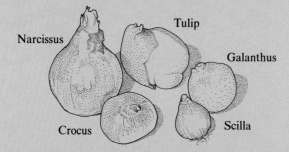

Narcissus

Tulip

Galanthus

Crocus

Scilla

popular bulbs—tulip, narcissus, crocus, galanthus, and scilla— are hardy bulbs. They are widely grown in northern areas of the United States, where they naturalize in lawns, beds, borders, and even in containers. Because these

begonia, and tuberose. They will naturalize in southern areas of the United States. Tender bulbs can also be grown for summer displays in cold-winter areas, providing they are lifted and stored for the winter.

AN EFFICIENT
FLOWER GARDEN

*When you have a small yard and little time
for gardening, good design and careful plant
selection are especially important. In this
lovely garden, sensible design and wise planting
conserve precious space, water, and time.*

In the evening, when Betty and Gerry Tietje come home from work, they are greeted by the beauty of their new garden. In the front yard bright beds of daylilies, coreopsis, sage, and lily-of-the-Nile highlight the house. In the backyard the fragrances of sweetshade and English lavender waft in through the windows, beckoning to them to come outdoors and enjoy the evening.

Less than two years ago the garden presented no such invitation. The yard had been landscaped with plants that were poorly suited to the site of their San Diego home. In front of the house a pair of enormous sweetgum trees (*Liquidambar styraciflua*) spread their greedy roots over the surface of the soil; what little grass would grow was so riddled with roots that it was nearly impossible to mow. A fence along the side of the house was overgrown with a rampant bougainvillea (*Bougainvillea* 'San Diego Red'). The Tietjes enjoyed the mantle of red bracts that covered the vine throughout the summer, but the thorny, fast-growing shoots made the narrow walkway between the fence and the home nearly impassible.

In the small backyard, bushes encroached upon a flat patch of grass. One of the largest plants there, mockorange (*Pittosporum tobira*) is a wonderful shrub for background plantings, but on this small suburban lot it overwhelmed the site. Another bougainvillea covered the chain-link back fence, blocking the view of the spectacular rocky canyon behind the house. Gerry Tietje had tried to grow a few azaleas, but they languished in the alkaline soil.

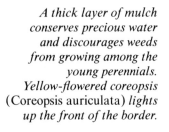

A thick layer of mulch conserves precious water and discourages weeds from growing among the young perennials. Yellow-flowered coreopsis (Coreopsis auriculata) lights up the front of the border.

When the Tietjes met Jim Stalsonburg, a garden designer and expert on low-maintenance, water-conserving landscapes, they had all but given up on their garden. They felt they had to move to a house with a larger garden before they could enjoy outdoor living. But the cost of a house in the San Diego area had quadrupled in the 15 years since they had made their purchase, and it seemed silly to move into a bigger home only a few years before their sons would be going off to college. "Would it be possible," they asked Stalsonburg, "to turn this yard into a place we could enjoy?"

Before Stalsonburg answered their question, he needed answers to a few of his own. By chatting with the Tietjes, he found out how they like to spend their time and got a feel for their preferences in garden architecture and plants.

He learned that, despite the Tietjes' desire for a floriferous garden, they really had little time for gardening. Both of them work, and what free time they have is devoted to their sons, to Boy Scout functions, and to church and social activities. Ideally, they wanted to use the garden as an extension of their home, to give their sons a place to bring friends, and to provide a space for parties. Originally from Wisconsin, they loved the soothing greenery of a shady woodland and delighted in the feel of a lawn underfoot. The mild, nearly tropical climate of San Diego stirred their hopes for year-round flower color.

Brick red daylilies (Hemerocallis hybrids) complement the warm tones of gloriosa daisies (Rudbeckia hirta 'Rustic Colors').

The sloping lawn and wrought-iron fence enclose the backyard without obstructing the view of the canyon.

For Stalsonburg, this presented quite a challenge. Time wasn't the Tietjes' only scarce commodity. Even without the overgrown plants, the lot was small. And water in San Diego is expensive and becomes more so all the time. Stalsonburg needed to create a comfortable garden that would make efficient use of the Tietjes' time, space, and water, while mimicking the lush woodlands of Wisconsin.

A Garden Remade

Before he began to design, Stalsonburg asked the Tietjes for complete freedom to remake the garden; none of the existing plantings could be sacrosanct. This idea met with some resistance; like most people, the Tietjes balked at the notion of chopping down mature plants. In the end they compromised, leaving two of five Italian cypresses in the side yard and allowing a healthy, well-placed purple leaf plum to remain in the corner of the backyard. After removing the rest of the overgrown plants, Stalsonburg brought in 30 cubic yards of topsoil. By mounding the imported soil for the beds and lawn, he relieved the flatness of the lot with some interesting topography and provided a much improved medium for the new plants.

A small bed in the corner of the backyard is simply planted with white lily-of-the-Nile (Agapanthus africanus) *and marguerite daisies* (Chrysanthemum frutescens).

To open up the backyard, Stalsonburg removed the chain-link fence and bougainvillea, thereby extending the yard to the rim of the canyon. To allow the Tietjes to enjoy the view without feeling dizzy, Stalsonburg created a slope from the patio up to the edge of the canyon—a rise of about 3 feet—topped with an open, wrought-iron fence. This slope screens the middle-ground view of the canyon rim, lifting the eye toward the horizon. Just outside the fence, he planted Aaron's-beard (*Hypericum calycinum*), a shrub with 3-foot arching branches covered in summer with bright yellow flowers, and trailing African daisy (*Osteospermum fruticosum*), a lilac-flowered bank cover. He also planted clumps of *Gaura lindheimeri*, a 3-foot willowy shrub with small pinkish white flowers that dance in the slightest breeze. The placement of these flowers where they can be seen through the fence creates a sense of enclosure without restricting the view.

Floral Efficiency

When choosing plants for this garden, Stalsonburg was careful to select those with a long season of bloom—or at least some kind of year-round interest. This is particularly important in a small garden, where every plant is on stage all of the time. Low maintenance, another important criterion, ruled out perennials that need to be staked, trained, and divided. Roses and other high-maintenance flowering shrubs were also out of the question.

Drought tolerance is Stalsonburg's specialty; he serves as a xeriscape consultant to the city of San Diego. Drought tolerant doesn't necessarily mean spiny cactus and drab clumps of gray foliage; some of the

Bright gloriosa daisies
(Rudbeckia hirta *'Rustic*
Colors') warm up this shady
spot. The seasonal color
provided by these and other
short-lived plants adds
variety to the beds from
year to year.

lushest plants in the Tietjes' garden can withstand dry spells surprisingly well. These plants thrive with ample water, but will endure drought once they are established. Stalsonburg used drought-tolerant species from all over the world in his design.

Along one side of the backyard he created a mounded bed punctuated by granite boulders. Daylilies (*Hemerocallis* hybrids) fill the front of the bed, producing yellow flowers from April to December. Behind the daylilies, lily-of-the-Nile (*Agapanthus* 'Peter Pan') sends up blue-flowered stalks among mixed African daisies (*Arctotis* hybrids). Society-garlic (*Tulbaghia violacea*) bears lavender flowers most of the year. The back of the bed is filled with the dense, fine foliage of yaupon (*Ilex vomitoria*) and grevillea (*Grevillea* 'Noellii'). Yaupon doesn't produce conspicuous flowers, but it is covered through the winter with tiny scarlet berries, which it bears without a pollinator. The pink and white flowers of grevillea are borne in clusters in early spring. On the other side of the wooden fence, the neighbor's bottlebrush and evergreen magnolia form a large-scale background for the Tietjes' flowers.

Adjacent to the patio outside the back door is a shady spot for moisture-loving plants. Babytears (*Soleirolia soleirolii*) creeps among the rocks in the low spot at the edge of the patio, thriving in the extra moisture that accumulates when the lawn is watered. A Japanese maple and birch give the Tietjes the woodland effect they love, shading *Rhododendron* 'Alaska', an azalea cultivar with pure white flowers that, along with the birch bark, glows luminously in the shade of the trees and

*Border penstemon
(Penstemon 'Cherry Glow')
blooms among upright
stems of lavender society-
garlic* (Tulbaghia violacea).

house. A pink-flowered Chinese-lantern (*Abutilon hybridum*) and ferns complete the lush woodland glade.

At the opposite end of the yard, Stalsonburg built a deck, covered at one end by an arbor. In an adjacent bed, sweetshade tree (*Hymenosporum flavum*) shades the deck and fills the air with honey-orange perfume. French lavender (*Lavandula dentata*), which blooms almost continually in this mild climate, adds another sweet fragrance. Society-garlic and daylilies link the bed to the planting across the lawn.

Stalsonburg designed these beds with room for the shrubs and perennials to expand. In the meantime, the Tietjes fill the spaces between the young plants with seasonal color. Multicolored border penstemon (*Penstemon × gloxinioides*), cream to red transvaal daisy (*Gerbera jamesonii*), violet-blue aster (*Aster × frikartii*), and blue swan-river daisy (*Brachycome iberidifolia*) are perennials, but the Tietjes grow them as annuals, pulling the plants when the flowers are finished. The true annuals in the beds include the luminous blue edging lobelia

The landscape designer softened the once-angular front yard with a curving path and rounded borders. A collection of flowering shrubs, perennials, and annuals ensures continuous color throughout the year.

(*Lobelia erinus* 'Crystal Palace'), scarlet sage (*Salvia splendens*), and soft salmon twinspur (*Diascia barberae* 'Ruby').

Climbing Color

Stalsonburg replaced the bougainvillea on the side fence with royal trumpet vine (*Distictis* 'Rivers'). Much more manageable than the bougainvillea but equally floriferous, this evergreen vine bears purple trumpet-shaped flowers with yellow throats. The foliage is attractive—deep green and glossy—and the shoots climb with tendrils. On the wall of the house opposite the trumpet vine is fragrant wonga-wonga vine (*Pandorea pandorana*). The wonga-wonga has shiny leaves and twining growth that, although fairly vigorous, is easy to keep in bounds. The flowers are light pink with brownish purple spots in the throat.

An Elegant Entryway

Stalsonburg completely reworked the front yard, removing the sweetgum trees and replacing the narrow L-shaped walkway that led from the top of the drive to the front door with an inviting brick-lined path curving up from the sidewalk.

Cigarplant (*Cuphea ignea*) edges a small bed along the front sidewalk. Throughout the summer and fall, it bears little tubular red flowers with dark bands near the white-tipped ends. Behind the cigarplants, lily-of-the-Nile (white-flowered *Agapanthus africanus* and dwarf,

blue-flowered *A.* 'Peter Pan') spread their strap-shaped leaves. The back of the bed is massed with yaupon and grevillea.

The large border in front of the home is filled with warm-colored flowers and backed by the neighbor's coral pink oleander (*Nerium oleander*). The rosy red flowers of autumn sage (*Salvia greggii*) appear in early summer and continue into fall. Several of these 4-foot-tall, gray-green shrubs are placed along the rear of the border, linking the planting to the bright hues of the overhanging oleander. Orchid rockrose (*Cistus × purpureus*), another grayish plant, bears papery reddish purple flowers with a red spot at the base of each petal. Blooming in spring, the orchid rockrose is a popular choice for drought-tolerant and seaside gardens. Coreopsis (*Coreopsis auriculata*) forms a 6-inch mat in front of the orchid rockrose; the Tietjes maintain its prolific display of yellow flowers from spring through fall by regularly removing the spent flower heads. (See Grooming the Garden, page 65.) Orange African daisies (*Arctotis* hybrids) also fill in the foreground. These plants bloom heavily from late fall to early summer, but scattered blossoms continue to open throughout the summer. Lily-of-the-Nile (*Agapanthus orientalis* 'Albus'), Marguerite daisies (*Chrysanthemum frutescens*), and society-garlic highlight the border with colorful flowers. Orange and rusty red gloriosa daisies (*Rudbeckia hirta* 'Rustic Colors') nestle among the granite boulders, which hide the tubes and emitters of the drip irrigation system.

Top left: Lavender-flowered aster (Aster × frikartii), *planted here with white-blooming lily-of-the-Nile* (Agapanthus africanus), *is one of the best perennials for western flower gardens. It blooms the year around in mild-winter areas if dead-headed regularly. Top right: Gloriosa daisy* (Rudbeckia hirta 'Rustic Colors').

Year-round interest, low maintenance, and long seasons of bloom make marguerite daisy *(Chrysanthemum frutescens),* star-cluster *(Pentas laceolata),* society-garlic *(Tulbaghia violacea),* astericus *(Astericus maritimus),* dwarf lily-of-the-Nile *(Agapanthus 'Peter Pan'),* lily-of-the-Nile *(Agapanthus africanus), and* daylily *(Hemerocallis hybrids) ideally suited to a small, easy-care flower garden.*

The Tietjes loved the birches around their home in Wisconsin, but the trees they planted around their San Diego home failed to thrive in the hot, dry conditions. To mimic the birches with a species better suited to the climate, Stalsonburg planted cajeput-trees (*Melaleuca quinque-nervia*), an Australian species with a weeping form and papery tan and white bark. Cajeput-trees grow quickly to about 25 feet, then slowly mature to 40 feet. The roots grow deep, allowing the tree to withstand drought and making it ideal for plantings near sidewalks and streets. In the spring and fall, cajeput-trees bear yellowish white flowers similar in form to the blossoms of bottlebrush (*Callistemon* species).

Automatic Irrigation

One of the greatest time savers in the Tietjes' garden is the automatic drip irrigation system. Controlled by a computerized clock, the system allows the Tietjes to set the exact number of minutes the water emitters should run and to establish a different program for each season. The amount of water each plant receives is controlled by the output of the emitter. Small plants are watered by a single emitter that releases ½ gallon per hour; a medium-size tree receives 5 gallons per hour from five 1-gallon emitters. Sprinklers, set to run at night when evaporation is low, are used to water the lawns.

Applying fertilizer with a drip irrigation system is easy. Once a month, Gerry Tietje pulls a small hose out of a sunken valve box and puts the end into a bucket of concentrated fertilizer solution. When he switches the system on, the fertilizer is siphoned from the bucket, mixed with the water in the correct proportion, and distributed to the plants.

Easy Maintenance

Once a week, the Tietjes' younger son mows and edges the lawns, a job that keeps him from his Boy Scout projects for no more than an hour. Once every three months or so, Gerry Tietje spends a day cutting back the permanent perennials to keep them fresh and floriferous, replacing the annual color, and attending to any adjustments needed in the irrigation system. The rest of the Tietjes' garden time is spent relaxing and entertaining their friends outdoors.

Mulches

Mulch, a layer of organic matter spread over the surface of the soil, helps plants in many ways. Mulch shades the soil, keeping it cool and moist, and this in turn allows roots to grow in the fertile top layers that are normally too warm and dry for roots. Mulch reduces evaporation, crusting, and erosion, and improves the fertility and structure of the soil. Mulch is also invaluable for weed control: It keeps most weeds from sprouting, and those that do grow are easier to pull.

Almost any organic matter can be used as a mulch; the kind you choose will depend primarily on what's available in your area. Some tried and true mulches are pine needles, homemade compost, and ground bark from fir, pine, or redwood trees. Leaves and lawn clippings make satisfactory mulches, provided they are composted first or spread thinly—no more than 2 inches deep. (If applied thick when fresh these materials may form an impermeable mat on the surface of the soil.) Also, do not use clippings if the grass has been sprayed recently with an herbicide. Some mulches to avoid are rice hulls, which are so light and fluffy that they are carried away by the wind, and peat moss, which mats together and repels water—if it doesn't blow away first. Avoid mulches that may contain weed seeds or other weed parts, such as clippings from a weedy lawn.

Apply mulch in the spring, when the soil is warm, after you've planted and after any early weeds have been removed. If you mulch too early, you will insulate the soil and it will not warm up as quickly. Spread the mulch 2 to 3 inches thick, tapering off toward the base of the plants. (A thick layer of mulch around the base of a plant encourages pests and diseases.) If the mulch has not been composted, lightly fertilize to compensate for the nitrogen used by the mulch as it decomposes. Add more mulch as necessary throughout the summer.

Mulches can also be used to insulate the soil to prevent frost heaving, the forcing of a plant from the ground when the soil alternately freezes and thaws. In the late fall, after the ground freezes, spread a thick layer of a fluffy material such as pine boughs or straw over the entire bed. The mulch will shade and insulate the soil, keeping it frozen until the spring thaw.

TINY TREASURES FROM MOUNTAINS AND MEADOWS

*What began as a means of coping with a rocky
site led to this gardener's discovery of the graceful
flowers from mountains and woodlands.
In her growing passion for rock gardening,
her vision of nature was transformed.*

When Catherine Hull first sank a shovel into the soil of her Massachusetts garden 10 years ago, she envisioned an English garden with a deep perennial border, but everywhere she dug, her spade struck bedrock. Although discouraged by the clank of shovel on stone, she soon found inspiration of another sort in a neighbor's garden. Her neighbor, whose house was built next to a cliff, had one of the most sensational gardens Hull had ever seen, filled with graceful plants and tiny flowers. Sitting in her friend's sewing room, she looked out of the second-story window and found herself face to face with a delicate orange alpine poppy (Papaver alpinum). *Although it was similar to the garden poppies she knew, to Hull this mountain species "had a kind of grace that only wild things have." Exploring the garden further, she discovered the shimmering apricot flowers of* Lewisia tweedii, *crimson blossoms on* Penstemon rupicola, *and sprays of white, pink, and yellow flowers borne above the silvery rosettes of saxifrages* (Saxifraga *species and hybrids*). *Thus was Catherine Hull initiated into rock gardening.*

Rock gardening, she found, is flower gardening on a lilliputian scale. The plants are rarely more than 10 inches tall, and most are diminutive tufts or flattened mats of fine foliage. The flowers are like jewels, enthralling in their simplicity, grace, and clear colors. Most of them are wild plants with proportions and colors untouched by the hands of hybridizers. Captured by the natural beauty of these tiny species, Hull began to view the traditional flowers she once loved as "rather heavy and overfed."

Creating a Rock Garden

Rocks, of course, are only one ingredient in rock gardening. The plants—mostly alpine species from high elevations—demand sharp drainage, air movement, cool temperatures, and plenty of moisture. Most species grow in full sun, but only if the air is cool. In New England, where summers are usually hot and humid, they need partial shade or a northern exposure. To create this environment, Hull had a great deal of work to do.

When Catherine and Harry Hull purchased their home on the north shore of Massachusetts, the garden had been neglected and was completely overgrown. Buried under the brambles were the bones of a woodland and rose garden designed in the 1930s by the noted landscape architect Fletcher Steele. A substantial level area was created between the house and the steep hillside by the use of deep stone retaining walls. Steele had used this level space for a wisteria arbor with stone pillars, two narrow lawns, a large stone-edged goldfish pool, and beyond, a row of dogwood trees. By the pool, a statue of Neptune set off the view of the bay, islands, and distant coastline. Over the years, however, many of these elements had been neglected or abandoned. The rhododendron and laurel became leggy and straggly in the depleted soil, wilting most of the

The lawn laps at the edges of the tufa island bed. Hull planned her garden so that the features of the original design—Chinese wisteria (Wisteria sinensis), *flowering dogwood* (Cornus florida), *and statuary— would frame the rock garden beds and borders.*

Top left: Alpines such as pink-flowering alyssum (Alyssum spinosum) *cascade down the dry stone retaining wall behind the long granite bed.*
Bottom left: Thrift (Armeria juniperfolia) *and lady fern* (Athyrium filix-femina).
Right: Carolina rhododendron (Rhododendron carolinianum) *blooms above a yellow mat of chrysogonum* (Chrysogonum virginianum). *The long-stalked, yellow flowers are hawkweed* (Hieracium maculatum).

summer; the clematis-and-rose border was diseased and unsightly; and the woodland garden down the hill was a jungle of bramble, poison ivy, brush, and twisted trees.

Several years of chopping, sawing, and digging cleared the way for well-behaved conifers and beds of alpines. Unlike some rock gardeners, whose perspective shortens to match the scale of their plants, Hull managed to create a garden that appeals to anyone, not just to other enthusiasts of alpines. Reinforcing the lines of the existing walls, pool, and lawn, she constructed raised beds for her treasured plants. To keep the beds from appearing to float, she planted each with a backbone of dwarf boxwood, conifers, and rhododendrons. In addition to providing a backdrop for the tiny specimens, these plants serve as visual stepping-stones to the larger trees and shrubs in the garden, linking the rock-garden beds to the rest of the landscape.

Still, each bed is a horticultural zoo. Rock gardening brings out a gardener's urge to acquire and experiment, to collect. This works in

Top left: Avens (Geum rivale).
Top right: Jonquil (Narcissus jonquilla).
Bottom left: Townsendia hirsuta.
Bottom right: Ring bellflower (Symphyandra wanneri) *and Rue anemone* (Anemonella thalictroides).

opposition to the principal rule of flower gardening, which dictates that masses of color are much more effective than spotty assortments of single specimens. But a rock garden serves a different purpose; the viewer moves more slowly and looks more closely. When Hull is visited by other collectors, she says they "can spend an hour going 10 yards." At this pace and proximity, the viewer can appreciate details of color and texture that wouldn't be noticed on a larger scale.

Another old axiom, that rock gardens should not be placed in view of the house, went right out Hull's window. The idea dates from the days of large formal gardens, when rock gardens were placed to be discovered by accident at the end of a long, winding trek across an estate filled with beds and borders of full-size garden flowers. Given the context, this rule made sense; a bed of dwarf geraniums and clumping saxifrages would never be noticed among towering foxgloves and sprawling baby's-breath. But in Hull's garden, the rock garden plants do not compete for attention. They are the premier attraction.

Stony Beds of Gravel and Grit

The centerpiece of the garden is a 50-foot-long mound placed prominently below the terrace and rear windows of the house. The front of the bed borders a small lawn; the back extends onto the top of a retaining wall. Most of the rocks on the property are natural granite outcroppings and stones, but in this bed Hull used tufa, a pale gray mineral quarried from a New York river gorge. Tufa is light and porous, and its surface invites exploration by tiny roots. Although expensive and difficult to obtain, Hull and other rock gardeners are devoted to tufa because so many alpine plants thrive in it. The pores hold plenty of water and air, and evaporation from the pocked surface helps keep the roots cool.

The tufa bed contains hundreds of species that glitter with exquisite flowers in April, May, and June. *Erigeron compositus* var. *discoideus,* a North American native with mauve flowers like small asters, combines wonderfully with the gorgeous blue trumpets of spring gentian (*Gentiana acaulis*). *Gentiana verna,* also commonly called spring gentian, has clear blue flowers that open flat. Columbines—not the tall garden forms native to woodlands and meadows, but the dwarf species that live on

Perennial candytuft (Iberis sempervirens) *brightens the tufa bed with dazzling white flowers. Near the center of the photograph is yellow alyssum* (Alyssum ovirense).

To fully appreciate a rock garden, it is best to get down and look closely at the specimens.
Top: Spring gentian (Gentiana acaulis).
Bottom: Columbine (Aquilegia saximontana).

cliffs and scree—include *Aquilegia akitensis, A. bertonlonii,* and *A. saximontana,* which all flourish in the rocky soil, forming dense clumps topped with blue and white flowers. One of Hull's favorite combinations is that of *Erinus alpinus* and dwarf dianthus (*Dianthus* species). *Erinus alpinus* makes a mound of bright green, sharply toothed leaves and 3- to 4-inch stems bearing rosy flowers. The dianthus is grown from seed and is quite variable, producing an assortment of pinks ranging from white to crimson.

Several drabas, compact plants with hairy leaves and usually with clear yellow flowers, bloom in the early spring. *Draba polytricha* is one of the earliest, bearing shining yellow flowers above a tight gray-green

Top left: Pink alyssum
(Alyssum spinosum).
Top right: Rockcress
(Arabis soyeri).
Bottom: Mossy saxifrage
(Saxifraga rosacea
'Sir Douglas Haig').

tuft. *Draba sibirica* has a more open habit than the others, with trailing stems and golden flowers on stalks up to 6 inches tall. *Draba dedeana* is one of the loveliest, with compact heads of pure white flowers borne 1 or 2 inches above a gray-green cushion of leaves.

The rockcress crucifers (*Arabis* species) also have compact cushions of foliage and white blossoms. *Arabis androsacea* has attractive flowers, but its silvery silken foliage is the main appeal. *Arabis ferdinandicoburgi* 'Variegata' is a dainty plant with large blossoms and compact clusters of leaves marked with yellow patterns.

Without saxifrages (*Saxifraga* species), an ever-popular genus with a name that means rock-splitting, Catherine Hull wouldn't consider her garden complete. From the Euaizoonia group—the encrusted saxifrages (named for the white edging on the leaves)—she grows the fine white-flowered hybrid, *Saxifraga × macnabiana*.

Top: Phlox (Phlox borealis). *Bottom left: Dwarf delphinium* (Delphinium tricorne). *Bottom right: Alyssum* (Alyssum ovirense).

Another group, the Kabschia saxifrages (also listed as Porophyllum saxifrages), have tight rosettes of fine foliage covered at the first hint of spring by rounded white, pink, or yellow flowers. Hull's collection includes several of the 30-odd species and a few of the hundreds of forms and hybrids of this attractive group. Mossy saxifrages, a group of species with flat, finely cut foliage, thrive in the shadier spots, bearing white, pink, or crimson flowers. *Saxifraga* 'Apple Blossom', a white form, and *S.* 'Sir Douglas Haig', a crimson hybrid, are but two of the more popular mossy saxifrages that bloom in her garden.

Hull also grows primroses (*Primula* species), another magnificent and varied genus. The *Primula auricula* of the Pyrenees and the Alps, one of the more dependable species, has fragrant, clear yellow flowers. *Primula hirsuta* (frequently listed as *P. rubra*) bears rose flowers with white centers. *Primula marginata* has lovely pale lavender or lilac

Top left: Lewisia
(Lewisia cotyledon).
Top right: Forget-me-not
(Myosotis alpestris).
Bottom: Azalea (Rhodo-
dendron *species*) *and
lily-of-the-valley*
(Convallaria majalis).

flowers and distinctive leaves edged with white, held at the ends of
branched, woody stems. Garden hybrid primroses are more widely
available than these species, but their enlarged size makes them too
bulky for the rock garden.

   In Hull's two raised granite beds, filled with outcroppings and
boulders of native granite, she grows some of her favorite plants for the
scree: species of *Lewisia, Penstemon, Draba,* and *Geranium,* to name
just a few. Also in the granite beds, clusters of tiny, fragrant white stars
top the twigs of garland flower (*Daphne alpina*) in spring. Later, showy
red berries are held against the gray-green leaves. In summer, the
lavender umbels of *Thalictrum kiusianum* top delicate feathery foliage.
Another lavender-flowered plant, *Ptilotrichum spinosum,* forms a
bushy, 12-inch globe of narrow-leaved foliage. A cascading species,
Dalmatian bellflower (*Campanula portenschlagiana*), has neat hanging

tufts of shiny green leaves and light violet bells. Many of these rock garden plants are dwarf species or cultivars of plants commonly used in full-size gardens. Another thing they have in common is a neat, restrained growth habit—invasive plants have no place in a rock garden.

Soil is critical to successful rock gardening. Hull mixes her own, blending equal portions of leaf mold, compost, and minerals (usually a mixture of sand and gravel). A nursery area at the side of the house contains eight bins for compost; Hull's compost contains manure from a local stable, washed seaweed, shredded oak leaves, and other organic debris raked from the garden and fed through a shredder.

Obtaining Rock Garden Plants

If you drive down to the local garden center and ask to see the alpine plants, chances are you won't get much more than a blank look; most nurseries don't carry them. Hull obtains plants through the mail from specialty nurseries, many of them located in the western United States, or through her membership in the American Rock Garden Society (ARGS) in Darien, Connecticut.

For many garden designers a pool or fountain is an essential feature in a garden. This pool is one of the original parts of the garden designed by Fletcher Steele. In past years, Hull has grown waterlilies and other flowering aquatic plants. Now she simply allows the pool to reflect the colors of the flowers along its edges.

Each year members of the ARGS collect, clean, and label seeds from the plants in their gardens and send them to the ARGS offices. Volunteers produce a list of all the seeds received. Included are the plant names and a code identifying the person who contributed the seeds. When Hull receives the list, she considers both the species and the source—some gardeners are better at plant identification than others—before making her selections. She rushes her requests to the ARGS, where the orders are filled on a first-come, first-served basis. Members may request up to 40 species; those who have donated seeds get 10 species free.

Hull also collects plants in the wild, but strictly in areas where it is permitted, and only with great care. Like all lovers of wild plants, she's a conservationist and views her efforts and those of other knowledgeable rock gardeners as a way to protect and increase endangered species. She'll only take a plant from a large, healthy colony, and then only if she's sure she can get it home safe and sound. Once the plants are established in her yard, she propagates and distributes them to other gardeners, thereby extending the species and reducing the need for further collection.

Seeds from the American Rock Garden Society are Hull's main source of plants for the garden. She raises the young plants in well-ventilated benches in the shade of tall trees.

Hull and her friends also trade plants, swapping sprigs and seedlings when they visit each other's gardens. Visitors to Hull's garden often return home with a clutch of tiny pots from her nursery. Rock gardeners become experts in packing and tranporting their little plants.

A garden planted in this way contains hundreds of stories, and is filled with the personalities of friends and memories of travels. Hull's interest in plants has led her to England, Scotland, Switzerland, Austria, Czechoslovakia, Korea, and Nepal, in addition to the mountains of the western United States. The plants in her garden are associated with a friend from the rock garden society, a neighbor down the road, or a botanical garden—associations that integrate her garden with her life.

Correcting Soil pH

The pH of a soil—its acidity or alkalinity—has a great effect on the health of plants. The pH scale ranges from 0 to 14; pH 7 is neutral. At pH levels below 7, the soil is acid; levels above 7 are alkaline. Most plants grow best in neutral or slightly acid soils (pH 5.5 to 7.0), but acid-loving plants such as azaleas, rhododendrons, and camellias don't grow well unless the pH is in the range of 4.0 to 5.5.

Although soil pH influences a number of processes in the soil, it affects garden plants mainly by decreasing or increasing their ability to absorb nutrients from the soil. Plants growing in soil that is too alkaline may be deficient in iron, manganese, phosphorus, or zinc, even if sufficient quantities of these nutrients are present. Interveinal chlorosis, a condition in which yellow areas appear between the veins of new leaves, is a common problem in soils where iron and manganese are unavailable to plants

because of too much alkalinity.

If the soil is too acid, on the other hand, phosphorus, calcium, magnesium, and other nutrients are less available to plants, resulting in stunt-

ing and poor root growth. To make matters worse, acid soils may contain toxic levels of manganese and aluminum—nutrients that become more available as the pH decreases.

Fortunately, you can easily adjust the pH of your soil. If you suspect that the soil is too acid or too alkaline, have it

tested by a laboratory or test it yourself with one of the kits available at garden centers. If the soil is too acid, a common condition in the eastern United States, add dolomitic lime. In addition to

raising the pH, dolomitic lime supplies calcium and magnesium, nutrients in short supply in acid soils. Fertilizing with nitrogen fertilizers containing nitrate (rather than ammonium or urea) will also raise the pH.

The clay soils of the western United States are often too alkaline, particularly for acid-loving

plants. To acidify these soils, apply soil sulfur, aluminum sulfate, or ferrous sulfate. Applying acidifying mulches such as conifer needles will also help. Maintain the acidity by fertilizing with nitrogen fertilizers containing urea or ammonium. These are usually labeled specifically for acid-loving plants.

The amount of sulfur or lime you'll need to add depends on the type of soil you have and how much you want to change the pH. If you have your soil tested professionally, the report will say how much to add. Also, the staff at a local garden center can usually recommend soil treatments that are tailored for your area.

Once the soil pH is in the proper range, you can be sure that the fertilizers you apply will be available to the plants. To learn more about fertilizing flowers, see Fertilizing the Garden on page 23.

EVERLASTING
COLOR

*In all but the mildest climates, flowers disappear
for the winter. This gardener continues to
enjoy the colors of summer, even when the ground
is frozen, in the arrangements she
creates with flowers she grows and dries.*

Early summer is without a doubt the richest season for flower color. Perennials, carefully trained and supported, reward the gardener's efforts with profuse bloom. Annuals, perhaps started from seed in a window, become so covered with blossoms that it's hard to spot the leaves. As summer cools into fall, the bright flower colors fade into memory, and the garden takes on the muted hues of the dormant plants.

But for Marie Torrens, the summer blooming season is just the beginning. During the summer, she harvests flowers, seeds, and fruits from her Albuquerque garden and hangs them up to dry. In winter, when her garden is faded and dormant, she continues to enjoy all the colors of summer, creating beautiful wreaths, baskets, and other fanciful arrangements with the dried flowers.

Rather than maintaining a separate, out-of-the-way cutting garden, Torrens plants the flowers she uses for arrangements among the flowering trees, shrubs, perennials, annuals, and bulbs in her spectacular backyard garden. In the early spring, the branches of forsythia (*Forsythia × intermedia*) are golden wands of color. Shortly after the buds burst open on the forsythia, bridalwreath spiraea (*Spiraea prunifolia*) becomes wreathed in pure white double flowers, and the branches of *Spiraea* 'Simplicity' and *Philadelphus × virginalis* 'Minnesota Snowflake' are clothed in clusters of single white blossoms.

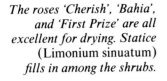

The roses 'Cherish', 'Bahia', and 'First Prize' are all excellent for drying. Statice (Limonium sinuatum) fills in among the shrubs.

'Color Magic' is one of the best hybrid tea roses. This popular variety is disease resistant but needs winter protection in cold climates.

On a larger scale, flowering and fruiting cherry (*Prunus* species), crab apple (*Malus* species), redbud (*Cercis* species), and Washington thorn (*Crataegus phaenopyrum*) spread flower-laden limbs against the deep blue spring sky.

Clumps of daffodil and crocus press up out of the soil under the flowering trees. *Narcissus* 'February Gold', a hybrid daffodil developed from *N. cyclamineus,* is usually the first to open. The petals of this flower bend backward from the short, wavy-edged cups. Torrens grows only bulbs that naturalize, but she feeds them heavily and is rewarded with prolific bloom. Recently she counted 900 blossoms in a clump originally started with just a few bulbs.

In the summer, scores of roses unfurl their buds in the beds and borders. Roses grow to perfection in the bright sunlight and dry air of the high desert. The plants are free of blackspot and rarely mildew. Torrens's favorite hybrid tea rose, 'Color Magic', opens from coral pink buds into 6-inch multicolored blossoms. When fully open, the flowers look hand-painted; strokes of deep coral define the edges of the petals, and dabs of yellow highlight the centers of the blossoms. For many years, this has been one of the best of the show roses.

Most varieties of Rosa rugosa *have flowers with a single whorl of petals, although hybrids with double flowers are also available.*

Torrens keeps in step with horticultural fashion by growing shrub roses. The increasing popularity of the shrub rose is well-deserved: A varied group consisting mostly of species roses and natural hybrids, they are tough plants that require minimal pruning and are generally disease resistant. Many have flowers with a single row of five petals, giving them a simple, delicate form. Some shrub roses only bloom once in the spring or summer, but many have a second, lesser bloom in the fall, and a few bloom throughout the growing season. Most have handsome habits and produce a decorative bonus of colorful hips or seedpods in the fall that last into the winter.

The rugosa rose (*Rosa rugosa*) is probably the best-known species in this group. Very hardy, it grows up to 6 feet tall with a 4-foot spread. Fragrant, single flowers bloom from spring to fall, followed by large, brilliant red hips. 'Delicata', a hybrid rugosa, graces Torrens's garden with pink flowers throughout the summer. Although she has given it plenty of room to grow, this variety is also ideal for small gardens, as it is easily kept to about 3 feet tall.

Austrian copper rose (*Rosa foetida bicolor*) bears single blooms, brilliant red-orange on the upper surface, yellow on the reverse. Grown since the sixteenth century, this variety originated as a sport (mutation) of Austrian yellow rose (*Rosa foetida*), which has pure yellow flowers and is also an excellent shrub rose. 'Thérèse Bugnet', a hybrid rugosa shrub that grows up to 6 feet tall, has light green foliage and double flowers that appear in cycles throughout the growing season. The red flowers turn pink and finally lighten to pale pink as they age, and they carry a delightfully spicy scent.

Statice (Limonium sinuatum), *available in a variety of colors, is a staple in dried flower arrangements. In the foreground is* L. sinuatum *'Apricot B. Shades', with blossoms of the hybrid tea rose 'First Prize' emerging from the center. Delicate sea-lavender* (Limonium latifolium) *creates a cloud of bloom in the background.*

Everlasting Color

Among these plants are the materials of Torrens's art. Strawflowers (*Helichrysum* hybrids) raise their yellow, pink, red, and multicolored heads to the sun; clouds of sea-lavender (*Limonium latifolium*) float above the soil like morning mist; and the orange pinecone heads of globe-amaranth (*Gomphrena haageana*) glow atop gray-green foliage.

Statice (*Limonium* species) is a staple plant in the florist trade; each year Torrens grows 70 to 80 plants in a rainbow of species and colors. Sea-lavender (*Limonium latifolium*), a species that resembles baby's-breath (*Gypsophila* species), transforms a bed of roses into a Valentine's Day bouquet. *Limonium bellidifolium* (also listed as *L. caspia*) 'Filligree', a popular cultivar with airy sprays of intricate purple-blue flowers, is a perennial often treated as a half-hardy annual, but Torrens grows it against a west-facing wall, where it survives the occasional 0° F winter temperatures without damage. German statice (*Goniolimon tartaricum,* often listed as *Limonium tartarica*), a pure white perennial species that makes a wonderful background and filler material in her wreaths, also grows in the west-facing bed, where it blooms very early. To get the whitest color, Torrens cuts the flowers when they are fully open. Annual statice (*Limonium sinuatum*) is available in a variety of colors; her favorites are 'American Beauty Pink', 'Apricot B. Shades', and 'Market Blue'. The yellow varieties aren't as clear as she'd like, but she finds 'Gold Coast' acceptable.

A rich assortment of new strawflowers (*Helichrysum* species) has breathed life into this familiar genus. *Helichrysum bracteatum* 'Bright Bikini Mixed' is a dwarf form ideal for bedding plants. It produces flowers in eight combinations of yellow, pink, red, white, and orange. To make sure she gets all the colors she needs for her wreaths, Torrens also orders the seeds by color; nearly a dozen different colors and shades are listed in seed catalogs.

Globe-amaranth (*Gomphrena globosa*), an annual, is also ideal for dried flower arrangements. Torrens especially likes the bright red flowers

Bottom left: Another statice, Limonium sinuatum *'Market Blue'. Bottom right: Perennial statice (*L. bellidifolium *'Filigree').*

and long stems of *Gomphrena* 'Strawberry Fields', available from Park Seeds. Another Park cultivar, *Gomphrena* 'Buddy', is popular for border plantings. The plants are compact, 6 to 8 inches tall, and create a tremendous mass of long-lasting purple flowers.

Winged everlasting (*Ammobium alatum* 'Grandiflora') has glistening silvery white petals with a golden center. The long stems are ideal for flower arranging but make the plant too ungainly for the flower border. Torrens grows it in the vegetable patch.

Top: Globe-amaranth (Gomphrena globosa *'Strawberry Fields').* *Bottom left: Strawflower* (Helichrysum bracteatum *'Bright Bikini Mixed').* *Bottom right: Winged everlasting* (Ammobium alatum *'Grandiflora').*

*Top left: The floribunda
rose 'Cherish' is
particularly good for drying.
Bottom left: English lavender
(Lavandula angustifolia)
is the species used for
perfumes and sachets.
'Munstead', pictured here,
is the most popular
dwarf form.*

Buds from the rosebushes appear in the wreaths as well. Most flowers are either too large or too delicate for drying, but the buds of small-flowered floribundas are ideal. Torrens picks them when they are just beginning to open and hangs them upside down to dry naturally. Some colors dry better than others. Reds blacken, and whites become muddy, but pink, coral, and orange flowers dry beautifully. Torrens is particularly enamored with 'Cherish', a pink cultivar, and has been very successful with the coral 'Bahia' and 'Cathedral', and the orange 'Marina'.

The perennial border is a rich source of flowers for arrangements. French lavender (*Lavandula dentata*) and dwarf English lavender (*L. angustifolia* 'Munstead') contribute foliage and flowers to wreaths and sachets. Pale yellow yarrow (*Achillea* 'Moonshine') is one of the first yarrows to bloom, flowering in late May in the foreground of the border. Double-flowered cultivars of larkspur (*Consolida ambigua*) soften the border and hold their color well when dried. The blue, white, purple, and lavender sprays of 'Pacific Giant' and 'Connecticut Yankee'

Flat-topped yarrow (Achillea *'Moonshine' and* A. *'Coronation Gold') blends well with McKana columbine* (Aquilegia *hybrids). Hybrid speedwell* (Veronica *'Blue Charm') provides a deep, cool background.*

hybrid delphiniums (*Delphinium* hybrids) also dry well when harvested early and hung upside down. Feverfew (*Chrysanthemum parthenium*) self-sows aggressively, but this Victorian favorite is ideal for old-fashioned arrangements. The globular flowers of pompom chrysanthemums (*Chrysanthemum × morifolium*) hold their petals nicely when dry. Dwarf goldenrod (*Solidago* species) dries well if the flowers are harvested before they open fully.

Pods, Hips, and Leaves

The large succulent flowers of tulips, irises, and peonies are not good subjects for drying, but their seedpods are interesting additions to arrangements. Like other flower gardeners, Torrens tries not to let her flowers go to seed, but if she doesn't dead-head them in time, she lets the pods develop. Tulip pods are light beige teardrops. The pods of spuria iris (*Iris spuria*) are soft tan, long, and flared at one end. Peonies (*Paeonia* species) have wonderful four-segmented pods that open like small flowers. Poppy seed capsules are classic subjects for winter

Top left: The flowers and foliage of crapemyrtle (Lagerstroemia indica *'Watermelon Red'*) *reflect the warm tones of common zinnia* (Zinnia elegans *'Pulchino'*). *Top right: Globethistle* (Echinops humilis *'Taplow Blue'*). *Bottom: Rose hips of* Rosa rubrifolia.

arrangements; the best are the ones with large seedpods, sold by the seed companies under such names as 'Gigantic Podded Mixed', but Torrens also finds uses for the smaller capsules of the Shirley poppy (*Papaver rhoeas*).

Torrens doesn't overlook her trees and shrubs when gathering materials. The small flat pods of redbud (*Cercis canadensis*) hold together well when dried. Rose hips accent the wreaths with bright shining red. 'Prairie Princess', a shrub rose, has lovely pink blooms in the spring, and the large, cranberry hips dry without crinkling. The fruit of 'Delicata' and *Rosa glauca* are also ideal for drying. The seedpods of crapemyrtle (*Lagerstroemia indica*) are ready for harvest in winter after they have opened.

The silvery leaves of silver spreader (*Artemisia caucasica*) and the woolly white foliage of dusty-miller (*Senecio cineraria*) set off the bright colors in Torrens's flower beds; when dried, the foliage has the same effect in the wreaths. The variegated sages (*Salvia officinalis* 'Tricolor') produce wonderful flowers in the garden, and their multicolored foliage combines with garlic, sage, shallots, red chiles, oregano, and lemon-thyme to make a lovely wreath for the kitchen.

Along the back border, the trumpets of white Easter lilies (Lilium longiflorum) *and golden enchantment lilies* (Lilium 'Matador') *are set off by silver spreader* (Artemisia caucasica).

A Homegrown Business

Ten years ago when Marie Torrens began arranging dried flowers, she was already an accomplished gardener and arranger of cut flowers. She had served as a master judge at flower shows for 13 years and had won many awards for her own designs. Until a friend suggested that they create dried flower arrangements for sale, her work with flowers had been strictly for pleasure.

Torrens spent several months creating wreaths and bouquets of dried flowers, corn, chiles, and other plant materials. She and her friend sent out over 600 invitations to the sale, enlisted the help of friends to host the party, hung the arrangements in Torrens's house, and hoped that people would come. When the doors opened on the day of the show, hundreds of people flooded into Torrens's home, and in less than an hour all of the arrangements had been sold.

Torrens's biggest challenge in creating her arrangements was in getting the flowers. The strawflowers she was able to find were all the same size, usually in poor condition, and available in only two colors:

In addition to flowers from her garden (top), Torrens's wreaths may contain chiles, garlic, corn, and dried seed-heads collected in the wild (bottom).

yellow and rust. She liked to work with blossoms on their own stems, but most of the commercially prepared flowers were on wire. The only statice she could find was purple, but she knew that white, pink, apricot, and yellow cultivars had been developed. Like vegetable gardeners who give up on mediocre market produce to grow their own delicious crops, Torrens started growing her own flowers, working them in among the other flowers in her garden and drying them in the garage and on the porch.

Torrens obtains flower seeds from popular mail-order seed companies, which in recent years have dramatically expanded their offerings of flowers for dried arrangements. She used to start the seeds herself in a hot frame, but she now prefers to employ a friend in the nursery business to start them for her in his greenhouse. In late spring, when the seedlings are ready, she transplants them into the garden.

Never-Ending Discovery

Flower arranging adds another dimension to Torrens's gardening, making it a learning experience even after 30 years of practice. "I hate to sell them," she says of her arrangements. "Every one I make is better than the one before." Part of the fun is experimentation. She's continually finding new flowers to dry, and she has been successful with plants reputed to dry poorly.

Best of all, she loves to dispel the widely held notion that the colors of dried flowers are muted and drab. Visitors to her home are astounded by the brilliant colors in her wreaths. When kept out of bright sunlight, the flowers last and last, extending the colors of a single summer into years of joy.

Drying Flowers

In the arid Southwest, creating arrangements of dried flowers is simple. Many flowers can be arranged when fresh and allowed to dry in place. In humid regions, however, the flowers become moldy or rotten if left to dry on their own. To keep this from happening, you can dry the flowers with heated air or use a dessicant (drying agent) such as silica gel.

Warm-Air Drying
Tie the flowers in loose bunches. A slip knot in the center of a 2- or 3-foot piece of twine can be used to tie the stems together, and it can be tightened as the stems dry and shrink. Knot the ends of the twine and hang the bunch in a dark, well-ventilated area. If the humidity is high, or if the air is cool, direct a current of warm air over the flowers with a fan heater. Place the heater at least 5 feet from the flowers; the air on the flowers should

be warm, not hot. To keep the area from over-heating, it's a good idea

to use a timer to turn the heater off and on.

A garden shed is an excellent place to dry flowers. If the shed is warmed by the sun, you won't need to use a

heater. Even the fan may be unnecessary if the shed is well ventilated. The airing cupboards built into the kitchens of older homes and apartments are also ideal for drying small quantities of flowers.

Dessicants
Some flowers, such as roses, lilies, and hydrangeas, need to be supported while they are drying to keep the petals from crinkling or rolling. Traditionally, flowers are buried in sand, but unless the sand has coarse, rounded grains, it can damage the petals. The best drying agent is silica gel, a sandlike material available from florist supply shops. Be sure to use a product intended for flowers; the silica gel sold for drying photographic and other equipment is too coarse.

Generally, the flower is removed from the stem before drying. The stem may be dried separately and glued back on the

flower, but most florists insert a piece of wire into the back of the flower and wrap it with stem tape. The flower may be buried face down or face up in the silica gel. Daisies and other open flowers with strong petals can be placed face down, but complex flowers like dahlias should be dried face up.

Techniques for burying the flowers vary, but in most cases you place the blooms on a layer of silica gel in the bottom of a box or deep tray and carefully pour gel over them, arranging the petals with a small paintbrush. The flowers should be completely covered. Tap the sides of the box to make the gel settle into any air pockets, and enclose the box in a plastic bag to keep the gel from absorbing moisture from the air. Most flowers are ready in three or four days, but large, fleshy specimens can easily take up to three weeks to dry.

FILLING YOUR GARDEN WITH FLOWERS

Exploring the world of plants is one of the great pleasures of gardening. A visit to the demonstration garden of your local nursery can provide a wealth of ideas.

Like the people who created the gardens described in the previous chapters, you can obtain plants for your garden from a variety of sources. In most cases, however, the best source of plants is your local nursery. In addition to selling plants and seeds, an increasing number of these nurseries have demonstration gardens where you can stroll among beds of mature plants in full bloom.

A visit to a demonstration garden is similar to a tour of a home garden. A demonstration garden reflects the personality of its designer and can be a wonderful source of inspiration and gardening ideas. A fine example of this type of demonstration garden is found at Gilberg Perennial Farms, located outside St. Louis, Missouri. This nursery offers visitors a chance to see perennials growing in a variety of conditions—from sun to shade, dry soil to small ponds. "Our goal is to demonstrate some of the possibilities of gardening with perennials," says Doug Gilberg, who designs the gardens with his wife, Cindy. What we've created here is essentially the same thing you would do in a home garden." Apparently, many of their customers agree, for the ideas in the Gilbergs' gardens are echoed in home gardens throughout the St. Louis area. In some cases, the Gilbergs' customers have duplicated entire beds from the nursery in their own yards.

More than just a showcase for their business, these gardens offer the Gilbergs a chance to experiment with new cultivars and color combinations. Using color to tie together the tremendous assortment of plants in the garden, the Gilbergs emphasize related hues of pink, blue, and violet. Dashes of brighter colors highlight the plantings, particularly in midsummer.

Moss-pink (*Phlox subulata*) is one of the first plants to bloom in the garden, making carpets of blue (*P. subulata* 'Emerald Cushion Blue'), pink ('Emerald Cushion Pink' and 'Sampson'), and white ('White Delight') beginning in early April. At first, the phlox is one of the only plants in bloom, but by mid-May many of the other perennials are producing flowers. An early bellflower, *Campanula glomerata* 'Joan Elliot', is covered with rounded purplish blue flowers borne atop leafy 2-foot stems. Cranesbill (*Geranium sanguineum*) begins blooming in June and continues without flagging in the summer heat; Gilberg grows both the magenta-flowered species and the soft pink variety *G. sanguineum* var. *prostratum,* also listed as *G. sanguineum* var. *lancastriense.* Daylilies (*Hemerocallis* hybrids) also bloom reliably despite the scorching summer weather. Blue sage (*Salvia* × *superba* 'East Friesland') bears deep blue spikes above cool gray-green foliage. Pineapple-scented sage (*Salvia elegans),* a tender late-blooming perennial, is sometimes nipped by frost before it can produce its fiery red flowers, but it is one of the best plants in the garden both for its color and for attracting hummingbirds.

Demonstration gardens surround the retail areas of the nursery, allowing visitors to see how the young plants in containers will mature and bloom.

Top left: The pink tinge in the purple spires of sage (Salvia × superba *'East Friesland'*) *is accentuated by a background of coralbells* (Heuchera sanguinea). *Top right: Speedwell* (Veronica incana).

Despite their interest in experimenting with flower color, the Gilbergs are even more inventive when it comes to combining leaf textures and colors. This they do, at least in part, by necessity. Most perennials flower for only a short period in early to midsummer. In home gardens, bulbs, annuals, and shrubs can be used to lengthen the blooming season and add variety to the garden, but the Gilbergs have chosen to show what can be done using only perennials. This is hardly a sacrifice; the richly varied leaves of these plants make the garden a wonderful place to explore even when few plants are in bloom.

Perennial grasses provide fascinating textural contrasts. The fine, upright foliage of Japanese bloodgrass (*Imperata cylindrica* var. *rubra*) frames the thick shoots of stonecrop (*Sedum spectabile* 'Autumn Joy'), and the reddish pink flowers of the stonecrop are enhanced by the ruby hues of the grass. Pale yellow *Coreopsis verticillata* 'Moonbeam' combines well with purplish fountaingrass (*Pennisetum alopecuroides*) and spiky blue oatgrass (*Helictotrichon sempervirens*).

Many broad-leaved perennials have variegated leaves that contribute silver, yellow, and white hues to the garden throughout the growing season. Snow-in-summer (*Cerastium tomentosum* 'Silver Carpet') spreads like a mirror beneath the white and green blades of *Iris pallida* var. *albovariegata.* Crowning the rigidly upright foliage of the iris are fragrant lavender-blue flowers. *Artemisia ludoviciana* 'Silver King' makes a 4-foot backdrop for purple clouds of meadowrue (*Thalictrum aquilegifolium*).

Top: Textural combinations can be as striking as any color scheme, as illustrated in this planting of yarrow (Achillea *'Moonshine'*), *large blue hair grass* (Koeleria glauca), *eulalia grass* (Miscanthus *species*), *sage* (Salvia × superba *'East Friesland'*), *and monkshood* (Aconitum *species*). *Bottom: A play of texture and color are created in this planting of Japanese bloodgrass* (Imperata cylindrica *var.* rubra) *and yarrow* (Achillea *'Moonshine'*).

Selecting Plants

Before setting out for a nursery—even a nursery like the Gilbergs'—read about the plants in the following encyclopedia so you can begin to develop ideas for your garden. The encyclopedia is devoted to herbaceous flowers—annuals, perennials, and bulbs—but you will also find general descriptions of the two most popular kinds of flowering shrubs, roses and rhododendrons. You may not find some of the plants mentioned in the previous chapters listed in the encyclopedia. These may be collector's items that are not easily found in the trade, or plants that grow only in a small geographic area.

The plants are listed alphabetically by botanical (Latin) name. Under each botanical name, you'll find the most frequently used common name. In the description that follows the names, you'll find information on hardiness, height, spacing, soil, exposure, flower color, blooming season, and other considerations.

Plant hardiness refers to the ability of the plant to withstand cold, and it is indicated by a zone number. Zone 10 is the warmest zone; Zone 1 is the coldest. These zone numbers were established by the United States Department of Agriculture (USDA) for the continental United States and the southern part of Canada. Refer to the USDA map on pages 132–133 to determine which zone your garden is in. Keep in mind that zone numbers are a very general guide and may vary depending on the microclimate of individual gardens. If you live in a cold climate, snow and mulch are excellent insulators; an early snowfall or thick covering of mulch (applied after the ground freezes) extends the hardiness of dormant perennials and bulbs. Without this protection, many plants will not survive the winter in cold climates.

This sunrose (Helianthemum nummularium) *has been given plenty of room to grow into an attractive mounded form.*

One of the challenges of gardening is anticipating how large plants will spread, and spacing them accordingly. Wherever possible, specific information has been provided to guide you in determining how to space plants. Spacing is also a matter of individual preference—how tight or

loose you want a planting to appear, how quickly you want the plants to fill in (and thus need pruning or dividing), and how much your budget will allow you to spend.

Ideally, when the plants are mature they should cover the soil completely. Newly planted beds or borders, if planted with the correct spacing between plants, will naturally look a little sparse, with more soil than plant showing. To create a full, lush garden, you may be tempted to place young plants closer together than recommended, but this can result in a formless jungle. When planning your garden, study the photographs and plant descriptions in the encyclopedia so that you can visualize how the garden will appear when the plants are mature. Sometimes nature will surprise you with a different picture, but those surprises are just a part of the discoveries that make gardening so enjoyable.

Dividing Perennials and Bulbs

Sooner or later, most perennials need to be divided. A typical perennial plant increases in size by producing new shoots and roots on the perimeter of the plant. After two to four years, the clump usually grows so large that it overruns nearby plants or dies out in the center.

In general, spring- and summer-blooming perennials are divided in late summer or fall, and fall-blooming perennials are divided in early spring. This gives the plants a full season to become reestablished before they bloom. In areas of the United States where winters are extremely cold (below -10° F), it's best to divide all types of plants in the early spring.

To prepare the plants and the soil for digging, water the bed a few days in advance. Cut the leaves of deciduous

plants to within 4 to 6 inches of the ground. Evergreens should not be cut back, but you should remove any dead foliage.

The dividing process is simple. First, dig around the clump on all sides and lift the plant, using a garden fork. If it is a strong, dense clump, you will need to split the plant into two or more pieces using a pair of garden forks. (Borrow the second fork from a

friend.) Place one fork deep into the clump and then insert the second so that the two are back to back. Use them as levers to pry the clump apart. If the roots are very woody

and won't come apart, you can cut them with a knife or shears—but this damages the roots, so cut as little as possible. If the plant has died in the center, remove and discard the old growth. Improve the soil with

organic matter and a handful of 10-10-10 fertilizer before replanting. Any extra plant pieces can be given away.

To divide plants with tuberous roots, such as dahlias and tuberous begonias, lift the clump and use a sturdy knife to cut through the crown. Separate the clump into tubers, making sure that each has at least one bud. (The buds are at the stem end.) Dust the cut surfaces with a fungicide containing captan, and place the tubers in a warm, dry place for a couple of days to allow the cuts to heal.

Plant them in the garden with the buds 2 inches deep.

Irises and other perennials with rhizomes can be lifted after flowering and the rhizomes cut into sections. Each section should have one fan of leaves. Discard leafless sections. Trim roots and leaves to about 3 inches, and immediately replant the rhizomes just under the surface of the soil.

ENCYCLOPEDIA OF FLOWERS

*Spark your imagination with the pictures
and descriptions in this plant encyclopedia.
The information will help you select
the right plants for your particular needs.*

Plant Climate Zones

These zones are based on mean
minimum temperatures and represent
only an *average* for areas within the
zone. Your location might be a zone or
two warmer than the map shows if you
live near a large body of water, or a
zone or two colder if you live at a high
elevation or on a north-facing slope.
Adapted from the USDA Plant
Climate Zone Map.

Range of Average Miminum
Temperatures for Each Zone

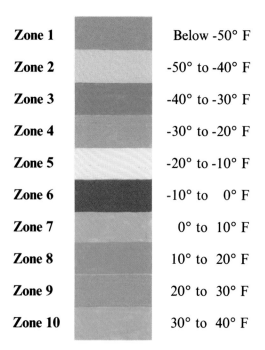

Zone 1	Below -50° F
Zone 2	-50° to -40° F
Zone 3	-40° to -30° F
Zone 4	-30° to -20° F
Zone 5	-20° to -10° F
Zone 6	-10° to 0° F
Zone 7	0° to 10° F
Zone 8	10° to 20° F
Zone 9	20° to 30° F
Zone 10	30° to 40° F

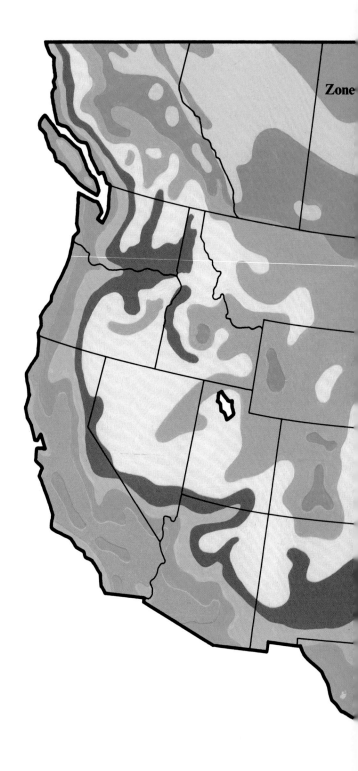

Zone

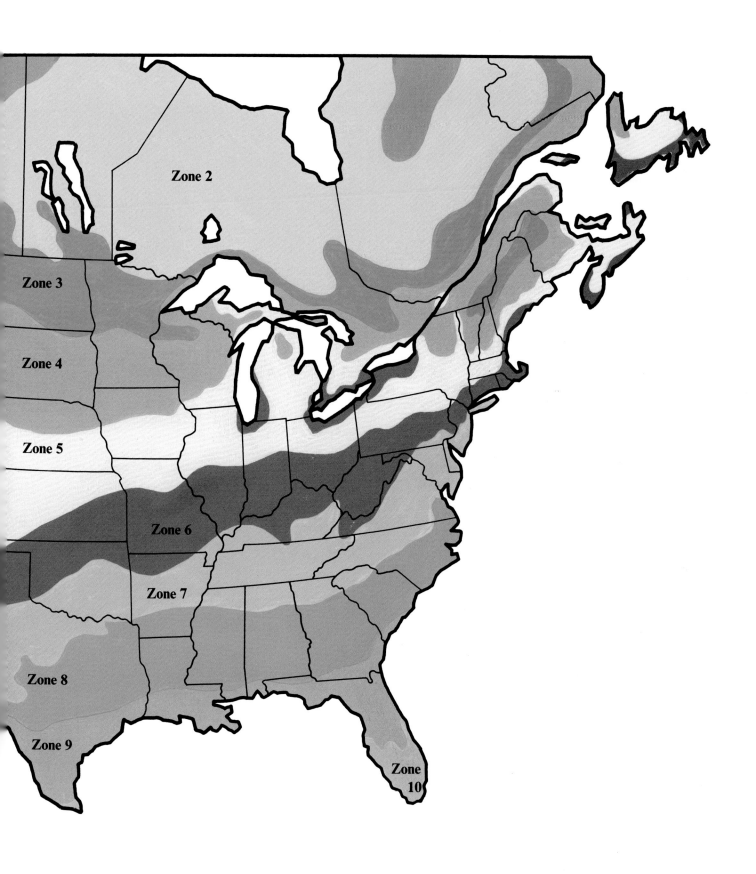

Acanthus spinosissimus

Acanthus species

Bear's-breech

Few perennials make more statuesque clumps than this fine Mediterranean native. Admired since classical times, bear's-breech foliage was even used as decoration on Corinthian columns.

Mature clumps can be 4 feet or more across. The leaves of *Acanthus spinosissimus* (sometimes listed as *A. spinosus*) are deeply divided and somewhat prickly. *A. mollis* is broader, smoother, and glossily green. Both have midsummer flower spikes, up to 5 feet high, that make a distinctive garden feature even when the flowers are spent and the plant is in seed. Individual flowers have purple hoods and broad white lips. When cut and dried, the spikes are valuable for large winter arrangements indoors.

A. spinosissimus (spiny bear's-breech) is the hardier of the two species. It succeeds, for example, in the herb garden at Cornell Plantations in New York state. A deep winter mulch of snow or leaves keeps this species safe to Zone 5. It emerges with renewed vigor the following spring. Snowdrop (*Galanthus nivalis*) or crocus (*Crocus* species) planted nearby can give interest to the area before the bear's-breech foliage takes its place.

In mild areas *A. mollis* can be invasive, spreading from underground suckers, and may need to be contained.

Bear's-breech is best planted from nursery pots in spring. Good drainage and sun are essential in the cooler limits of its range; in warmer areas it makes a fine plant for up to half shade. In either area, slugs and snails can be a problem.

A single specimen clump of either bear's-breech looks fine as a focal point in the garden, but it should also be considered as a plant to build dramatic associations around. Plant it behind the strong evergreen leaves of winter-begonia (*Bergenia* species) and *Yucca* species and frame it with the spires of grassy *Miscanthus* species to create a memorable garden picture.

In areas where *A. mollis* is unlikely to survive outdoors throughout the winter, it can be used as a dramatic container plant for patio or deck. Three plants in a half-barrel soon join together and flower in midsummer. Withhold water as soon as top growth is touched by the first frost and store the container, almost dry, in the garage over winter.

Achillea millefolium 'Cerise Queen'

Achillea filipendulina

Achillea species

Yarrow

The yarrows are valuable perennials with a range of garden uses. The biggest and best known is *Achillea filipendulina*, fern-leaf yarrow, which sends up strong 4-foot-high stems above its clumps of feathery foliage. These stems carry mushroom-shaped heads of tiny yellow flowers that maintain their bright yellow color for several weeks and their shape and texture throughout the fall. Cut at any stage, they are among the best material for dried winter arrangements indoors.

In windy gardens the plant may need staking. It is sensible, therefore, to choose the smaller cultivar 'Coronation Gold'. More dwarfed but in the same pattern is *A.* 'Moonshine'. Here the elegant tussock of leaves is a soft gray-green,

making a perfect foil for the heads of pale sulfur yellow flowers. Only 2 feet high, this is a fine front-of-the-border plant that looks good throughout the season. While *A. filipendulina* is hardy anywhere (it is from the higher elevations of Asia Minor), 'Moonshine' is a little more delicate but does well to Zone 5. If you are adventurous, try it in colder areas with good winter snow cover.

What these species must have is an open position and perfect drainage; heavy, wet clay soils in spring spell death. Also avoid too much competition in a packed border.

The common yarrow, *A. millefolium,* is less choosy but still needs an open site. Many gardeners know this as a lawn weed and thus

seldom see its white flower heads because they are mowed off. Selected forms such as 'Fire King' and 'Cerise Queen' emphasize the pink tinge that often occurs in the wild. Sturdy 1½-foot-high stems make a robust clump in the open position it needs. Again, good drainage is essential. Common yarrow survives to Zone 3.

A. ptarmica is known as sneezewort in its European home, where it grows with loosestrife in marshy ground, so its garden needs are very different from its relations described above. Kept moist, it grows well in most garden soils. The best form is the 2-foot-high 'Angels' Breath' with its mass of pure white flower sprays throughout summer. Like common yarrow, sneezewort survives to Zone 3. One word of caution: It is quite aggressive and can squeeze out its less robust neighbors in the border.

Aconitum napellus

Acidanthera bicolor

Acidanthera bicolor

Peacock orchid

Such a contrived common name
hints at the exotic appearance of
the flowers, but it does not indicate
that this is, in fact, a gladiolus relative. Native to Ethiopia, it is just as
easily grown as its cousin. Any decent garden soil suits it, as does up
to a quarter shade; more shade
than this results in a lot of leaf and
little flower.

The typical gladioluslike corms are
planted in late spring when the soil
has warmed up; 6 or so planted 1
foot apart make a fine clump. Ribbed swordlike foliage soon develops,
but the first flowers do not open
until early August. They continue,
however, until the frosts of fall.

Each 3-foot spike of hooded white
flowers is a marvel of quiet beauty.
Long tubes open into milk white
petals with a deep purple throat;

this and the soft, haunting fragrance,
especially strong in the evening,
make it quite distinct from gladiolus.

In Zone 9 the plant is fully hardy.
Elsewhere, although experience
may show it unnecessary, corms are
best lifted before hard frost and
stored dry over winter. It is worth
collecting the little cormels at the
base of the corms for planting in
future years.

Aconitum species

Monkshood

Related to buttercups from cool,
temperate areas of Europe and
Asia, monkshood is hardy throughout most of North America, even
to Zone 3. Its tuberous roots are
invariably poisonous, as names
such as wolfsbane (for the yellow
A. vulparia) indicate. With flowers
mostly in shades of blue and
purple, monkshood can fill the role
of delphinium, if not quite so
grandly, in gardens where the latter
prove difficult. Species vary in
height from 3 to 6 feet and bear
long-lasting flower spikes.

Monkshood needs a soil that does
not dry out. Fortunately, it grows
well in some shade, so summer
moisture is more easily provided.
As it is among the first perennials
to start growing in spring, division
is best in late fall, when the clumps
become overcrowded. Seven plants
to a square yard make a fine clump
in a year or two.

Actaea rubra

If spring division is essential, do it as soon as the ground is warm to ensure that broken roots (which are inevitable) regenerate at once. The divisions must be kept watered to prevent the soft, early foliage from wilting. Without this care monkshood does poorly and, although unlikely to die, it will not build up worthwhile flowering stems. A whole season is thus lost.

Flowers of all the species have a domed upper petal that gives monkshood its name.

The flowers of *A. × bicolor* are half purple-blue and half white, and they are carried on branching sprays in midsummer. The species is about 4 feet tall, but there are some modern, named cultivars that are more compact and grow only 3 feet high.

Late in August, *A. variegatum* blooms with flower hoods that are distinctively high. The mainly blue flowers with creamy yellow tips are borne on strong wiry stems about 5 feet high. *A. napellus,* the common monkshood, blooms at the same time. The deep blue flowers are tightly packed on the central spike. If the spike is removed as soon as the flowers are past, another secondary display often follows. The pale pink form 'Carneum' is especially good in the cool, moist Northwest.

A. carmichaelii comes from the far eastern part of Asia where Asia almost meets Alaska. This late bloomer begins to open in mid-September and, unless hard frost intervenes, it is still good a month later. Some forms can reach 6 feet, but this species is usually around 4 feet high and is marvelous towering above Japanese anemone (*Anemone japonica*) and Korean chrysanthemum (*Chrysanthemum rubellum* hybrids).

Actaea species

Baneberry

As a buttercup relative, baneberry is predictably poisonous, but makes a fine ornamental garden plant nonetheless.

Native to much of northern North America, baneberry is completely hardy, certainly to Zone 3. As a woodland plant, it prefers some shade. In May the clumps of wiry, 18-inch stems with elegantly cut leaves show off heads of fuzzy cream-colored flowers. These give a pleasant, though short-lived, display, but the attractive fruit that follows is the prime reason for cultivating the plant. A leafy, organic, slightly acid soil is best and it should stay moist. Summer drought, although not a killer, causes early leaf drop.

A. rubra carries spikes of brilliant scarlet berries that ripen in late June and carry on into September.

Actaea alba

Adonis vernalis

A. alba has equally striking white fruit, each with a black spot, giving the plant its alternative name of doll's-eyes. These are at their best from August on.

Both baneberries look lovely interplanted with red and white oriental lilies, creating a flower and fruit combination that is most unusual. *A. alba* and *Lilium speciosum* 'Album' are planted together for a white combination and *A. rubra* and *L. speciosum* for a red combination. Both plants enjoy moist conditions and acid soil, but some lime is acceptable if plenty of humus is added.

Adonis species

Pheasant's-eye

The common name is of no help here, as it refers to a very different red-flowered species for which the genus was named: Adonis was the beautiful youth of Greek mythology who was killed by a boar and whose drops of blood brought forth a brilliant scarlet flower.

Adonis amurensis is a yellow-flowered species from Japan, where it has been grown for centuries, often as an early forced pot plant. A number of forms, both single and double, exist and are gradually becoming available in North America.

The plant is eventually over a foot high but begins in spring as a cluster of flower buds at ground level.

Quickly the stems extend and golden yellow flowers open, 2 inches across, each backed with a fuzz of bracts like love-in-a-mist (*Nigella damascena*). Deeply divided, elegant foliage follows. A few twigs pushed in the ground around the base of this plant keep it from flopping outward.

This charming plant likes half shade in soil that does not dry out and places where it does not become crowded by more aggressive plants. It succeeds in Zone 5 with the usual snow cover protection. Similar in habit and hardy to Zone 4 is its northern European equivalent, *Adonis vernalis,* also yellow-flowered and a foot high.

Agapanthus campanulatus

Aegopodium podagraria 'Variegatum'

Aegopodium podagraria

Goutweed, bishopweed,
ground elder

Because they identify one of the most aggressive weeds known, goutweed, bishopweed, and ground elder are names that spell horror to many gardeners. Like so many weeds, including dandelion and chickweed, *Aegopodium podagraria* is an import from northern Europe.

However, there is a 9- to 12-inch, cream- and green-leafed form called 'Variegatum' that, although able to colonize ground quickly, is much less vigorous and makes a fine ground cover. It is best in confined areas or under established shrubs where cultivation is neither needed nor desired. Planted among conventional evergreen foundation plantings, it relieves the monotony

remarkably well. One great virtue is that it grows in shade and can be used right up to the trunks of mature trees where grass usually will not grow.

Flowering stems, resembling those of its relative Queen-Anne's-lace (*Daucus carota*) appear in July but are infrequently produced. Since they add little to the scene, they are best removed along with any foliage that reverts to green. Variegated goutweed is hardy to Zone 3 and does well in most garden soils. When planted in a humid climate, the plant exhibits leaf blight. Foliage affected by blight can be mowed and new foliage will quickly grow back.

Agapanthus species

Lily-of-the-Nile

For a century or more this has been a classic container plant for setting out on grand summer terraces. Its cantaloupe-sized heads of clear blue stand 3 feet above the clumps of glossy, strap-shaped leaves. Despite the common name lily-of-the-Nile, *Agapanthus africanus* is, in fact, from South Africa. Its container plant role remains valid, but it is hardy only in California and Florida, and storing such a large evergreen plant presents a problem in today's smaller homes.

A. orientalis is evergreen in warm Zones 9 and 10 and deciduous to Zone 7. It has blue or white spherical heads in midsummer. Even hardier are the newer selections derived from *A. campanulatus*. Often

Agastache foeniculum

Agastache mexicana

smaller in both stature and bulk—to about 2½ feet—they are available in all shades of blue from pale sky to thundercloud. Well mulched in winter, these plants have been known to survive to Zone 4. They should be tried more often in warm corners of the yard.

Lily-of-the-Nile does well in most soils that do not dry out in summer. Although it takes shade, the flower heads lean awkwardly toward the sun. It associates particularly well with gray foliage plants such as *Artemisia* species and dusty-miller (*Senecio* species).

Agastache species

Horsemint, giant hyssop, anise hyssop

The name horsemint has a connotation of coarseness that is misleading regarding this useful, aromatic perennial. It grows in any well-drained garden soil in full sun and can take the place of bergamot (*Monarda* species), if less spectacularly, in areas of very hot summers where bergamot fails.

Giant hyssop makes 3-foot-high clumps of mintlike leaves with fat spikes of dark pink to purple flowers in July and August. Often they continue into September and even the dead heads are attractive unless broken down by snow. They combine well with Japanese anemone (*Anemone japonica*).

The most common species is *Agastache foeniculum* or anise hyssop (*foeniculum* means fennel or anise, referring to the scent of

the leaves). It is a prairie plant, hardy to Zone 6 and probably in even colder areas if it has a cover of snow or light leafy mulch as added insurance.

A. mexicana is taller and more broadly branched with clear pink flower spikes throughout summer. Less hardy, as its name suggests, it is a good perennial for the dry Southwest and should be treated as a garden annual in colder areas. Its aromatic leaves have a refreshing lemon scent that is released if you crush a leaf.

Cuttings from nonflowering side shoots are easily rooted in late summer. They should be over-wintered in a frost-free (not too warm) greenhouse and kept barely moist. Growth soon develops in spring, but watch for whitefly, which can quickly destroy the plant.

Alcea rosea

Ageratum houstonianum 'Blue Danube'

Ageratum houstonianum

Flossflower

Pussyfoot or flossflower is a valuable summer annual, providing a soft-textured effect, as the common name suggests. Hairy leaves are topped with heads of powder-puff flowers 1 to 2 feet high. These are usually in some shade of blue, although white and pink forms are available. Blue combines particularly well with gray-leaved plants and pale yellow flowers; dusty-miller (*Artemisia stellerana*) and golden marguerite (*Anthemis tinctoria* 'E. C. Buxton') make fine perennial companions.

Flossflower is native to southern Mexico and south into Guatemala, and it should thus be treated as a tender annual. Sown indoors, it cannot be planted out until all likelihood of frost is past. Then almost any garden site is suitable; avoid full shade (up to half shade is acceptable) and plant in soil that is neither too dry nor too wet.

Flossflower is another of those annuals subjected to the breeders' obsession with dwarfness; while tight little 6-inch balls have a use in carpet bedding, they offer little to the general garden scene. There is now a renaissance of desirable taller forms with a much longer season of flower.

Alcea rosea

Hollyhock

The church-steeple spires of holly-hock are an inevitable part of every romantic cottage-garden picture, towering above the rosy-cheeked children playing by the back step. Hollyhock is no less beautiful in reality, and deserves a renaissance.

Originally from Asia Minor and hardy to Zone 5, hollyhock likes well-drained soil in full sun. In such a location, against a warm wall or backed by tall shrubs, hollyhock is a dependable perennial that makes a fine show in July.

In the competition of the mixed border, in richer soil, it often becomes soft and prey to rust disease. In such a spot the more recent

Alcea rosea

Alchemilla mollis

quick-maturing types, sown in-doors in February, are best used as annuals, but then the typical old-fashioned look is lost.

Hollyhock needs and deserves its own spot, where a clump of spikes 8 or 10 feet high can gradually open their mallow flowers, avail-able in every soft color but blue. Double-flowered forms in the same range of colors also exist and are good as a contrast with the singles. Solid colors are not always offered but it is possible, with such a quick-maturing plant, to select your own seed from desirable plants and gradually develop your own strain in the desired color.

Alchemilla mollis

Lady's-mantle

This is by far the best of the lady's-mantles and comes from Asia Minor. It is hardy to Zone 3 and has a place in almost every garden. Its role is as a broad edging plant, bordering a path or fronting other mixed perennials in the flower bed.

A. mollis makes 12- to 18-inch clumps of soft gray-green foliage that is attractive throughout the season. After rain, lady's-mantle is especially beautiful when droplets of water are held by the leaves and glisten in the sun like so many beads of mercury; the beads run to-gether when touched. The flowers, individually tiny, come in soft yel-lowish green billowing heads in June, perfectly complementing the

leaves. They are excellent compan-ions for blue- and purple-flowered associates.

Lady's-mantle will grow in any but the wettest soil through summer, although drought reduces its lush-ness. In warm areas at least half shade is necessary. Often denigrated as invasive, self-sown seedlings are, in fact, usually a welcome bonus. The problem is easily prevented, however, by cutting off old flower heads before they set seed. This also encourages further fine foliage to develop later in the growing season.

Allium giganteum

Allium christophii

Allium species

Onion

For those who are accustomed only to onions that are fried, baked, or made into sauce, it may come as something of a shock to realize how many of the onion tribe are extremely ornamental garden bulbs. They are mostly sun-lovers from the temperate Northern Hemisphere. In any more than about a quarter shade, flowering is reduced and stems are apt to lean toward the light. Ornamental onions are hardy to Zone 4 and probably in colder areas; they are used with great effect in the bulb garden at Chicago Botanic Garden.

All the bulbous onions show their Asian steppe origin in rapid spring growth and early summer rest. Good drainage is essential. *Allium* species should be planted as soon as bulbs become available in autumn, the bigger species 6 inches deep

and the smaller proportionately less. Of the dozens of species, the following are commonly offered.

A. aflatunense has drumsticklike heads of tiny flowers, deep lilac in color and held on 3-foot stems in early June. Following the late tulips, this species is valuable for lengthening the season of spring bulbs or for planting among summer bloomers such as daylily (*Hemerocallis* hybrids). The leaves die away so quickly that there is little competition. *A. giganteum* is similar, but 4 feet high. Appearing a month later, it is a wonderful, if expensive, summer bulb.

A. caeruleum, with its clear blue flowers and hardy bulbs, is an uncommon species. The open heads

are held 15 inches high in early summer. It is wise to apply a winter mulch in colder areas.

A. christophii (often sold as *A. albopilosum*) is called stars-of-Persia and is one of the joys of June. Only 18 inches high, the heads can be almost half that size across and are made up of star-shaped, amethyst-colored flowers, each just touching the next—giving a light yet solid effect. When the heads become dry, they maintain their shape for months in the garden or indefinitely if brought indoors.

A. karataviense is another wonderful Asian species in which the foliage is the major attraction. The mauve apple-sized heads are borne in June on 6-inch stalks that push up from a pair of broad gray-green leaves with a purplish cast.

A. moly, the lily leek, is a Mediterranean species with smooth, grayish leaves and foot-high stems of

Alstroemeria aurantiaca

Allium schoenoprasum

bright yellow flowers that appear in June. It is a common and easy plant from the same area as *A. nea-politanum,* the daffodil onion, which has 18-inch stems carrying heads of shining white star-shaped flowers, each accentuated with a dark eye.

A. schoenoprasum, or chives, is a plant of rocky stream banks in northern Europe. Everyone with an herb garden knows that as long as moisture is available this species stays green. It is a fine edging plant with clumps of grassy leaves and heads of purple flowers in June and July. Both leaves and flowers can go into the salad bowl.

A. senescens, mountain garlic, is from central Europe eastward to northern Asia. It grows well to Zone 3, if not in colder areas. Because nomenclature is rather confused, plants offered under this name can be surprisingly different. The best form is separated as *A. senescens* var. g*laucum,* which has tufts of grayish leaves that are twisted and curled and give an almost undersea effect; the little drumsticklike flower heads, only 1 foot high, are not unlike thrift (*Armeria maritima*) and continue the marine analogy. The pale rose flowers, at their best in August and September, look good with the late-summer stonecrops (*Sedum* species) and have a long season of interest. Even when dead, the flower heads maintain their shape into winter.

The bulbs of mountain garlic are bottle-shaped and group themselves on a fleshy base as they increase, giving the typically tufted habit. Almost any soil or planting spot suits them, excepting extremes of damp, drought, and shade. Too much competition from adjoining plants reduces the distinctive effect.

Alstroemeria species

Peruvian-lily

Where it succeeds, the Peruvian-lily is among the most delightful perennials that can be imagined. Strong, wiry, 3-foot-high stems carry wide heads of elegant lily blooms that are long-lasting both in the garden and as cut flowers. Of the dozens of species, very few are available, but are worth every effort to obtain. The new hybrids are appearing on the cut-flower market.

In spite of the common name Peruvian-lily, *Alstroemeria aurantiaca* comes from Chile. Both brilliant orange and bright yellow forms exist. In each case the petals are marked with darker stripes and dots. The plant reaches about 3 feet in height and flowers from late June through July. Hardy to Zone 6, it needs a warm spot by the

Alstroemeria Ligtu hybrids

Amaranthus caudatus

house and a good winter mulch at the limit of its range. In safer areas it can even be invasive and succeeds among shrubs in half shade. Soils must not stay wet in early spring.

The Ligtu hybrids (*A. ligtu* × *A. haemantha*) are also of Chilean origin. Here the flowers come in an extraordinarily wide range of colors: creamy pink, coral, salmon, and soft orange. All are beautifully marked and borne in June and July on sheaves of stems up to 4 feet high. Hardy to Zone 7, these hybrids are often difficult to establish, and 2-year-old container-grown seedlings planted in spring are best. Both the fleshy roots and young stems are very brittle and must be treated with care.

A. psittacina is the parrot-lily, whose unusual red flowers with green tips always cause comment in July when they bloom. This species

is seldom more than 2 feet high. As a native of the upper elevations of Brazil, it is on the edge of hardiness in North America, although safe enough to Zone 8. A good winter mulch and a leafy soil often allow it to succeed up to two zones cooler. It is worth every effort.

Having flowered in midsummer, Peruvian-lily quickly goes dormant, and prominent positions will need a scattering of quick-maturing annuals to fill the gap. Use either directly sown seeds—love-in-a-mist (*Nigella damascena*) and pot marigold (*Calendula officinalis*) germinate almost at once—or small plants from a late greenhouse sowing. Care must be taken not to injure the Peruvian-lily's delicate, fleshy roots.

Amaranthus species

Love-lies-bleeding, prince's-feather

Among the biggest annuals grown, this plant is ideal for dramatic effects. Sow in place or plant out from trays 1 foot apart. Any sunny spot will do, and in rich soil the plant increases wonderfully. As with most summer annuals originating in the tropics, it succeeds in all zones that can give at least three hot summer months. Root rot can be troublesome in wet soils.

A. caudatus is love-lies-bleeding or tasselflower. Up to 5 feet in height, the deep crimson flower spikes cascade forward like so many velvet-plush bellpulls. Later, the stems take on a similar color. A lime green form is popular with flower arrangers. Both can be dried for indoor winter arrangements. They must be gathered as soon as the

Amaryllis belladonna

Amaryllis belladonna

majority of the main tassel is mature. Being somewhat fleshy, they seem to continue to mature even after they are cut.

The related *A. tricolor* is variously called Joseph's-coat, fountainplant, or prince's-feather. It produces showers of brightly striped leaves in all shades of red, green, and pink on thick fleshy stems 5 or more feet high. The flowers are not exciting. Both of these plants are grown in their tropical homes as food plants and are similar to spinach.

Amaryllis belladonna

Belladonna-lily

One of the loveliest of the South African bulbs, this is a plant for warm areas. The big daffodil-like bulbs are planted in full sun when dormant in July and August. Following the first rain, belladonna-lily quickly thrusts up its 2-foot stems of clear pink, lilylike flowers that darken with age to crimson. The first flowers open in late August and continue until early October. They are richly and strangely scented, not unlike old-fashioned pear-drop candies. The ground-level, strap-shaped leaves come after the flowers and continue until the following spring, turning yellow and going dormant by May.

Such a growth pattern explains why belladonna-lily is not for cold areas (Zone 8 is probably the limit)

and why it is not convenient to lift the bulbs after they flower; greenhouse space in winter is too precious for a few leafy bulbs. In the warmest zones it will naturalize in the light shade of trees and looks wonderful growing through low ground cover, such as English ivy. Plants that flower after their leaves have gone to rest invariably have a naked look unless the gardener carefully plans some suitable accompaniment. In a sunny spot gray-leaved plants such as dwarf lavender (*Lavendula* species) or lavender cotton (*Santolina chamaecyparissus*) are ideal, as is catmint (*Nepeta* × *faassenii*), which offers some late flowers if sheared earlier.

Amsonia tabernaemontana

Anaphalis margaritacea

Amsonia tabernaemontana

Bluestar

This is not a dramatic species but a subtle and interesting perennial originally from the southeastern United States; the fact that it has escaped from cultivation up the East Coast demonstrates its hardiness. With a winter mulch, applied early, it is safe even to Zone 4 and possibly beyond.

Elegant clumps of 2-foot stems are clothed with narrow, willowlike leaves. In June these are topped with heads of pale, almost ice blue, star-shaped flowers. Related to periwinkle, bluestar has the same twisting petals.

Although the flower display is neither spectacular nor long-lasting, the plant retains its tidy shape and, as a bonus, by mid-September the foliage turns as clear a yellow as the willow leaves it resembles.

Fronted by a band of perennial evening-primrose or sundrops (*Oenothera tetragona*), whose leaves turn a rosy red, it creates a bright fall picture in small gardens where the usual autumn-coloring trees are too large to plant.

Bluestar grows well in half shade and succeeds in any but the wettest of soils.

Anaphalis species

Pearl-everlasting

Essential to any garden in which perennials play a part, pearl-everlasting is important especially in moisture-retentive soils where most gray-leaved plants fail. This plant will even take part shade without losing its shape and texture.

Anaphalis margaritacea is a native to much of eastern North America and thus hardy to Zone 3. Clumps can reach 3 feet in height, the stems topped with sprays of papery white daisies with a yellow eye. The effect is long-lasting in the garden and later in dried arrangements.

With wider leaves that are green on top and white underneath and that originate from felted white stems is *A. cinnomomea*. This is about the same size as *A. margaritacea* but is tighter in habit. From India, it is

Anaphalis triplinervis

Anchusa azurea

less suitable for colder areas of North America, but safe enough to Zone 5.

A. triplinervis is only half the height of its cousins but just as easy to grow. They all look fine with the late-summer displays of stonecrop (*Sedum spectabile*) and Japanese anemone (*Anemone japonica*).

Since most of the gray and silver plants are of Mediterranean origin and of doubtful hardiness, pearl-everlasting is particularly valuable in the colder zones. Also, the foliage has value longer than that of most other flowering plants. Although usually employed to tone down brightly colored flowers in the border, *A. triplinervis* makes a fine formal edging to paths by itself.

Anchusa species

Bugloss

Anchusa azurea is one of the few border plants with pure true-blue flowers and thus should be forgiven its coarse bristly leaves, inelegant habit, and erratic lifestyle. The flower spikes are those of a giant forget-me-not (3 feet high in 'Loddon Royalist', the best form) and at their best in June, the time of bearded irises (*Iris* species) and lupines (*Lupinus* species). These two plants help to mask the gawky stems of bugloss. Pale yellow and white bearded iris make a perfect color complement. The iris cultivar 'Pinnacle' is worth searching out and combining with bugloss, as are similar yellow and white color combinations available in lupines grown from seed.

As a Mediterranean naturalized in the southwestern United States, this borage relative needs good

drainage and full sun. Even then it may need replacing every other year. It is generally hardy to Zone 5, given good conditions. Cold, wet soil in spring spells death.

A charming cousin is *A. capensis* from the Cape of South Africa. A biennial, it is grown as an annual from early spring-sown seeds. Its tidy foot-high domes of clear blue, white-eyed flowers bloom throughout summer. As with summer annuals, it can be grown in all zones; only the length of the frost-free period restricts the show. Again, such a brilliant blue is enhanced by soft yellow and white, two colors available now from petunia (*Petunia* hybrids).

Anemone pulsatilla

Anemone blanda 'Radar'

Anemone species

Windflower

The windflowers are among the most beautiful and diverse of garden flowers. The bigger species are Asian and, although of Chinese origin, are known as Japanese anemones; they have been grown and prized in Japan for centuries. Several species names (*Anemone hupehensis, A. japonica, A. vitifolia*) may appear in catalogs, but those offered are most likely to be hybrids. Hence the name *A.* × *hybrida* occurs as well.

Clumps of grape-leaflike foliage put up nearly bare flower stems in late summer. The first to open, in late August, are apt to be the shortest; the pink 'September Charm' is one of the best, about 3 feet high. Later come types like the superb 5-foot 'Honorine Jobert', white-flowered and raised as long ago as 1858.

All Japanese anemones have cup-shaped flowers, up to 3 inches across, in white or shades of pink, and lit up by golden stamens in the center. The blossoms can be single or double and they all flower for weeks on end.

Japanese anemone enjoys a good garden soil that neither dries out in summer nor lies wet in spring when growth begins. It takes up to half shade and is excellent with other perennials and in front of shrubs. Successful to Zone 5, it needs some winter mulch in the north.

A. pulsatilla is the pasqueflower of European limestone uplands. It has two seasons of beauty. In spring it opens its flowers almost at ground level; the cobwebbed cups of royal purple have gold stamens. After pollination, the flower stems elongate and hold silvery-haired seedheads a foot high above the elegant leaves. Pasqueflower is easy to grow in any well-drained site to Zone 3; full sun is necessary to ensure compactness.

A. coronaria is the originator of the multihued florist anemones seen in shops in early spring. These are the De Caen and St. Brigid types. Even in the wild, at the windswept elevations of Crete, pink, purple, and blue forms grow together. The dried tubers are planted in autumn in a sunny place and the parsleylike leaves and flowers appear over a long period in spring. Zone 6 is safe, but with good winter snow cover it can be grown to Zone 4.

A. blanda is one of several little spring-flowering windflowers from the woodlands of Europe. (Others to look for are *A. apennina* and *A. nemorosa*.) Sky blue is the typical color, but pink and white forms exist. The little tubers are planted a couple of inches deep in early fall in leafy soil where they will not be disturbed. Along with snowdrops (*Galanthus* species) and squill (*Scilla* species) they make a charming ground cover under shrubs. These windflowers are hardy to at least Zone 4.

Angelica archangelica

Anigozanthos flavidus

Angelica archangelica

Angelica

Slices of the green candied stems of this old European herb used to be the common and delicious decoration on cakes; tasteless plastic strips seem to have taken their place, but angelica remains a spectacular garden biennial. From small seedlings that overwinter happily to Zone 3, an enormous clump of leaves develops in the second year and sends up a 6-foot stem of spherical heads. First lime green, the flowers turn straw brown and remain statuesque for weeks.

A group of 3 to 5 plants placed 2 feet apart is enough for most gardens. After this, it is simply a matter of leaving the self-sown seedlings where they appear in desirable spots. Any soil but the wettest is suitable. This is one of the few culinary herbs that will accept more than half shade. It looks particularly good behind old-fashioned roses and with foxglove (*Digitalis* species) at the back of a half-shady border.

Anigozanthos species

Kangaroo-paw

There are several species of these strange Australian natives: *Anigozanthos manglesii* is usually red-flowered, as is *A. coccinea,* while *A. flavidus* is yellowish green. But as they are all similar in form and cultivation, they can conveniently be described together. Availability is somewhat erratic so they should be snapped up by those able to grow them.

Kangaroo-paw is for the fortunate gardener in Zone 8 and above. From tuberous roots the plant makes a clump of narrow leaves, somewhat like a rigid Siberian iris. Being evergreen, the foliage is valuable throughout the year. Give kangaroo-paw full sun and a peaty

Anthemis tinctoria

Anthemis tinctoria

soil that neither dries out nor lies wet in winter—the usual criteria for delicate plants.

In July branching stems rise 3 to 4 feet high, producing long-lasting sprays of unusual and distinctive flowers. The curved tubes are furry and end in a star of petals supposedly resembling the toes of a kangaroo's paw.

Hybrids are gradually becoming available in a wide range of delicate colors and different sizes. They should be tried wherever the climate permits. Kangaroo-paw also makes long-lasting cut flowers for the home.

Anthemis species

Golden marguerite

Anthemis tinctoria is one of the best early-summer daisies. From clumps of foliage as divided as parsley come a profusion of flowers that last for several weeks. 'Gralloch Gold' is brilliant yellow; 'E. C. Buxton' is a cooler lemon yellow that is much easier to use and is particularly effective with the tall herbaceous phloxes (*Phlox* species). Paler still are 'Wargrave Variety', 'Powis White', and 'Moonlight'. All grow to 3 feet and should be cut down after flowering in June to mid-July to encourage foliage growth and a perennial habit. They are from Central Europe and safe to Zone 3. Provide a well-drained soil and full sun; a light winter mulch is helpful.

A. cupaniana is another sun-lover, but from maritime Italy, where it keeps its wide mats of silver filigree foliage throughout the year. It is for mild Zone 8 climates and

above; elsewhere, overwinter the easily rooted autumn cuttings. White daisies cover the plant in June, and if sheared a second, although less spectacular, display occurs later. It is especially useful as a ground cover foil for spring bulbs, whether as a perennial or part of a spring bedding scheme. It also makes a fine gray mat for the bare autumn flower spikes of belladonna-lily (*Amaryllis belladonna*) or nerine (*Nerine* species) to grow through; their silver-pink trumpets are a perfect accompaniment.

Antirrhinum majus

Aquilegia caerulea

Antirrhinum majus

Snapdragon

Among the most traditional of old cottage-garden plants, snapdragon is a perennial when planted in a sunny spot in the milder zones. It grows for three or four years as long as rust disease does not strike. It is usually a well-branched plant with spikes of pink to purple flowers. The furry lower lips close the flower tubes and pollinating insects must pry them open. They also can be squeezed at the back to make snapping dragons. New open-mouthed flowers, which resemble the tubular flowers of foxglove or penstemon, do not offer this traditional pleasure and lose much of their old-fashioned charm.

It is common to grow snapdragon as a summer annual. It grows in all zones if planted when the soil begins to warm up. It can also take a couple of degrees of frost without harm. Modern forms come in all colors except true-blue and full red and vary in height from 6 inches to 4 feet. In windy gardens the tall forms need staking and are best replaced with medium-sized types. Any normal garden soil and site suits them, but excellent drainage is essential.

In the wild, snapdragon grows in the cracks in rocks and old walls, where it thrives on a diet of lime mortar. Such plants become woody at the base and go on for years. To extend the show and allow side shoots to take over, prevent seed formation by removing any spent flower spikes.

Aquilegia species

Columbine

The seventy or so species of *Aquilegia* found around northern temperate regions vary from tiny alpines for the rock garden to robust plants for the border. All share the distinct flower shape—chubby bells with curved spurs behind each petal—and elegant gray-green lobed leaves.

A. caerulea, a lovely large columbine from the Rocky Mountains, is the state flower of Colorado. To 2½ feet in height, it carries its sprays of elegant, long-spurred flowers in late June and July. The typical color, as the name suggests, is blue, but a blue that varies from mist to deep sky. There are color variants—white, yellow, and red—that have been collected in the wild. With such a range, it is not surprising that this species is used in

Aquilegia flabellata 'Alba'

Aquilegia 'McKana Hybrids'

hybridizing. Under winter snow the species is safe to Zone 5.

A. canadensis is one of the most familiar columbines. It is found in wild woodlands over most of North America east of the Rockies. On stems up to 2 feet high, the red and yellow flowers begin in May and last through June. The show is prolonged by half shade and a soil that does not dry out too soon. It is hardy to Zone 3.

A. chrysantha is a tall plant, sometimes over 3 feet, from Arizona and New Mexico, with clear yellow flowers and distinctively long spurs.

While the true species needs at least Zone 6 conditions, its qualities have been brought into a number of garden-bred strains that are offered as Long-spurred hybrids under various names. These are much more suitable for general garden use to Zone 5 (they have been known to survive to Zone 3) and are easily raised from seed sown in spring.

Hybrid columbines flower in June and early July and come in an amazing range of soft colors: blue, violet, red, pink, yellow, cream, and white. If seed is not required, stems should be cut down as soon as the flowers are spent. Often you can encourage a few late flowers this way and the plants are strengthened for the following year.

Although columbine's height makes it suitable for a back position in many borders, the lightness of the stems is better appreciated

if plants are brought forward and placed a foot or so apart. Full to three-quarters sun in any ordinary garden soil will suit; too much moisture in early spring is apt to ruin any plant that has successfully overwintered.

A. flabellata is a small Japanese species only 18 inches high. The flowers are soft lilac with yellow-tipped petals whose strongly hooked spurs illustrate the origin of the botanical name: *Aquila* means eagle. This Asian species is hardy at least to Zone 5 as long as the winter snow cover is adequate.

Arabis caucasica 'Snowball'

Arabis caucasica 'Variegata'

Arabis species

Rockcress

There may be some botanical doubt as to the correct name of *Arabis alpina* (mountain rockcress) but it is generally used for one of the commonest of all rock garden plants and may actually be *A. caucasica*. Whatever the name, the foaming white, foot-high hummocks that tumble over dry walls and along the front of borders in spring are one of the best sights of the garden year.

From the mountainsides of many areas of Europe, it grows well to Zone 3 if snow cover is constant. Without the snow cover, the gray-green leaf rosettes look extremely miserable by the end of winter and their flowering capability is reduced. In colder climates, a few evergreen boughs laid over clumps is worthwhile insurance.

As a plant of rocky places, *A. alpina* is very intolerant of wet soils; good drainage in full sun is essential if the plant is to give its best. While it is in no way aggressive and does not run underground, it is certainly not a plant for associating with tiny, choice alpines in a specialist's rock garden. It is better to plant it with spring bulbs, such as the smaller tulips that enjoy similar situations and don't have to be lifted each year. Add some ornamental onion (*Allium* species) and this combination gives an almost labor-free display until early summer. Clip the rockcress after flowering is finished to encourage further leaf rosettes and a tightly clumping habit.

White is the typical color, but as with many old garden plants a number of forms have been selected that must be propagated by cuttings or by carefully pulling old plants apart and replanting immediately. Pink- and red-flowered types and a useful variety with cream-edged leaves are also available.

A. caucasica or wall rockcress is grayer with longer leaves and a more compact habit. It has the typical cross-shaped flowers of the genus—fragrant if you can get down to its level. From southeastern Europe's stony hillsides, it needs the same perfect drainage as is provided by a rock garden or wall. A winter mulch in cold areas is wise.

Argemone mexicana

Arctotis stoechadifolia var. *grandis*

Arctotis stoechadifolia var. *grandis*

Blue-eyed African daisy

This lovely African daisy is one of the most distinctive of a wide range of daisy-flowered plants for which South Africa is renowned. The hot, dry summers and moist, mild winters of its native habitat clearly indicate the plant's needs. These include a frost-free climate, full sun, and good soil drainage. Under these conditions, it is a proper perennial with woody lower stems that go on for several years. Only the warmest zones provide the perfect home.

Fortunately, its growth and development is quick enough for it to be grown as a tender annual. Sow it indoors in spring with petunias, marigolds, and other annuals, then plant it outside when all chance of frost is gone. Plant it in the sunniest spot or the flowers will not open. The soil must also be warm and well drained.

Under these conditions, the plant develops soft, dandelionlike leaves that are densely woolly underneath. The wonderful 3-inch daisies are blue-violet and cream on top with bronze on the reverse.

Argemone species

Mexican poppy

Few easily sown annuals have such a distinct form and presence as the Mexican poppy. It is wild to much of the Caribbean and has become a naturalized weed in the subtropics around the world. But this does not detract from its garden value in any way.

Argemone mexicana is a tall, branched annual, up to 3 feet under good growing conditions, with smooth gray leaves and veins etched with pale blue markings. Leaf tips are extended into spines, but the plant is not aggressively prickly. As with many poppy relatives, a yellow sap runs from broken stems. Flowers up to 3 inches across are exquisite bowls of clear yellow; they begin in early summer and continue for weeks. Prickly seed capsules extend the interest.

In areas with hot summers, seeds can be sown outside after the last frost. Otherwise, sow indoors to

Arisaema triphyllum

Arisaema triphyllum

give them a good start. Full sun and a well-drained soil are necessary.

Another species, equally well worth growing, is *A. platyceras*. It has bigger, white flowers and needs similar conditions. Both species look good with their geographical neighbor, the California poppy (*Eschscholzia californica*).

Arisaema triphyllum

Jack-in-the-pulpit, dragonroot

There is always fascination with members of the arum family whether they are exotic climbers from tropical jungles or common native woodlanders like this one. Although many people see jack-in-the-pulpit as a companion to wakerobin (*Trillium* species) and wild ginger (*Asarum* species), it is also a highly distinctive garden plant at every stage of its growth pattern.

In early spring a purplish spear pushes through the leaves, gradually unfolding in May to a typical arum flower with its purple-green hood enclosing the central yellow spadix—Jack in his pulpit. Some forms have distinctive white- and green-striped hoods. As the flower fades, the fine arrowhead leaves—1 to 2 feet high—develop. By August the head of brilliant orange-red berries has formed. These berries are poisonous.

Such a plant typical of deciduous woodlands requires a leafy soil and at least half shade. It is hardy to Zone 4. Choose a prominent position with other woodland plants, above which it will stand statuesque and eye-catching.

Arnica cordifolia

Armeria maritima

Armeria species

Thrift, seapink

This is one of those plants that evokes the memory of some wild form seen on a mountain hike. The common species, *Armeria maritima,* has an enormous geographical range: the coasts of northern Europe and around the Mediterranean and along the Pacific Coast of North and South America down into Chile. Although there are variants, once brought into cultivation they become very similar.

Thrift makes a tussock of little grassy evergreen leaves that grow from low woody stems. In June leafless flower stalks 6 inches to a foot high carry knobs of pink or almost-white flowers. When finished, these can be clipped off, leaving a tidy little dome of leaves.

In well-drained soil, thrift is useful as an edging plant. It is also effective in dry walls and rock gardens.

With snow cover in winter, Zone 3 is the lower limit of its range. Taller in flower and with longer, broader leaves is *A. pseudoarmeria.* This species comes from maritime Portugal and is less frost tolerant. It makes more of a show in the garden and is suitable for borders. Like all seaside plants, thrift must have full sun. Established clumps can last for years.

Arnica species

Arnica

The range of garden-worthy members of the daisy family native to North America seems endless, and arnica is yet another. With some 30 species around the temperate world, the genus is often found at higher elevations. *Arnica cordifolia,* from both sides of the Rockies, is among the best. Distributed from the Yukon to California, hardy strains of the plant are available for northern gardens.

Above a low clump of soft, heart-shaped leaves grow 18-inch stems bearing large, clear yellow daisies. The effect is much like that of leopard's-bane (*Doronicum* species), unaccountably delayed by a couple

Artemisia absinthium

of months. You can prolong the show noticeably if you pinch out the dead flowers to prevent seed production.

Other species, such as *A. montana* and *A. chamassonis,* are also worth growing on the edge of woodland and other areas where highly bred garden plants would be out of place. All are hardy to Zone 3.

Artemisia species

Wormwood, absinthe, southernwood

Although related to daisies, the flowers of *Artemisia* species have little individual beauty. However, their foliage color, texture, and ability to combine with other, brighter plants make them essential in almost every garden. There are almost two hundred species, mainly from temperate areas of the Northern Hemisphere. Those listed here are the most ornamental. Their aromatic qualities have taken several into the category of medicinal and culinary herbs: Absinthe and tarragon are two examples.

Gray foliage and aromatic leaves almost always mean the need for full sun and well-drained soil, and species of *Artemisia* are no exception. While the species commonly grown are mainly herbaceous, dying down each fall to an overwintering rootstock, a couple are almost subshrubs.

A. abrotanum is southernwood, oldman, or lad's-love, names evolved from past times when it was grown at English cottage doors to be brushed by every passerby for its scent. The leaves of this shrubby plant are feathery and gray-green. There seem to be two forms, one that reaches 6 feet high with feathery plumes of brownish flowers, the other that is lower and best kept clipped into a soft hummock. Zone 5 is probably its limit.

A. arborescens is also shrubby, a wonderful plant for Zone 8 and warmer areas. Coming from the cliffs of southern Greece, it is not very frost tolerant. It is so easily rooted from cuttings that it is worth overwintering indoors and planting out in summer, or using as

Artemisia ludoviciana 'Silver King'

Artemisia stellerana

a container plant. When thriving, it becomes a 6-foot-high shrub of strongly aromatic, silvery, lacy leaves that look superb in the fall with nerine (*Nerine bowdenii*) and belladonna-lily (*Amaryllis belladonna*).

A. absinthium is known both as absinthe and wormwood—the one name indicating its use as a constituent of various liqueurs, the other its use as medicine. Although less shrubby, in its best forms it is a European rival to the Grecian species, and one that succeeds at least two zones colder (to Zone 6). Plants reach 2½ to 3½ feet in height. The long sprays of tiny gray-yellow flowers make a fine pattern but are best removed as soon as they are spent to encourage more silver leaves.

A. lactiflora is very different and out of place with the other species mentioned here. It is a strong, tall border plant from China with divided green leaves up 6-foot-high stems that are topped with heads of tiny cream flowers in August. It is good with purple phlox (*Phlox* species) and survives into Zone 5 and sometimes beyond.

A. ludoviciana is a native white sage that grows well in an herbaceous border. Usually about 3 feet high, its running roots soon build up a wide clump whose stems have white, willowlike leaves topped with plumes of grayish flowers in July and August. 'Silver King' and 'Silver Queen' are good cultivars and both do well to Zone 4.

A. schmidtiana is a lovely Japanese plant that forms a symmetrical 18-inch dome of silver filigree foliage ending in tiny, grayish white flower heads. To maintain its shape, it needs an open position without competitors. A few twigs pushed into the ground around the outside prevent the clumps from flopping open in the middle. Trimming the plant back will also help slow this trend. With good snow cover, growing it in Zone 4 is entirely possible. It is good planted with small spring bulbs that disappear as it develops.

A. stellerana is the dusty-miller from Siberia, and thus is hardy throughout most of North America. In warm areas it keeps much of its foliage over winter. Unscented, felted, lobed gray leaves are carried with tiny yellow flowers on velvety stems.

Arum italicum 'Pictum'

Arum italicum

Italian arum, cuckoo-pint

This is the common southern European equivalent of North America's jack-in-the-pulpit (*Arisaema triphyllum*). It has outposts in England and seems remarkably frost tolerant to at least Zone 5. The flowers bloom in May with a yellowish, hooded spathe and a purple central spadix inside. However, the foliage is the principal reason for growing this plant.

In the fall, arrow-shaped leaves develop from the tuberous root. They grow a foot high despite the cold weather to come and, depending on the severity of winter, either continue to increase or wait for better times in spring. In northern areas, without snow cover, the above-ground foliage dies and new leaves emerge in spring.

A particularly lovely cultivar known variously as 'Pictum' or 'Variegatum' has narrower leaves marbled gray and cream and is prized for use with small flower arrangements. It is worth searching for and displaying in a prominent position.

'Marmoratum' is another fine cultivar, with the broad arrow-shaped leaves of the species and veins irregularly marked with gray, just like polished marble.

Soon after flowering, the leaves die, leaving a drumstick of brilliant berries. These are poisonous, as are those of jack-in-the-pulpit. This is not necessarily a reason for leaving them out of the garden; children should be taught never to touch fruits they do not recognize.

Italian arum is a plant of woodland edges and olive groves, and thus needs at least half shade and a leafy soil.

Asclepias tuberosa

Aruncus dioicus

Aruncus dioicus

Goatsbeard

From North America as well as northern Europe and Asia, goatsbeard is one of the most statuesque of perennials, presenting a fine show for months. First, a 3-foot clump of fernlike foliage develops, then the flower spikes push through, doubling the plant's height in early July. The spikes become feathery plumes of tiny cream flowers, rather short-lived in the male plant (the sexes are separate in goatsbeard), while the female develops green seedpods that are excellent when dried for winter arrangements. Uncut, the plant maintains its skeleton in winter, elegant throughout the season.

Goatsbeard is successful at least to Zone 4, and it grows well in full sun or even half shade as long as the soil does not dry out. A single clump can spread to 4 feet across, so it makes a fine specimen plant for the back of the border or the edge of a lawn.

Where space is limited, a charming form called 'Kneiffii' is an excellent substitute. Only half the size, it has finely divided leaves and produces an elegant effect for several summer months. It should be brought right to the front of the border.

Asclepias species

Butterflyweed

With so many gardening books extolling the virtues of English gardens, it is a comfort to meet a plant that succeeds so much better here than there. But then it should: *Asclepias tuberosa* is the brilliant butterflyweed native to many areas east of the Rockies, where it enjoys locations with full sun and good drainage. (At Royal Botanic Gardens, Ontario, wild butterflyweed does better on the edge of the railway tracks than in the nearby carefully cultivated gardens; it likes the cinders.) The plant is hardy to Zone 4.

Two-foot-high stems of narrow leaves with the typical poisonous milky sap of most of the genus carry almost flat heads of vivid, glowing orange flowers in late July and August. This is not an easy

Asphodeline lutea

color to use, but it looks good with the smaller silver artemisias such as *Artemisia schmidtiana.*

A. curassavica is a tender South American treated as an annual in most climates. It has some of the brilliance of its hardy cousin, although with flowers tending more to red. It is a 3-foot-high, widely branched plant that creates a fine pattern through summer. The show culminates in the long pods and silky seeds typical of the genus that float across the garden on the autumn air. These can overwinter and germinate even in Zone 6.

Asphodeline species

Yellow asphodel, king's-spear

These common plants of rocky places and often poor soils are found all around the Mediterranean.

Asphodeline lutea has clumps of long, grassy, blue-gray leaves that form strong flower spikes 3 or even 4 feet high. The scented flowers open in May or June (earlier in southern areas), displaying yellow stars among the darker bracts. They are replaced by berrylike fruit that turns from green to brown. It remains attractive throughout summer or until gathered for drying in winter arrangements indoors.

The paler yellow flowers of *A. liburnica* bloom slightly later. Less common, it needs to be sought out from specialist nurseries or grown from seed. It will take three years to flower and then remain a long-lived perennial.

As its habitat indicates, *Asphodeline* species needs perfect drainage (fleshy roots soon rot if standing in water) and as sunny a spot as possible. It does poorly when crowded with other plants; even in the wild it seems to stand alone, statuesque in its rock-strewn home.

Although a southern plant, yellow asphodel thrives in Zone 6 and, given a mulch if natural snow cover is uncertain, seems safe enough beyond this. Certainly it is a plant worth some extra effort.

Planted with smaller spring bulbs, yellow asphodel extends their season and responds well to a similar dry summer rest later on.

Aster novae-angliae

Aster × *frikartii*

Aster species

Michaelmas daisy, aster

There are literally hundreds of *Aster* species strewn around the world (only Australia seems exempt). Of these hundreds, a number are valuable garden plants. All can be considered hardy (if given a snow cover in colder areas) in well-drained soils throughout most of North America, although in the coldest areas *A.* × *frikartii* should be lifted and stored over the winter.

A. alpinus, from mountainsides of central Europe and Asia, is not a typical michaelmas daisy either in form or season. Seldom exceeding 1 foot in height, the narrow-leaved stems bear heads of fine yellow-eyed daisies in late spring. Ray florets can be white, pink, blue, or purple depending upon the cultivar. All are simple, easy plants for rock gardens or the border front.

A. ericoides is a native heath aster. It is a wiry, 2-foot plant producing

good twiggy growth early in summer. It continues to look green and fresh until September, when it becomes at last a starry cloud of typically white daisies. Pale blue and pink forms are available occasionally. Do not cut down the plant until spring, as its stems remain elegant even after dying.

The New England aster (*A. novae-angliae*) is much bigger, often 5 feet high, and rather coarse. Despite its name, which originated from the earliest collections, it is wild from Vermont to Alaska and down to New Mexico. Stems of rough, lank leaves have broad sprays of semidouble daisies, typically pinkish purple. There are cultivars with clearer colors—for example, the lovely old 'Harrington's Pink', which is also more compact.

A. novi-belgii is an East Coast plant that grows wild from Newfoundland to Georgia; it runs from underground rhizomes and can be a pest. It reaches 1 to 4 feet in height.

In the last century or so a vast number of asters have been bred; they vary in height from little over 1 foot up to 5 feet, and in color from white through all the pinks to rosy red and through the blues to violet and purple. It is best to visit a local nursery to make your selection. The plants like a moist, but not wet, soil and are best divided and replanted every other year to provide a wonderful show in September.

In 1920 a Swiss plant breeder introduced three cultivars of *A.* × *frikartii,* of which 'Mönch' (the name of a famous mountain) remains the best. It is also the best perennial aster. A 3-foot plant of clear blue that flowers for months from July on, it needs and deserves all the care you can give it.

Astilbe × 'Gloria Superba'

Astrantia major

Astilbe species

Astilbe

Although sometimes called perennial spiraea, this plant is not even in the same plant family. Astilbe is the accepted botanic and common name for a dozen or so wild species, mainly from Asia, and their hybrids (forms of *Astilbe* × *arendsii*) that are some of our most valuable perennials to Zone 4.

Woody rhizomes push up and unfurl bronze, scaly, fernlike leaves late in spring. This makes a fine foliage ground cover from which pyramidal spikes of tiny flowers develop and open from June into August, depending on the forms selected. Colors are white through all the pinks to purple and crimson;

the dark colors often are enhanced by bronze-tinted foliage. These types are usually up to 3 feet high; *A. chinensis* 'Pumila' is ideal for smaller gardens at half this height; it still works well as a ground cover.

Astilbe enjoys moist or even boggy conditions and it looks wonderful next to water. It prefers a rich soil and half shade. Astilbe associates particularly well with Japanese primrose (*Primula japonica*) at the start of the season and the dark-leaved *Ligularia* species later on.

Astrantia major

Masterwort

Originally from Europe and Asia, masterwort is not a dramatic plant but it has a definite, quiet distinction. Above a ground cover of smooth grape-leaf–shaped foliage, flower stems rise 2 feet, dividing and carrying little flower heads that look like formal posies made for the occupants of a Victorian dollhouse. Each is a dome of tiny white flowers surrounded by a collar of green bracts; flowering is at its best in late June and early July.

Masterwort is a woodland-edge plant that needs half shade and summer moisture or it will wilt. In leafy soil it spreads by underground rhizomes. Self-sown seedlings may occur as well. It is probably safe to

Aubrieta deltoidea

Zone 4 and possibly beyond (often a garden has protected corners or a microclimate much more encouraging than the basic zone number suggests).

Specialist nurseries may offer other masterworts and they are well worth searching out. 'Variegata' is a brightly variegated form of the common species. *Astrantia maxima* is a wonderful plant with clear, rose-pink flowers. This species needs good soil and some care to keep going.

Aubrieta deltoidea

Aubrietia

An added *i* creates the common name for one of the best-loved of all rock garden plants. Many gardeners are familiar with the tumbling, 6-inch-high clumps of brilliant purple, lavender, or pink falling over dry stone walls in April and May and making some of the brightest shows of the season.

Aubrietia is native to rocky slopes on hillsides of the eastern Mediterranean. This and the invariably alkaline soil there give clear directions to cultivation in gardens: good drainage, some lime in the soil, and full sun. As always, limits of climatic zone relate directly to snow cover being sufficiently permanent during periods of intense cold. This snow cover acts as a protective insulator. Given this condition, aubrietia is a must for any garden keen on its spring show.

Plants should be clipped after flowering to encourage a tight habit and a solid bank of flowers the following spring. Aubrietia is best planted as young seedlings in May and June. There are named forms that are true to color, but unless they are to be used as the ground cover for a color-coordinated spring bulb display, it is sufficient to grow the mixed packets from seed. All colors, as well as single and double forms, occur.

Aurinia saxatilis

Baptisia australis

Aurinia saxatilis

Basket-of-gold, goldentuft, madwort

In addition to these rather exotic common names, this splendid spring-flowering plant often keeps its old botanical name *Alyssum saxatile* on many nursery lists. The wide-spreading, 9-inch mats of grayish leaves become entirely hidden in April and May by sheets of brilliant, little, yellow flowers; these are often rather fierce in effect, and the softer creamy yellow cultivar 'Citrina' is worth searching out. Unlike the species, which seeds itself with abandon, this and other, more compact cultivars must be propagated by cuttings.

In dry walls, nonspecialist rock gardens, and the front of sunny borders, basket-of-gold shares top honors with aubrietia (*Aubrieta*

deltoidea) and rockcress (*Arabis* species). In fact, these plants overlap geographically in their native southeastern European homes. In the garden, what suits one will suit the other and they combine to make a brilliant show with spring bulbs.

The only concern in using this plant is a colorless summer. Lavender (*Lavandula* species), artemisia (*Artemisia* species), and pinks (*Dianthus* species) can be added to the same sunny site to create interest in succeeding months.

Baptisia australis

False-indigo, wild-indigo

There are over thirty distinct species of *Baptisia,* all of them pea-flowered perennials native to North America. Several are very worthwhile garden plants, although they are used more often in English gardens than in their homeland. However, *B. australis,* the blue false-indigo, is grown on both sides of the Atlantic.

It is one of those perennials, like peony (*Paeonia* species), that once established thrives for decades and is best left alone. Each year in June, strong 4-foot-tall stems with gray-green leaves bear lupinelike spikes that bloom a soft, deep blue. The blossoms develop into fat pods, and throughout the summer the plant makes a good companion to other flowers. At the first frost, the

Begonia tuberhybrida

Begonia semperflorens-cultorum
'Whiskey'

leaves and pods turn velvet black and can be brought indoors for dried arrangements.

Any deep garden soil and sunny spot suits blue false-indigo. A few twigs pushed into the ground around the clump help to hold the plant together and a light clipping over when flowering is done will produce a formal dome of foliage. Of course, this occurs at the expense of seedpods. The plant is hardy, under snow, to Zone 4.

Begonia species

Begonia

There are over a thousand wild begonias. They are so prized by gardeners that over ten thousand cultivated forms are recorded and more appear each year. Begonias are native to the tropics and subtropics of both the Northern and Southern Hemispheres, especially in South America and Asia.

With such a warm habitat range, it is surprising to consider any begonia a garden perennial, but *Begonia grandis* from Malaysia, China, and Japan is hardy to Zone 6 and, with a good winter mulch, possibly beyond. Its secret is that, while the lush, leafy adult plants succumb to winter, tiny bulblets survive and quickly build up new plants each year. These seldom appear before the end of June. With moisture, tiny plantlets appear and in a few weeks grow to 2 feet high. They have the typical off-center begonia leaves, which are pale green above

and burgundy beneath. By August hanging sprays of pink flowers begin and these continue until frost. *B. grandis* takes half shade in a leafy, moist soil and it looks wonderfully exotic with the smaller plantain-lilies (*Hosta* species).

More common in gardens, although more trouble to grow, are begonias that are long-lived indoors but are treated as annuals outside.

One group, known as the *B. semperflorens-cultorum* hybrids, is derived from a number of tropical South American species. These are the wax begonias, which are especially valuable since they are among only a few summer annuals to accept shade; in fact they need it, along with a leafy, moist soil. Planted when all chance of frost is past, they flower without a break until fall in all zones. Flowers range from white through all shades of

Begonia tuberhybrida

Belamcanda chinensis

pink to rosy red and the foliage is pale green to dark bronze. Height varies from a few inches to over a foot tall.

The second major group is known as the *B. tuberhybrida* hybrids. These are the tuberous-rooted begonias, which are often grown as container plants but are also successful outside in a spot sheltered from wind and heat. They need a rich, leafy garden soil. Plant them when growth is well advanced. Vast numbers of flowers, double or single and in every shade except blue, bloom throughout the summer. They can be grown in all zones that have three months of warm weather.

Belamcanda chinensis

Blackberry-lily

There are few iris relatives whose fruiting display is as distinctive as their flowers, so blackberry-lily is valuable for its two seasons of interest.

Swordlike leaves develop in spring from the overwintering rhizomes. Above these, 3- to 4-foot-high zig-zagging stems carry buds that open into sprays of red-spotted orange flowers from July onward. By the time the last flowers have opened, the first have changed to pecan-size fruit that splits in succession to reveal rows of brilliant, shiny black seeds—giving the plant its common name. These often remain unshed until Christmas if the flower arrangers can be kept at bay.

Blackberry-lily is from China and Japan. It succeeds in full sun in well-drained spots, surviving to

Zone 5 with a winter mulch. In Virginia it seeds itself in open woodlands. The plant is useful for extending the season in a spot where spring bulbs have gone to rest. Blackberry-lily is apt to be attacked by the iris borer, a larva that eats young flowering stems and ruins the anticipated display. If iris borer is a problem in your area, apply an insecticide dust containing carbaryl or malathion weekly from the time the first growth starts until early June.

Recently some selections and hybrids with yellow flowers and a variety of spotting have become available. These are worth every effort to find.

Bletilla striata

Bergenia cordifolia

Bergenia species

Winter-begonia, Siberian-tea

There are so few garden perennials with evergreen foliage that *Bergenia* species is particularly valuable. It has woody rhizomes at ground level that produce roundish leathery leaves, often over 6 inches across. Most turn a fine, burnished bronze as the cold weather approaches. As the seasons change (this can occur anytime from January to May depending on the area), tight heads of flowers start to appear. These first open down among the leaves and then extend up to a foot in height, branching as they go. The plant will take almost any soil in sun or shade, but overrich soil makes it soft and too lush.

Winter-begonia (no relation to true begonias) is *B. ciliata,* an exquisite but rather tender species from northern India, where it grows on moist rock faces. The big leaves are hairy on both sides and around the edge. Its blush pink flowers appear early. Although hardy to Zone 6 and beyond, it needs protection from spring frosts after growth has begun, since the young foliage is very delicate.

B. cordifolia and *B. crassifolia* are from Siberia and thus hardy, under snow, to Zone 3 at least. A cover of evergreen boughs is essential where snow is erratic beyond Zone 7.

Bletilla striata

Hardy orchid

Few of the so-called hardy orchids look particularly orchidlike unless you closely examine their tightly packed spikes of flowers. *Bletilla striata* is an elegant exception for gardens in Zone 8 or warmer areas and for warm courtyards in Zone 7. From temperate China and Japan, the plant requires a good, leafy soil that does not dry out in summer.

Usually bought as dried bulbs, hardy orchid is best started indoors in pots in a cool spot and planted outside after the last frost. It needs protection from heat and performs best in a half-shaded location that is kept moist.

Well-grown plants reach 2 feet high and develop fine, pleated, irislike leaves and graceful sprays of 1-inch flowers of the color often called orchid purple. They are good

Bletilla striata

Brachycome iberidifolia

Brachycome iberidifolia

through June and sometimes into July. There is also a white form occasionally offered that is charming but less showy.

A clump of hardy orchid rising airily above little woodland-edge carpets of epimedium (*Epimedium* species) and the smallest plantain-lilies (*Hosta* species) always catches the eye and is worth every care.

Brachycome iberidifolia

Swan-river daisy

In the five distinct areas of the world in which a Mediterranean type of climate exists, annual members of the daisy family make a big impact on the spring flora. Quick to germinate with the first autumn rains, they grow throughout the mild, wet winter and burst into a blaze of flower in March, continuing until they succumb to a strong summer sun.

Swan-river daisy is an Australian example of this distinctive lifestyle. The 1½-foot-high plant makes a wide, much branched, little dome of foliage covered with small, bright daisies in a range of purples and blues. In California, it can be grown in the same way as in Australia. Elsewhere it needs to be treated as a tender summer annual. In areas where summers are short,

sow the seeds indoors and then plant the seedlings outside. In areas where June to September are frost free, sow directly in the ground.

All the annual daisies, whatever their origin, need well-drained soil and full sun. Swan-river daisy is perhaps the best annual daisy in the blue-flowered range. It looks lovely with the yellows and oranges of the South African daisies, including *Ursinia, Dimorphotheca, Venidium,* and *Osteospermum* species. The summer garden could be filled with these daisies, their flowers opening with the sun and closing at night, the reverse of the petals often in striking contrast to the fronts. Easily grown from seed, this is an exciting group of plants deserving greater use.

Browallia speciosa

Brassica oleracea 'Dynasty Pink'

Brassica oleracea

Flowering kale, ornamental cabbage

The problem with most garden annuals is that, originating from the tropics, they turn into compost at the first hard frost. With real winter still a couple of months away, the garden is stripped of most of its color. Ornamental cabbage fills this autumn gap wonderfully.

The wild cabbage, *Brassica oleracea,* native to western European cliffs, has given rise to an extraordinary range of vegetables. These include broccoli, cauliflower, kale, cabbage, brussels sprouts, and this highly ornamental form.

From seeds sown in spring, a typical 1-foot cabbage plant develops and gradually assumes brilliant colors. Depending upon the selection,

it can be variegated with white or cream leaf edges or, more spectacularly, entirely pink or purple. With the leaves tightly arranged in a perfect rosette, the effect is that of old-fashioned roses laid upon the ground.

Ornamental cabbage is best planted in late summer to replace annuals, or used in large containers. It grows in all zones, but the effect is short in northern climates.

Browallia speciosa

Bush violet

Although well-known as a house-plant, bush violet is relatively new as a summer annual for the garden. In its home in the mountains of Colombia, it is a 5-foot-high perennial. Selections and cultivational methods have turned it into a 1- to 2-foot annual that is valued for its clear blue flower color.

Bush violet is grown like any tender tropical in the summer garden. Plant only after all frosts are over and the ground is warm. It will cover itself with tubed, wide-lipped flowers (rather like small flowers of the tobacco plant, a relative) until the fall. Like all annuals, it needs moisture and plenty of fertilizer to continue the show. Bush violet grows in all zones and is limited

Brunnera macrophylla

only by the length of summer. Up to half shade (or more in hot areas) is acceptable.

Having a naturally lax habit, bush violet lends itself well to hanging baskets and, if well-maintained, develops into an almost complete sphere of blue by early September. It can be left outside as long as frosts do not threaten—this may be until Christmas in the far South. In the North, frost can arrive just as the basket of bush violet is at its peak. Bring it indoors and hang it in a sunny window for a few more weeks. A cool greenhouse or sun room can prolong the pleasure into the new year. In the garden, bush violet combines well with perennials in the front of the border.

Brunnera macrophylla

Perennial forget-me-not

Perennials that flower at the same time as late-spring bulbs (which are also perennials, of course) are extremely valuable in the garden. The texture and shape of the foliage contrasts well with the narrow leaves of the bulbs. The heart-shaped leaves of *Brunnera* species is excellent for this purpose.

B. macrophylla comes from the Caucasus mountains and Siberia and, under a mulch of snow or pine boughs, does well to Zone 4. It needs a leafy soil and is a good dry-shade plant under deciduous trees. During the hottest summer weather, it needs some moisture to keep from wilting.

Airy sprays of bright blue forget-me-not flowers appear in late April and May above the developing leaves. Pink lily-flowered tulips are a perfect accompaniment in form

and color, an association that can remain for several years without renewal.

As the plants flower, the foliage continues to grow. By midsummer, the 18-inch domes of heart-shaped leaves form an excellent shade-loving ground cover. Although clipping off the dead flower heads may be desirable in the interests of tidiness, a few should always be left to produce seeds. Young self-sown plants help to ensure continuity. Extra plants can be moved to begin other groupings or passed on to grateful friends.

A variegated form exists and should be sought out. Although it is more delicate, its cream and white leaves with blue flowers make a lovely picture in May. Occasionally it reverts to green leaves, and these should be removed.

Calceolaria integrifolia

Caladium × *hortulanum* 'Postman Joyner'

Caladium × *hortulanum*

Angel-wings, fancy-leaved caladium

This is another relative of the common wild jack-in-the-pulpit, but one that is a truly tropical plant. There are over a dozen species native to tropical South America. They all have tuberous roots and produce stemless plants with all the leaves growing straight from the tubers. But what leaves! Even in the wild they can be red with a green border, variegated green and white, or spotted gray and cream.

The most distinctive types have been bred and selected to produce the range now known as the fancy-leaved caladiums. These make plants 1 to 2 feet high with broad arrow-shaped leaves held at right angles to their stems. Looking like so many patterned heraldic shields, they can be pink, red, salmon, or variously variegated. One of the

most beautiful has almost pure white leaves, only the veins and a narrow margin being green.

Angel-wings must have a hot summer, rich soil, and plenty of moisture in at least half shade. It should be started indoors and planted outside only when soil and air temperatures are likely to stay about 70° F.

Calceolaria integrifolia

Slipperflower, pouchflower

The common names refer to the inflated lower lip of the flower. In some strains these have become so large and extraordinarily spotted that the plants look like a convention of multicolored toads.

All species of *Calceolaria*, some five hundred of them, are from Central and South America. One or two from Patagonia are rock garden plants for West Coast gardens, prized by specialists. The Chilean *C. integrifolia* is shrubby and grows well in Zone 9 gardens, making a 4-foot-wide dome (and almost as high) of soft hairy leaves covered for months from May onward with showers of little yellow pouched flowers marked with darker spots.

In areas where the plant cannot be expected to overwinter (although, cut down in autumn and mulched well, it may surprise you), cuttings

Calendula officinalis 'Art Shades'

can be rooted easily in late summer and kept in a cool spot until the following spring. Planted in any good garden soil in a warm location shaded from the midday sun, it soon builds up much like fuchsia (a compatriot from temperate South America) to a flowering plant by midsummer. It often survives to Zone 5.

Calendula officinalis

Pot marigold

Not to be confused with the marigold from Mexico (*Tagetes* species), this is one of the typical annual plants of old English cottage gardens, sowing itself in borders and cracks of paving and dry walls. It has been used medicinally, and the brilliant petals also serve as a coloring agent for butter and other foods.

The rough, rather coarse leaves have a distinctive scent entirely different from the pungent Mexican species. The loose, 2-foot-high plant has 2-inch-wide, yellow-eyed, orange daisies. Pot marigold has been a subject for breeding and selection for a couple of centuries and now double forms are available, some with flat, and others with quilled, petals, in a range of colors from cream to the most glaring orange.

In its southern European home and in gardens to Zone 8, fall germination of seeds is common. These seedlings can take a few degrees of frost and begin to flower in April and May. In less favored areas, seeds are sown directly in the ground or started indoors and planted outside later. With careful dead-heading, flowering continues well into the fall. Allowing some seed production by any hardy, or even tender, annual and watching for chance seedlings the following year is one of the delights of gardening. So often a plant or two turns up in a paving crack or other corner, softening hard lines—something that could not otherwise be arranged. Use any soil but the wettest and grow in full sun.

Caltha palustris

Callistephus chinensis 'Color Carpet Blue'

Callistephus chinensis

China-aster

This is one of the stalwart annuals of the late summer garden. A native of China, it exhibits a number of forms and flower colors even in the wild. Flowers can be white, pink, or all shades of bluish violet, with single and semidouble forms occurring together. It is not surprising that plant breeders have worked on this already genetically variable stock since its introduction to the West in the 1730s, to produce an extraordinary range.

The typical China-aster is a widely branched, 2-foot-high plant bearing 3- to 4-inch flat flowers with the conventional yellow-disk center. Although forms close to this original type are still available and remain among the best for general use, there are also intensely double, pom-pom flowers, and others with quilled petals. Size now varies from 3-foot-tall types with an open habit to tight little dwarfs no more than 6 inches high.

In climates with four frost-free months, seeds can be sown outside and a good show expected in August and September. Otherwise, and for earlier flowers, treat China-asters like other annuals sown indoors and planted outside near the end of May or when spring frosts are past.

Unfortunately, China-aster is susceptible to many diseases and insects. Select cultivars that are resistant to wilt, root rot, and viruses, and spray for disease-bearing insects. It is also best not to plant it in the same location two years in succession.

Caltha palustris

Kingcup, marshmarigold

This perennial is native to North America from Alaska to Newfoundland south to Tennessee. It also extends across northern Europe and Asia. One of the most delightful flowers of April and May in the wild, kingcup is worth bringing into the garden if its requirements can be met. Coming from wet bogs and watersides, it needs a constant supply of moisture in the early part of the year. Because the plant goes to rest by August, it does not matter if the soil dries out a bit later on. With enough water, half or three-quarters shade is acceptable and helps to keep the plant lush. It grows to Zone 3 and possibly even colder climates.

The double-flowered form is most valuable as a plant that enjoys wet and soggy spots. Although many plants become huge and coarse in this situation, this one never does.

Camassia leichtlinii 'Atrocaerulea'

Camassia leichtlinii

Growth begins when the spring thaw is complete, and soon the heads of shiny green, marble-sized buds push up to 2 feet high. In the spring sun, they catch the light and glint across the garden.

As the flowers fade and columbine-like seedpods take over, the leaves extend and provide a bright hummock for the next three months. Kingcup associates well with other bog plants, especially the Asian primrose (*Primula japonica*) and, later, astilbe (*Astilbe species*).

Camassia leichtlinii

Camass

This is a West Coast plant growing wild from British Columbia to California, yet with a winter mulch, it is hardy to Zone 5, and probably beyond.

Camass is an elegant lily relative. From overwintering bulbs, the lax leaves begin to develop early in spring, putting up fine flower spikes in late May and early June. These are 4 feet high with starry flowers extending up the elegant spire. The normal form is white, but geographical variants and garden selections include flowers that are pale to deep blue, soft yellow, violet, and white. There is even a double form in which the starlike flowers have become rosettes.

Although it often naturalizes to some extent in lawns, camass needs a good garden soil if it is to produce eye-catching flower spikes. Plant a dozen or so bulbs 9 inches apart and 9 inches deep in fall, mulch, and then just leave them alone to increase. Only when the clump becomes so crowded that the size of the flower spikes begins to diminish is it necessary to divide the bulbs.

A spot in full sun is needed (shade exaggerates the already limp leaves) at the back of the border. There it can die off, as it does by late July, hidden by other plants in the border.

Campanula glomerata

Campanula medium

Campanula species

Bellflower

There are almost three hundred species of bellflower strewn around the temperate areas of the Northern Hemisphere. They vary from tiny alpine plants with threadlike stems to robust perennials 6 feet tall. A considerable number have been brought into cultivation and worked upon by plant breeders to extend the range even further. All of the species discussed here grow to Zone 5 in full sun and some species are even hardier. All need ordinary garden soil that is not too wet.

Campanula carpatica, from the Carpathian mountains, makes a clump of bright green leaves covered in June and July with wide, open, cup-shaped flowers. Unlike most bellflowers, the blooms of this plant face upward. *C. carpatica* is only a foot high and therefore needs a front-of-the-border spot. Its color ranges from white through all the blues to deep violet.

C. glomerata is known as the clustered bellflower. This name describes well the concentration of typical bell-shaped flowers at the top of the leafy stems in June and July. The best form is 'Superba', intensely violet-blue and 2 feet high. Other clustered bellflowers vary from white to pale purple and from 1 to 3 feet in height. They are native to Europe, including Great Britain, and to northern Asia.

Much bigger is *C. lactiflora* from the Caucasus mountains. It has the advantage of thriving in sun or shade and even seeds itself under trees without becoming invasive. Strong stems up to 5 feet high carry huge branching heads of lilac flowers in late June, when it looks splendid with shrub roses. If deadheaded, a second display often takes place in the fall. A pink cultivar, 'Loddon Anna', and a dwarf one, 'Pouffe', are sometimes available.

C. medium is Canterbury-bells, one of the loveliest of old-fashioned biennial garden flowers. Sown in June, it overwinters as a flat, leafy rosette that thrusts up rough stems with wide bell-shaped flowers early the next summer. These are available in all shades of pink, blue, or white. There is also a cup-and-saucer form in which the bell sits on a petal-like base. Coming from southeast Europe, Canterbury-bells needs a well-drained soil and a good winter mulch in cold areas.

C. rotundifolia is the harebell or bluebells of Scotland, although it isn't restricted to that country. There are wild forms all around the Northern Hemisphere. This elegant little plant has foot-high stems of typically blue, nodding bells throughout summer. Although it will take light shade, a sunny location helps to keep it compact. Harebell makes a charming picture growing out of paving or leaning from a dry wall.

Canna × generalis

Canna × generalis

Canna × generalis

Common garden canna

The striking silhouette and spikes of exotic flowers have been a part of subtropical bedding schemes since Victorian times. In warm Zone 9 climates, where the fleshy rhizomatous roots are not killed by winter frosts, canna is of immense value for this effect. But it is in the colder climates that it truly stands out, offering an exotic vision of the South for three summer months.

Garden canna was produced by interbreeding several wild species from Central America. The range is now enormous. They all have paddle-shaped leaves carried on fleshy 3- to 6-foot stems topped by a spike of lily flowers in brilliant yellow, pink, and scarlet—often spotted in contrasting shades. The old bronze-leaved form with small red flowers is a superb foliage plant at all stages of growth and invaluable for filling empty spots in the perennial border.

In Zone 6 and warmer areas, the rhizomes can be planted in rich, moist soil in full sun after the last frost. In colder areas, garden canna should be started in pots and planted outdoors as soon as the soil is warm enough. Three or five plants set a foot apart make a spectacular flowering clump by the end of summer.

Caryopteris × clandonensis

Bluebeard, blue-spiraea

For Zone 5 and warmer gardens, bluebeard is one of the most valuable of late-summer shrubs. After being cut to the ground in a hard winter, it behaves as an herbaceous perennial and regenerates from the rootstock. The plant should be tried more often, as long as it is well protected by a mulch in winter.

The product of two Asian species, bluebeard originated as a chance seedling in a garden in Surrey, England. It has produced several cultivars, including 'Kew Blue'. Bluebeard is a 3-foot-high shrub, often bigger across, with aromatic, gray-green leaves. Starting in August and until the leaves fall, every leaf axil carries a bunch of little flowers like those of verbena (*Verbena* species). These range from pale to dark blue. After turning

Caryopteris × clandonensis

Catananche caerulea

brown, the seedheads make an interesting pattern into winter. It is best to cut the shoots back by half their length in spring.

Bluebeard needs a well-drained spot in full sun. Meadow-saffron (*Colchicum* species) makes a particularly good accompaniment; in spring its lush leaves enliven bluebeard's bare branches and in fall its pink-purple goblets are seen against the blue haze of the shrub.

Catananche caerulea
Cupid's-dart

There are very few hardy perennial everlastings and this is the only one with colorful flowers. Thus it has a living role in the garden and a post-mortem one in winter arrangements indoors. As a native of hot Mediterranean hillsides, cupid's-dart needs a sunny location and perfect drainage. Its hardiness is doubtful beyond Zone 6, although a good snow cover before deep-soil freezing extends the range. Overly rich soil makes the plant lush and even more short-lived than it already tends to be.

Cupid's-dart makes a clump of grayish grassy leaves that produce masses of wiry stems carrying double, daisy flowers. These are typically lavender-blue with a darker center held in a papery base. Immediate dead-heading helps the display last from July well into late summer. There is a white form and one with white-edged blue flowers. The robust 'Major' with deep violet-blue flowers is probably the best, and grows 2 feet high.

The rather thin growth of cupid's-dart is helped by the gray foliage of *Artemisia* species planted nearby, but cupid's-dart does not do well with too much competition and can be easily shaded-out and lost.

Celosia cristata 'Century Yellow'
(Plumosa group)

Catharanthus roseus 'Little Rose'

Catharanthus roseus

Madagascar-periwinkle

Once included with the true periwinkles (*Vinca* species), this tropical subshrub is very distinct in all but flower shape. Originally collected from Madagascar in the 1750s, the plant has become naturalized throughout the tropical world. In cultivation it has long been a favorite container plant for the greenhouse, propagated by cuttings. New forms that grow true from seed have been bred, and Madagascar-periwinkle has taken on new importance as a valuable summer annual.

A bushy plant, it grows to 2 feet tall and has shining leaves. Forms with typical pink blooms are available, as are those with white or rose flowers, with or without a contrasting eye. All have the usual rotate

petals of the family. Madagascar-periwinkle needs to be started very early in the year in considerable warmth, and it is generally better bought potted, to be planted when all danger of frost is past and the soil has warmed. It thrives in all but the driest soils and is one of the few summer annuals that remains floriferous in shade. It does well in all zones with a hot summer.

Madagascar-periwinkle is poisonous (but there is no attractive fruit to encourage experimentation) and contains over sixty different alkaloids whose extracts are marketed commercially as drugs for cancer therapy.

Celosia cristata

Cockscomb, feathered-amaranth

Some of the most brilliantly colored summer annuals come from this tropical plant, native to Africa and South America. Brilliance does not necessarily make a good garden plant, however, and unfortunately breeders of cockscomb (*Celosia cristata*) have often let their taste for the bizarre get out of hand. On a dwarf plant a few inches high and meagerly furnished with undistinguished leaves sits a strange assemblage of individually tiny flowers compressed together into something that indeed resembles a fat cockscomb or brain coral. The colors, which can be bright yellow, orange, or crimson, are often mixed in the same seed packet.

Another, much more attractive face is seen in the Plumosa group, known as feathered-amaranths.

Centaurea cyanus

Centaurea dealbata

This group is as graceful in form as cockscomb is awkward. Here tiny flowers in the same color range are carried on flamelike spires, feathery in texture and elegant in outline. The taller types, often over 2 feet high, are the most attractive and bloom from early summer until the frosts of autumn.

As tropical annuals, they are started indoors and planted outside after all danger of frost has passed. They succeed anywhere if given a few warm summer months and good, rich garden soil in full sun.

Centaurea species

Knapweed, bachelor's-button, cornflower, mountain bluet

There are almost five hundred wild *Centaurea* species concentrated in southern Europe and Asia Minor. Many of these are valuable annual or perennial garden daisies, usually with hard, knotlike flower buds whose shape remains after the flower petals have died.

C. dealbata has a green upper leaf with a gray-green underside. It produces 2-foot-high daisies that are a lovely pink or lavender with a silvery cast. The combination of pink and silver is charming. A perennial from the Caucasus mountains, the plant is hardy to Zone 5. Like the other members of the daisy family, it does poorly in wet soil and needs full sun to keep the flower stems strong and upright.

Bachelor's-button or cornflower (*C. cyanus*) is a thin Mediterranean annual up to 3 feet high. Grayish stems and narrow grayish leaves are topped with fringed daisies in a range of clear colors: blue, pink, or white. All are delightful. This is a hardy annual because in Zones 8 and above it germinates in autumn, and flowers, as it does in its native home, in early spring. In cooler areas it can either be started indoors and planted outside later or sown in place as soon as the soil is fit to work. Flowering begins in June and continues until fall if the plant is dead-headed. Cornflower

Centaurea macrocephala

Centranthus ruber

needs good drainage in full sun and, like pot marigold, will often shed its own seeds and come up year after year.

The name *C. macrocephala* means "big head." Native to the Caucasus mountains and hardy at least to Zone 5, this plant has strong straight stems 3 feet tall. Clusters of hard, green, almost golf ball–size buds enclosed in papery bracts open into yellow-fringed daisies. The plant is useful for winter drying as well as for its garden effect. It grows easily in any sunny spot and can become invasive if allowed.

Mountain bluet (*C. montana*) is smaller and quite useful in the front of the border. From Central Europe, it is hardy to Zone 3 in dry soil. Less than 2 feet high, it produces blue or white flowers in June at the same time as lupine (*Lupinus* species) and the first flush of catmint (*Nepeta* × *faassenii*).

Centranthus ruber

Red valerian

Native to cliffs and rocky slopes of western and southern Europe, red valerian has a penchant for lime that has made it almost an inevitable part of castle and monastic ruins. In these locations it sends roots deep into stony crevices to feed on the lime-based mortar with which the castles were built.

On these walls the plant looks entirely at home. Its 3-foot-stems of gray, glaucous leaves and heads of tiny, bright pink flowers make a perfect dome 3 feet across. There is a white form and one called 'Atrococcineus' that is deep coppery red. The length of bloom, which begins in late June, depends on the climate.

As the description of its habitat makes clear, red valerian must have light, perfectly drained soil in a sunny position. It has become naturalized—some would say a weed— in parts of coastal California, and

thus is not for the coldest areas. Zone 6, with a winter mulch, is probably its limit but such a doubtfully hardy plant should be at least tried if it is available. It cannot be emphasized too much that zone numbers are a very general guide and that the microclimate in individual gardens, combined with a little extra effort, can bring success despite the advice found in books.

Ceratostigma plumbaginoides

Cerastium tomentosum

Cerastium tomentosum

Snow-in-summer

The genus *Cerastium* includes some high alpines cherished in specialists' rock gardens as well as some common weeds, such as mouse-ear chickweed.

Snow-in-summer is a lovely garden plant that becomes weedy when not watched carefully, especially in mild areas. It comes from the mountains of Italy, where it runs under and over rocks, and it can spread alarmingly in the garden. Thus, it is not for the type of rock garden that holds tiny treasures. It is excellent as a continuing floral display when the robust spring carpeters such as aubrietia (*Aubrieta deltoidea*) and alyssum (*Aurinia saxatilis*) are gone. It also does well combined with the stronger creeping bellflowers (*Campanula* species). At Wave Hill Garden, New York, overlooking the Hudson River, it is allowed to scramble

through shrubby cinquefoil (*Potentilla atrosanguinea*), making a lovely white and yellow picture.

Snow-in-summer makes wide clumps of gray stems and leaves a foot high that carry a wonderful show of pure white, 1-inch flowers in midsummer. These are widely bell-shaped and face upward. Full sun in a well-drained soil provides the necessary conditions. If the plant runs under stones, it is hardy to Zone 5 and sometimes 4; otherwise it will survive to Zone 6.

Ceratostigma species

Hardy plumbago, leadwort

The true plumbago, with its flower heads the color of the summer morning sky, is for the warmest zones only and the envy of all who cannot grow it. This relative, although very different, does offer something of an alternative with its blue flowers.

Ceratostigma plumbaginoides, the hardy plumbago, is only a foot and a half high and, although it runs underground, seldom becomes invasive. Its purplish stems and shiny leaves produce a good ground cover. In August, bristly heads develop a sequence of short-lived flowers that continue until the frosts of autumn. As temperatures drop, the leaves turn bronze and purple, so the season ends in a dramatic way.

Native to stony slopes in western China, the plant needs good drainage. It grows in the sunniest spot in

Ceratostigma willmottianum

Chasmanthe aethiopica

the front of the border but will also take partial shade. Like snow-in-summer (*Cerastium tomentosum*) it is effective roaming through the stones of a dry wall. In a suitable position and with a winter mulch it is hardy to Zone 5.

A related species is the shrubby *C. willmottianum*. This marvelously blue-flowered, 4-foot-high plant is worth trying in Zone 6 and warmer areas in a protected spot.

Chasmanthe aethiopica

Chasmanthe

This elegant gladiolus relative from South Africa is suitable only for the warmest zones. From flattened corms very much like those of the gladiolus (*Gladiolus* species), pleated leaves push through the ground in autumn, encouraged in California by the first fall rains. By early spring the 3-foot flower spikes start to show, opening their first flowers in May and sometimes earlier. Bright orange with a red flush, the flowers are narrow with an elongated, overhanging upper lip and long, protruding stamens.

Chasmanthe needs a well-drained soil and a sunny location. It associates well with belladonna-lily (*Amaryllis belladonna*) and nerine (*Nerine bowdenii*)—both of which flower before their leaves appear—by giving their bare stems the benefit of chasmanthe's early leaves.

In Zone 8 and colder areas, chasmanthe corms can be overwintered and planted in spring when the soil warms up and frosts are over. However, in colder regions the bright fresh foliage, welcome in a southern winter, is less distinctive in the rush of summer growth all around.

Chelone glabra

Cheiranthus cheiri

Cheiranthus cheiri

Wallflower

One of England's favorite cottage-garden plants, wallflower blooms with the spring bulbs and brings a wide range of unusual colors to the early garden scene. In the wild it is truly a flower of walls, sharing historic ruins with red valerian (*Centranthus ruber*) and other plants that relish a lime soil and perfect drainage. A little evergreen sub-shrub 1 or 2 feet tall with bright yellow spikes of flowers, wallflower is similar to stock (*Matthiola incana*) and, like it, deliciously scented.

Forms with double flowers and colors from palest cream through orange and apricot to dark blood red are available, varying in size from less than 1 foot to more than 2 feet in height.

Although a perennial, wallflower is normally grown as a biennial. Seeds are sown indoors in May and the seedlings later transplanted outside a foot apart, or the seeds can be sown directly in the ground. In cold climates, the plants are moved in fall to their overwintering position, where they are to flower. In Zone 6 they survive most winters outside but are best overwintered in frames and replanted, almost in flower, for their May show. Alternatively, a few plants, three to an 8-inch pot, can be grown in a cool greenhouse and brought indoors for their ravishing scent as they flower in February.

Chelone species

Turtlehead

This is a widely distributed North American native growing in marshes from Newfoundland south to Georgia and west to Minnesota. It is useful in the mixed herbaceous border to give color and interest later in the season.

Chelone glabra can reach 6 feet in height but is seldom seen above 4 feet. It makes a stiff, yet handsome, clump with spikes of white or pale pink two-lipped flowers that are strangely reminiscent of a turtle's or snake's head. Aster (*Aster* species) and the fall-flowering stonecrop (*Sedum* species) combine well with turtlehead.

Two shorter relatives are *C. lyonii* and *C. obliqua*. These have stronger-colored, rose-purple flowers and are well worth trying, although they

Chelone lyonii

Chionodoxa luciliae

may not be quite as hardy. Under a mulch of snow, the common turtlehead is safe to Zone 3.

Turtlehead is native to marshy or boggy ground and does best in an ordinary garden soil as long as it does not dry out during the growing season. It takes half shade, which helps to conserve moisture, as does a spring mulch of compost or other well-rotted organic material.

Chionodoxa luciliae

Glory-of-the-snow

Few plants are so suitably named. Both in the wild and in cultivation, glory-of-the-snow pushes up its leaves through the spring snow-melt, and as the sun warms the soil its flowers open wide, almost touching the snowbanks around. Not that such a chilly frame is essential: The plant is as effective in February in California as it is two months later in Zone 3.

Typically associated in the garden with crocus (*Crocus* species), monkshood (*Aconitum* species), and other small early-spring bulbs, it differs from blue scilla (*Scilla* species) in having wider, open flowers and a white base on each bright blue petal. Three or four flowers the size of a quarter appear on each stem, which is about 6 inches high.

Leaves extend further after flowering, so it is wise to interplant glory-of-the-snow with some later, bigger bulbs to mask the declining foliage.

Although full sun is desirable at flowering time, it does not matter if shrub or tree shade develops later overhead. By then, the bulbs will have built up their strength for the following year. One small clump may be charming, but glory-of-the-snow is best naturalized in as large a number as can be afforded. Plant the little bulbs 3 inches deep and 6 inches apart and they will increase rapidly in good, well-drained soil. *Chionodoxa luciliae* is the best of the six species, all from southeastern Europe and Asia Minor.

Chlorophytum comosum (in front)

Chrysanthemum coccineum

Chlorophytum comosum

Spiderplant

There is probably no more common houseplant than spiderplant and none easier to grow and propagate. But this in no way detracts from its value in its variegated forms as an ornamental.

Spiderplant needs little introduction. The foot-tall clump of wide, grassy green leaves, striped with white or yellow, springs from a tuberous rootstock. It throws out long stems that produce new plantlets at their tips. These root as they touch moist soil, making propagation immediate and easy.

As a South African native, spiderplant is a garden perennial only in Zones 9 and 10. Its leaves blacken at the first frost, but as a summer foliage plant it is as useful in the garden as it is indoors in winter. Its green and white stripes

brighten dark corners and combine splendidly with wax begonia (*Begonia semperflorens-cultorum* hybrids) and impatiens (*Impatiens* species). Spiderplant prefers some shade because it bleaches a bit in the hottest spots. It is also superb for hanging baskets and containers, since the stems of young plantlets cascade over the side.

The tuberous roots make spiderplants very resistant to drought, but summer watering produces the most attractive plants.

Chrysanthemum species

Chrysanthemum, pyrethrum, Shasta daisy, feverfew

Depending on the botanical authority used, there are between one hundred and two hundred *Chrysanthemum* species, strewn mainly around the Northern Hemisphere. The disparity is caused by a great variation among chrysanthemums, which is sometimes used as a means to create separate genera. Basically, the chrysanthemum is a daisy with aromatic foliage. It can be an annual, herbaceous perennial, or shrub, with a vast range of types in between. These have been extended immensely by careful selection and breeding.

In the case of the florist's chrysanthemum (*C.* × *morifolium*), breeding has taken place over many centuries. It is the product of several Asian species that were prized in China and Japan long before

Chrysanthemum × superbum

Chrysanthemum coccineum 'Brenda'

being brought to the West, where breeding has been even more extensive. Although potted chrysanthemums and cut flowers are seen blooming all year round, this is arranged through controlled artificial lighting that simulates shorter daylight hours. In the garden the plant naturally flowers in late summer and fall. A potted mum can be planted outside after the blooms fade, but it is unlikely that it will do much. A florist's chrysanthemum that will perform outdoors must be sold specifically for that purpose.

Forms range in height from 1 to 4 feet, come in most soft colors, including white, yellow, pink, and bronze, and can be single- or double-flowered. Solitary show flowers are created by disbudding sprays of flowers, but this is unnecessary for garden bloomers.

Any decent, well-drained soil in at least three-quarters sun suits the chrysanthemums described here

(unless stated otherwise). With a winter mulch, plants survive to Zone 4.

One of the simplest florist's chrysanthemum types is *C. nipponicum,* a Japanese species with a dome of dark, 3-foot-high glossy foliage that becomes hidden in September by masses of white daisies. This is a useful foliage plant at the front of the border for several months before the floral display begins.

Very different is *C. coccineum* from Asia Minor. Known as pyrethrum, its flower heads are one of the sources of the commercial insecticide bearing that name. In the garden, pyrethrum makes clumps of pale green, ferny foliage and puts up 2-foot-high stems with wide pink, white, or red daisies from June on. The first flush coincides with bearded iris (*Iris* species) and

lupine (*Lupinus* species). Full sun and good soil with perfect drainage are necessary. Do not crowd pyrethrum plants or they will grow poorly. Pyrethrum is hardy down to Zone 5 with a winter mulch. Even with care, however, the plant is apt to be short-lived.

The easily grown Shasta daisy, *Chrysanthemum × superbum* (also listed as *C. maximum*) is a product of two Iberian species. From the dark green ground-hugging foliage come strong stems 2 to 4 feet high carrying fine white daisies in late June and July. Double types lack the typical yellow eye. If deadheaded, side shoots extend the show. Growing conditions are the same as for pyrethrum but the Shasta daisy will take Zone 4.

Feverfew (*C. parthenium*) is a short-lived perennial from southeastern Europe that has naturalized in parts of North America. The name feverfew suggests a medicinal value, but only in recent years has

Chrysanthemum parthenium

Chrysogonum virginianum

the plant been shown to have curative properties for some migraine conditions. Feverfew is started from seed indoors under glass and planted out in spring. It grows 2 to 3 feet high and throughout the summer produces sprays of white daisies with yellow centers. The cultivar 'Aureum' has bright golden yellow foliage. Feverfew reseeds in light soil in sun or shade to Zone 5.

The traditional white marguerite is really a shrubby chrysanthemum (*C. frutescens*) also known as parisdaisy, although it is native to the Canary Islands. Propagated by cuttings, it is a useful, near-permanent resident in warm gardens, as well as an invaluable container plant in colder areas. The original white, single daisy type has been extended into double, as well as yellow and pale pink, forms.

Chrysogonum virginianum

Chrysogonum

It is surprising that this charming little native sunflower relative has not been given a common name. "Always gold" or "green and gold" might be proposed because they are almost never out of flower during the growing season. Originating from Pennsylvania south to Florida and Louisiana, chrysogonum is not a plant for the coldest areas, but it can be grown to Zone 5 with a winter mulch.

The plant makes a low hummock of hairy leaves resembling those of black-eyed-susan (*Rudbeckia hirta*). They are hardly above the ground before the appearance of the first golden daisies, which are 1½ inches across. As the season progresses, the flowers continue to bloom and the stems get a little higher, but never more than a foot tall. Chrysogonum may be hidden

in the fallen leaves of autumn or even by the first snowfall before it gives up for the year.

This persistent little plant is happy in any good garden soil that is neither too wet nor utterly dry in summer. It is a plant for the front of a prominent small border, raised bed, or rock garden, where it can get the attention it deserves. It is effective growing above low ground covers, with small spring bulbs in temporary attendance.

Clematis integrifolia

Cimicifuga racemosa

Cimicifuga species

Bugbane

This wonderful buttercup relative is like an enormous baneberry (*Actaea* species) without the bright berry display. Bugbane doesn't need it. Rising above its clump of finely divided leaves late in the season are tall, long-lasting spires of creamy bottlebrush-shaped flowers.

Cimicifuga racemosa, which originates from Ontario south to Tennessee, is one of the plants called black cohosh, and was once used medicinally by Native Americans. Although this role has disappeared, *C. racemosa* has a modern role as a valuable border plant for late July to August flowering. Above the leaves rise 5- to 6-foot-high leafless stems that produce an airy and arresting effect. The dried seedheads that develop remain elegant for weeks.

C. simplex, from Siberia and Japan, is only 4 feet high. It flowers into, and sometimes beyond, October, ending the season with its white fluffy spires. 'White Pearl' is a good cultivar.

Bugbane likes a deep, rich, leafy soil and half shade. Plenty of moisture is essential if the plant is grown in full sun. With winter mulch, it grows to Zone 4.

Clematis species

Virgin's-bower, clematis

With over two hundred species from both the Northern and Southern Hemispheres, *Clematis* species offer a wide range of desirable plants for North American gardens. They are best known as climbers for walls and for scrambling through other shrubs, but there are also nonclimbing species for the herbaceous perennial border. These take ordinary garden soil in full sun.

C. heracleifolia is a rather coarse subshrub (its name means "leaves like hogweed"), but it makes a striking statement in the garden. From a woody rootstock grow 3-foot-high stems with three-lobed leaves. In July these develop clusters of flowers in their axils. Unlike the usual wide, flat clematis flowers, these are more like pleasantly scented English bluebells (*Endymion non-scriptus*) in color and shape. Occasionally there are one

Cleome hasslerana 'Alba'

Clematis viticella 'Venosa Violacea'

or two selected forms that have brighter blue flowers. Native to northern China, with a winter mulch it is hardy to Zone 4 and perhaps beyond.

C. integrifolia comes from southern Europe and therefore is safe enough in Zone 5 with a mulch or snow cover. This plant is a couple of feet high with opposite pairs of leaves. In late June violet-blue nodding flowers, not unlike the color of a turk's-cap lily (*Lilium martagon*), appear. The display is charming, but short-lived. Both of these nonclimbing clematis need the support of a few sticks around the clump to keep it together and to maintain height and shape.

C. viticella, from southern Europe, is a scrambling plant that climbs by twisting its leaf stalks around any support it meets. Once there, it is attached for good, so any training must be done before the plant has made up its own mind. In spite of this habit and its ability to reach 10 or 12 feet in height, the plant is almost herbaceous. Young stems start to emerge from near ground level as soon as the soil warms up. This plant can be trained up an arbor or against a wall, or it can be allowed to romp through a stout shrub. Beginning in June and continuing off and on until September, flowers up to 2 inches across bloom in a wide range of colors from white, through the blues, to pink and purple. Double-flowered forms with an old-world charm are also available. Any good garden soil in at least half sun is suitable. Zone 4 is probably the limit.

Cleome hasslerana

Spiderflower

One of the most useful of summer annuals, spiderflower grows quickly and gives height and form to blank spots in the garden.

The plant is from Brazil and Argentina and therefore must be grown indoors and planted outside when all danger of frost has passed. It succeeds in all zones with a warm, reasonably long summer, often reseeding itself and flowering the following year only slightly later than newly planted spiderflowers.

The plants quickly build to a widely branched form 4 feet high and clothed with pale, fingered leaves. Each prickly stem ends in a flower head that elongates from July to frost and continuously produces pink, purple, or white flowers resembling a daddy longlegs. It is a fine long-lasting cut flower. The

Colchicum speciosum

Cleome hasslerana

long seedpods turn purplish and are part of the display.

Spiderflower does well in any good garden soil in full sun. It needs moisture, since drought dwarfs the plant unacceptably. It is one of those annuals whose skeletons becomes woody enough to withstand fall frosts and, although dead, it maintains an interesting shape well into winter. Be cautious of the thorns when you decide to pull it up.

Colchicum species

Meadow-saffron, autumn-crocus

Despite the common name, *Colchicum* is not a crocus. Apart from being botanically unrelated, its growth pattern is so different that it fills a very distinct garden use.

Most species come from southern Europe and Asia Minor. From tuliplike bulbs they push their wonderful flower display directly out of the bare ground in September and October. Each blossom, up to 4 inches across, is like a narrow, pink or purple wineglass. Dozens of flowers may come in succession from just a couple of mature, established bulbs.

After the flowers are gone, a leaf bud appears and gradually unfolds into a rosette of 16-inch leaves like those of plantain-lily (*Hosta* species). These last until the plant goes to rest the following May. In Zone 6 or colder areas (meadow-saffron

is probably safe to Zone 4), the leaf bud remains unopened until spring, when the shining lushness of the leaves is quite impressive.

All species are good, but *C. byzantinum* and *C. speciosum* are especially so. They accept any soil but the wettest and a spot in full sun.

The dry bulbs of meadow-saffron are often found flowering right on the shelf in garden centers, so it is not surprising they are sometimes called wonder bulbs. Even at this stage you can plant them out in the garden, placing the top of the bulb 2 inches below the soil surface.

Coleus × hybridus 'Pink Rainbow'

Consolida ambigua

Coleus × hybridus

Painted-nettle, coleus

The brilliant leaf colors of coleus have been enjoyed for centuries as houseplants propagated from cuttings. Now you can grow attractive, faster-maturing types as annuals in the garden.

Hybrid painted-nettle is derived from several species native to Indonesia and the Philippines. Square stems and paired leaves indicate their dead-nettle or mint family relationship, as do the spikes of little blue-hooded flowers. These are so insignificant compared to the leaves that they are often pinched out to encourage more foliage.

Even in the warmest zones, painted-nettle rarely overwinters and is best started indoors each year. Buy new seeds or maintain especially attractive forms by rooting cuttings. Plant outside only when the soil has warmed and all danger of frost

has passed. In half or even full shade in moist soil, painted-nettle makes a bushy plant up to 2 feet high with patterned leaves of every conceivable color but blue. With such potential variation, it is wise to choose named types so that you know what you are getting.

The rainbow types can be dwarf, remaining under 1 foot in height, or semidwarf, growing to 2 feet. A packet of mixed seeds produces plants that are entirely red, pink, bronze, or salmon, each with a green edge, or cream with green splashes, and so on. Seed of each form can also be obtained from the corresponding plants.

Consolida ambigua

Larkspur

In almost every way except for differences of petal configuration, larkspur is an annual delphinium (*Delphinium cultivars*), a genus with which it was once merged. These botanical considerations have no effect on cultivation and the two groups can be considered together.

Larkspur is an annual of Mediterranean origin, and there, with other natives such as pot marigold (*Calendula officinalis*) and pheasant's-eye (*Adonis annua*), it germinates with the autumn rains to grow slowly over winter and flower in the spring. After setting seed it dies in the drought of summer.

Gardeners in Zone 9 can successfully imitate this natural pattern outdoors. Elsewhere, treat larkspur as a typical summer annual and

Convallaria majalis

sow indoors. If there are four decent summer months ahead, you can sow directly in the ground.

Fernlike leaves and a narrow spike in a range of pastel colors make larkspur one of the most loved of summer annuals. If you remove the central flower spike, side shoots often bloom. It is a good cut flower and retains its color and petals when dried. Depending on selection, height varies from 1½ to 3 feet. Provide well-drained soil in full sun.

Convallaria majalis

Lily-of-the-valley

Native to Central and Western Europe, lily-of-the-valley has been cultivated as a garden plant since time immemorial. It is renowned for its scent—penetrating, sweet, and entirely distinct.

Lily-of-the-valley is also one of the best (and occasionally invasive) of all ground-cover plants for shady sites, succeeding even under black walnuts, traditionally the most inhospitable of spots. It grows in any soil to Zone 4 under a mulch of winter snow.

From rhizomes running a couple of inches underground, the purple shoots push up in April or May and open to a pair of fresh, shining leaves. To one side (not between them, as is usual) a narrow stem of beadlike buds appear. These soon

open into hanging bells with a wonderful scent that permeates the spring garden.

As the flowers fade, the foliage extends. As long as the soil remains reasonably moist, the green carpet continues until fall. Then the leaves turn yellow and die, and a few spikes of bright red berries light up. These, it should be warned, are poisonous. The plant contains glycosides which are used medicinally.

Lily-of-the-valley has double and pink-flowered forms and one with cream stripes on the leaves, but none is more beautiful than the single white type.

Coreopsis tinctoria 'Baby Sun'

Convolvulus tricolor

Convolvulus tricolor

Annual morning glory,
dwarf morning glory

There are over two hundred species of *Convolvulus,* native to most areas of the temperate world. Among them are some delightful southern European perennials and small shrubs (such as the silver-leaved *C. cneorum*) suitable for warm gardens. There are also some beautiful, but noxious, weeds suitable for none.

Dwarf morning glory is a charming 6- to 9-inch annual, native to hot rocky banks in southern Italy, Sicily, and other parts of the Mediterranean. Wild plants have wide, trumpet-shaped, three-colored flowers as the name suggests. Pale blue petals shade to yellow and then to white in the center.

Selection and breeding have produced tighter, more floriferous plants with brighter blue flowers.

In California and other warm-winter areas, autumn-sown seeds germinate quicker and the overwintering plants flower in early spring, as they do in their native homes. In colder areas seeds can either be sown indoors and the plants put out when the soil is fit (they can take a couple of degrees of frost without coming to harm if gradually hardened off), or sown directly in the ground and the seedlings thinned to 6 inches apart. Dwarf morning glory needs a sunny place in the front of the border.

Coreopsis species

Coreopsis

Of the hundred or so species of coreopsis strewn across North and South America (and even a few in Africa), several are useful garden plants. All are native to the central United States and are among the easiest plants to grow, giving a summer-long show of yellow daisies above light, fernlike foliage. As with almost all daisies, coreopsis needs full sun and, although it will often survive summer drought in a good soil, regular watering gives the best results.

Coreopsis tinctoria is the annual species of this recommended trio. Up to 4 feet in height, it has flowers that are typically bright yellow with a bronze central zone. Selected forms accentuate one color or the other. Sow indoors or seed directly in the ground when the soil starts to warm up. The plant often appears in catalogs as the genus

Coreopsis verticillata

Corydalis lutea

Calliopsis, but botanically it belongs here. The annual coreopsis, or tick-seed, is also used in wildflower mixtures for broadcast sowing.

C. lanceolata is a rather short-lived perennial 2 feet in height with lovely yellow flowers 3 inches across. *C. verticillata* is an excellent long-lived perennial 3 feet tall, with smaller flowers than *C. lanceolata* but more of them. The cultivar 'Moonbeam' has lemon yellow flowers. Other named forms include 'Golden Shower', which has warm yellow flowers, and the dwarf 'Goldfink', a 15-inch plant with brilliant golden blooms ideal for the front of a sunny border. Perennial coreopsis survives to Zone 4 under winter snow.

Corydalis species

Corydalis

There are three hundred or more of these charming poppy relations (although very unpoppy-looking) strewn around the Northern Hemisphere, with a few strange ones in South Africa. The most common is *Corydalis lutea,* from Europe, which grows well in shady, moist spots to Zone 5 and probably well beyond if the winter snow cover is good.

It's an unassuming little plant that makes mounds of pale, lacy, filigreed foliage less than a foot high, with short spikes of yellow, spurred flowers like tiny snapdragons. Individual plants seldom last more than a couple of years, but before dying they set so much seed that young plants appear in the most unexpected places, providing splashes of soft color throughout the summer.

Corydalis is lovely with the blue navelwort (*Omphalodes* species) in early summer.

Other species are worth looking for. The Siberian *C. nobilis* is a strong 2-foot-high perennial for early color in woodland sites. *C. tuberosa,* sometimes called fumewort, colonizes well and looks good with the smaller spring bulbs. Its soft, pinkish purple color is unusual so early in the season.

Crambe cordifolia

Cosmos bipinnatus

Cosmos species

Cosmos

Like its close relation the dahlia (*Dahlia* cultivars), cosmos grows in the southwestern United States and down into the tropics. Some have tubers; it's worth looking for the tuberous, almost black-flowered *Cosmos atrosanguineus,* which smells of chocolate. It must be treated like a dahlia: Lift the tubers in autumn in Zone 8 and below and store them in a cool place in barely moist peat over winter.

The typical garden cosmos is usually a late-flowering annual that looks best from August until frost. From seeds sown indoors in spring and planted outside when all danger of frost has passed, it makes a tall (to 5 feet or more), widely branched plant with feathery foliage and big yellow-eyed daisies. *C. bipinnatus,* 3 to 5 feet tall, has flowers that are white to pink or crimson. *C. sulphureus,* 2 to 3 feet tall, has yellow to orange blooms. All species require good soil in full sun.

Breeders have created earlier-flowering types, but the timing of bright cosmos flowers late in the season when other flowers have faded is one of their best attributes. Dwarf types with a compact bushy habit only a couple of feet high are now available, but they lack the grace of the original cosmos.

Crambe cordifolia

Colewort

This is one of the largest herbaceous plants for the garden. A single, deep-rooted specimen takes up at least 25 square feet of garden border. If given the required space, it makes one of the most dramatic flower shows of late June and July.

Colewort comes from the Caucasus mountains and succeeds in deep, rich soil to Zone 5 and, with a good mulch, beyond. Above a great clump of dark green leaves 6 feet high, widely branched stems develop and become covered with white star-shaped flowers. The effect is like that of a vast baby's-breath. The scent is either disgusting or delightful, depending on the recipient.

Treat colewort as a specimen for an isolated spot and enjoy its month of glory, or place it at the back of the border behind late-flowering plants like cosmos (*Cosmos* species) or cannas (*Canna × generalis*).

Crocosmia masoniorum

Crinum × powellii 'Krelagii'

Crinum × powellii

Crinum-lily

Enormous crinum-lily bulbs, shaped like small footballs, produce top growth of similarly impressive size. But crinum-lily is only for the warmest areas of North America: Zones 9 and 10. Where it succeeds, it makes an impressive pattern with bear's-breech (*Acanthus* species) and cannas (*Canna × generalis*), which also enjoy sunny positions in the garden.

Crinum × powellii is a hybrid between two species from South Africa, and is a better garden plant than either parent. Plant the bulbs so that the long fleshy necks extend about halfway above ground. From these emerge the long wavy-edged leaves. Three bulbs placed 1½ feet apart create a clump 4 or 5 feet across and almost as tall.

In midsummer, smooth stems push up to 4 feet tall and display heads of long-tubed flowers. Each is lilylike and delightfully scented. They open over a long period, beginning in late June and continuing for many weeks if the soil remains moist.

The typical flower color is rose-pink, but lighter and darker forms, as well as a beautiful white one, have been selected. In areas on the edge of its safe range, a winter mulch of rich compost is wise. So too is a constant watch for slugs and snails, which find its leaves irresistible.

Crocosmia **species**

Montbretia

This is a lovely, easy-to-grow gladiolus relative that comes from South Africa and is hardy to Zone 7 with a good winter mulch. Unfortunately for colder areas, it doesn't adapt well to the conventional treatment of autumn lifting, winter storage, and replanting in spring. This is because it grows from strings of semiattached corms and does not make the big self-contained corms as does gladiolus (*Gladiolus* species). Nonetheless, it is worth trying to store the corms in barely moist peat in a cool spot over winter.

An established clump of montbretia makes sheaves of long, pleated leaves with wiry stems 2 feet high. In late summer they carry small lilylike flowers. The most common type is *Crocosmia × crocosmiiflora,* a hybrid produced

Crocus tomasinianus

over a hundred years ago by the famous French nursery firm Lemoine. It has bright orange flowers that are yellow in the tube and marked with dark red. It does well in sun or shade and can even become invasive in moist soil.

C. masoniorum is larger, growing to 3 feet high. Unlike the other species, whose flowers either look forward or even decorously downward, these brilliant vermilion blooms crowd the arching stem tip and face upward. Tone down this eye-catcher with gray foliage or complement it with purple-leaved plants. It should be planted in full sun only.

Crocus species

Crocus

No spring is complete without the joy of crocuses blooming at the very beginning of the gardening year. Both the species crocuses and the Dutch hybrids look best planted in masses or clumps. Their welcome flowers never reach more than 6 inches high.

Crocus is a relative of iris (*Iris* species) and has three stamens as opposed to the six of meadow-saffron or autumn-crocus (*Colchicum* species), which is related to the lily. Plant crocus corms in the fall a couple of inches deep in places where they can be left undisturbed. They will increase over the years if allowed to by squirrels, which consider crocus a gastronomic treat.

There are almost eighty distinct species native to rocky slopes and alpine meadows of southern Europe and Asia Minor, and all are worth growing in the garden. They are hardy to Zone 4 or beyond.

Crocus chrysanthus is widespread in southeastern Europe and in cultivation has produced a number of lovely forms. The flower buds push above ground in late January in the south. They emerge elsewhere as soon as the thaw sets in. The little goblet-shaped blooms are feathered on the outside with purple, gray, or bronze and open to blue, yellow, or cream with bright orange at the center. The grassy foliage that follows should not to be cut off until it withers naturally.

C. tomasinianus from Yugoslavia has pale lavender buds opening to warm lavender inside. It is one of the best for mass planting under shrubs. More robust are the Dutch hybrids, which are available in mixtures of single colors—yellow, white, and purple—and striped.

Cuphea ignea

Curtonus paniculatus (in back)

Cuphea ignea

Cigarplant

This is one of a number of plants—perennial and even shrubby in its native subtropical or tropical home—that must be treated as an annual because it curls up and dies at the very thought of frost. Impatiens, petunias, and begonias are typical of this group. Although worked upon by plant breeders until they bear little resemblance to their wild ancestors, their antipathy to frost is unaltered.

The charming little cigarplant, on the other hand, is the same plant introduced in 1845 from Mexico, where it can still be found. Unchanged by cultivation, it makes a little 3-foot bush carrying inch-long tubular flowers throughout the season. Blossoms, which are sealing-wax scarlet with a black-and-white tip, look like miniscule cigarettes, newly lit.

Although it can be grown from seed sown early in the year, the cigarplant is usually overwintered from cuttings taken in September. In full sun in a good garden soil, it succeeds anywhere summer annuals grow. It will not perform well under drought conditions or in very short northern summers.

Curtonus paniculatus

Aunt Eliza

The appealing common name has nothing to do with anyone's long-dead relation but is a malapropism for this plant's other botanical name, *Antholyza.* It is another of those invaluable South African iris relatives that make such a strong silhouette under the right conditions.

If the plant is to be a permanent perennial, it needs a moist soil, full sun, and a location in Zone 8 or above. In colder areas, plant the corms 7 inches deep when the soil has warmed in spring, as is done with gladiolus (*Gladiolus* species), and lift them in fall. Aunt Eliza does well in northern Scotland, so it should survive in the colder zones of North America if deep snow cover is certain.

Strongly ribbed swordlike leaves stand vertically to 3 feet high, and from the center of each sheaf grows

Cyclamen hederifolium

a branching spray of flowers resembling those of montbretia (*Crocosmia* species). With their curved trumpets and orange-red color, they make an especially striking show in late summer.

Aunt Eliza combines well with the even taller bugbane (*Cimicifuga* species) and monkshoods (*Aconitum* species), bordered perhaps with fleshy-leaved stonecrop (*Sedum spectabile*).

Cyclamen hederifolium

Ivy-leaved cyclamen, neapolitan cyclamen

The big florist's cyclamen derives from the beautiful but frost-tender *Cyclamen persicum* and is safe only in warm southern gardens. Fortunately, the charm of the genus is fully displayed in the hardiest of them all, the ivy-leaved or neapolitan cyclamen.

This is a native of several parts of southern Europe, especially Italy, where it grows in the leaf litter of deciduous and even evergreen woodlands. This explains its ability to accept full shade and its need for some protection from the midday sun.

Cyclamen grows from flattened disk-shaped tubers, which in the case of this species can reach 6 inches across in old specimens. Those for sale are usually only a quarter of this size. Plant them

during their summer dormancy just below ground level with the smooth side down (roots and shoots grow from the upper surface). In late August the little pink or white shuttlecocklike flowers appear and continue well into October. As they decline, the beautifully marbled, surprisingly frost-tolerant leaves expand. In mild areas they make a fine winter ground cover. In Zones 5 and 6 full leaf development does not occur until spring.

Dahlia 'Rosello'

Cypripedium calceolus var. *pubescens*

Cypripedium species

Lady's-slipper, moccasin-flower

Of all the native plants, these lovely wild orchids never cease to amaze. They grow in southern gardens and by the roadside in parts of Ontario.

Lady's-slipper needs the apparently contradictory conditions of a peaty, leafy, lime soil. It also needs moisture since it comes from moist areas on the edge of woodlands. Although it takes full shade, a gleam of spring sunshine does wonders for the rather somber flowers.

Cypripedium calceolus has hairy, 2-foot, pleated leaves that unfold in spring to put up a stem of one to three uniquely shaped flowers: four wide, yellow petals around a bronze, slipper-shaped pouch. The display lasts for only a couple of weeks in late spring, but the lovely plant is worth the effort required to grow it successfully.

C. parviflorum is sometimes regarded as a subspecies of *C. calceolus.* Visually it is distinct, with long maroon or chocolate petals twisted like old-fashioned candy canes.

Under snow cover, lady's-slipper is hardy to Zone 3. In hot gardens *C. californicum* is a better choice. This 2½-foot plant has pale yellow petals and a pink-tinged central slipper.

The grandest lady's-slipper is *C. reginae,* which grows in boggy woodlands in the northeastern United States and Canada. A 3-foot-high plant, its pink and white flowers are one of the marvels of late May.

Dahlia cultivars

Dahlia

The first *Dahlia* species were collected in Mexico and sent to the royal botanical garden in Madrid in the late 1700s, when Mexico was still a Spanish possession. The tuberous-rooted plant offered the misplaced hope of a new source of food. Although this did not work out, its potential as a garden flower was quickly recognized and in less than fifty years dozens of named forms were bred, especially in Britain, France, and Germany.

Interest in the dahlia has continued unabated ever since, with many thousands of cultivar names recorded. As with any popular garden plant, almost as many names drop out of the list as are added. Specialist nurseries still offer an amazing range of types. In the wild some species can reach 20 feet in height

Dahlia 'Cup O' Tea'

Dahlia 'Larks Ford'

and, although this is possible in the warmest gardens, it adds little but amusement to the garden scene.

Garden dahlias are typically from 1 to 6 feet in height and must be treated as tender annuals in Zone 8 and below, since the foliage blackens at the first fall frost. Young plants are set out after the frosts are over and the soil has warmed. They quickly build up a number of hollow, fleshy stems and paired leaves with a distinctive smell. Dead-heading, irrigation, and feeding ensure continuous flowering throughout the season.

Although wild dahlias have single daisy flowers, their propensity for doubling was noticed by the Aztecs long before they were collected by

Europeans. Now every variation seems possible, from singles with or without an anemonelike center, to such intensely double forms that the flower looks almost the same from behind as from the front. Petals are flat, quilled, or fringed on flowers ranging from 1 inch to 1 foot in diameter. There are dahlias in every color and combination of colors other than true-blue.

The extremely dwarf bedding types do little for the honor of the genus. The dahlia's real role (in addition to providing an almost inexhaustible supply of cut flowers) is as a robust plant for the back of the border. Medium-sized flowers stand up to weather best. Choose cultivars that require a minimum of staking.

The plant needs full sun in good garden soil that is kept moist throughout summer drought. By the end of the season, it makes

a collection of fleshy-rooted tubers. Lift the tubers carefully, with 6 inches of stem remaining, and store them in a cool, frost-free place in barely moist peat throughout winter. Pot them in April and they will quickly grow large enough to plant out after the ground has warmed up. Tubers must always have a bit of stem attached—this is where the dormant buds are located.

Dianthus barbatus

Delphinium 'Piccolo'

Delphinium cultivars

Delphinium

The towering spikes of delphinium have been a mainstay of the traditional herbaceous border for a century. No other garden plant produces as wonderful a range of blue flowers, although blue is no longer the only color. Purple, lavender-rose, soft red, white, and yellow now exist, and often the flowers have a black central eye that looks like a bumble bee caught in the act of pollination.

The large-flowered hybrids are now a long way from the European *Delphinium elatum*, the major parent, and the years of breeding for size have inevitably produced plants that need special care in cultivation. However, given a rich, well-drained soil, full sun, and protection from slugs, 6-foot-high spikes are easily possible. Five to seven plants placed a foot apart produce a magnificent spectacle in July. They should be staked. If cut down after flowering,

secondary spikes often appear in September. Delphinium is hardy under snow to Zone 4.

While many named cultivars propagated by cuttings and true to color are available, there are also fine strains that are raised from seed. If sown early in spring, a first flowering occurs by fall.

In windy gardens the smaller belladonna hybrids or the tiny 'Blue Butterfly' are a better bet.

Dianthus species

Carnation, pink, sweet-william

In the wild, *Dianthus* is a species concentrated in the limestone uplands of central and southern Europe. With such a heritage the cultivational needs of perfect drainage and full sun become quite obvious.

D. barbatus, sweet-william, is an exception to this general rule. Native to the Pyrenees and the Balkans, it is grown as a biennial and likes a richer environment. With seed sown in May, it builds up clumps of narrow leaves that overwinter and start to put up flowering stems the following May. By June each plant is an 18-inch dome of color, a myriad of starry flowers in white and all shades of pink, red, and purple, often with the edges in another color. Blooming directly

Dianthus chinensis 'Snowfire'

Dianthus deltoides

after the spring bulbs and before the summer annuals have bulked up, sweet-william makes a fine show just when it is needed in Zone 6 and above. It is also a superior cut flower. Sweet-william dies after blooming, so summer-flowering plants should be at the ready to fill in the gap.

Carnation (derived originally from *D. caryophyllus*), and pink (mainly from *D. plumarius*) are now so similar they are virtually indistinguishable. In general, pink flowers in June and carnation follows, but they overlap considerably and both bloom into the fall.

Typically, carnation, which ranges from 1 to 3 feet tall, has very double flowers and a powerful scent. Some, such as 'Old Crimson

Clove', date back to the sixteenth century, while the white-flowered 'Mrs. Sinkins' is a comparatively modern mid-Victorian. These named types are raised from cuttings pulled off the old plants in September. Plants root fairly well if you simply push the stems into the ground and place a little sand around the base. From seed, the color range spreads through pinks and purples to yellow, buff, and white.

Pink is a good plant for the front of sunny borders to Zone 5. Spilling forward onto paving, its gray foliage associates well with English lavender (*Lavandula angustifolia*) and old-fashioned roses. Unfortunately, it does not grow well in the humid southeast.

D. deltoides is the maiden pink from Europe. It makes low hummocks—about a foot tall—of brilliant starry flowers in June and

seeds itself most satisfactorily (but never aggressively) in dry walls, rock gardens, and cracks of paving.

The rainbow pink, *D. chinensis*, has probably been changed the most by modern plant breeding. This Chinese species has been transformed into yet another summer annual with fringed flowers in a wide range of colors (no blues, no good yellows) on 6- to 9-inch plants. They are available in single colors—scarlet, coral, pink, and white—and in mixtures. Most have a contrasting eye. Since it is native to a temperate climate, you can plant it even if frosts are still likely as long as you harden it off, and it won't turn to mush at the first fall frost. Some plants will even overwinter.

Diascia barberae

Dicentra spectabilis

Diascia barberae

Twinspur

Diascia consists of a group of about fifty South African foxglove relatives only recently making its mark in North American gardens. It is a very worthwhile mark for Zones 8 and warmer areas. *D. barberae,* twinspur, is the most generally available species, but others are beginning to appear.

Twinspur reaches 18 inches in height, but as it usually flops forward the effect is less. Although twigs pushed around the clump hold it up, the plant is best placed in front of the border, where it can

behave naturally. Provide up to half shade in any normal garden soil and you will be rewarded with spikes of soft, pink, flat-faced flowers from early summer onward.

If raised from seed, twinspur starts flowering later, but it can be over-wintered as rooted cuttings taken the previous fall. In the warmest zones, the plants overwinter outside and just need clipping over when the flowers decline. After a short rest, they start all over again.

Dicentra species

Bleedingheart, lyreflower

Both common names evoke admirably accurate images of *Dicentra spectabilis* when seen from a distance, with its arching stems hung with pink heart-shaped buds or lyre-shaped open flowers. A closer examination—you must gently pull the flowers open—miraculously gives a third name: lady-in-the-bath.

Whichever name is used, this is one of the most beautiful perennials in late spring. The fleshy stems are 2½ feet tall and an established clump grows to 3 feet across. Leaves are like a giant corydalis (*Corydalis*

Dicentra spectabilis

Dicentra eximia

lutea) elegantly divided with a grayish cast. Bleedingheart reaches its full beauty when its dangling rosy flowers are blooming, but even when these are gone, the foliage remains attractive before going to rest in July or August. The white-flowered form with paler foliage is just as lovely and breeds true from seed.

Native to Japan and other areas of the Far East, the plant is remarkably at home in North America in almost full shade or in moist soil and full sun. It is in a cool woodland that bleedingheart is at its best and lasts longest. There, it seeds

itself but never becomes invasive. It is a good cut flower—you could never have too much bleedingheart.

Equally beautiful, although on a lighter scale, is *D. eximia,* one of North America's most gardenworthy wildflowers. Known as turkey-corn or wild bleedingheart, it comes from mountain areas from New York to Georgia. It is hardy to Zone 4 under a winter mulch.

Wild bleedingheart likes the same conditions as its Asian cousin, and once established is almost continuously in flower from late May until September. Its pink to purple lockets hang from arching stems above grayish, divided leaves.

The western bleedingheart, *D. formosa,* should also be sought out. There are several fine named cultivars. 'Bountiful' is almost crimson

in color and 'Silver Smith' is white with very gray foliage. 'Adrian Bloom' originated in England and is able to take more sun than the species as long as it is well-fed and well-watered. All of these delightful plants are ideal for planting with the smaller spring bulbs, whose dying foliage is suitably hidden by the developing leaves of bleedingheart.

Dictamnus albus

Dictamnus albus 'Purpureus'

Dictamnus albus

Burning-bush, gasplant

This is an extremely variable, long-lived perennial with a natural distribution from Europe east to China. Although cultivated since Roman times, there is no record of who first discovered the volatile properties of this plant. On a warm, still summer evening you can hold a flame close to the flower spike and ignite the plant's volatile oils; this does not harm the plant.

Dictamnus albus is a fine, strong, 3-foot-high plant with aromatic leaves that are attractive but can cause irritation and blisters on sensitive skin. It is best not to weed around the plant with bare arms, especially on a warm day. Sun seems to increase the skin's sensitivity. In late June the top third of each stem holds a spike of pink, purple, or white flowers with long stamens. The seedpods that follow give shape and interest to the plant in the fall, and the stems should not be cut down unless required indoors for dried winter arrangements.

Seeds are tricky to germinate and the young plants are slow to develop, taking three years to flower.

It may be five years before a good clump is built up, but once established you have it for life. Apply an annual mulch of well-rotted compost to keep burning-bush healthy. Place it carefully in the garden—it does not do well when divided or moved to a new location.

Burning-bush needs full sun in a deep, well-drained soil. Zone 4, with a winter snow mulch, is the limit for this plant.

Dierama pulcherrimum

Dierama pulcherrimum

Wandflower, angels-fishing-rods

Although wandflower is a good common name, a more descriptive alternative is angels-fishing-rods. It is one of the most beautiful and striking of the host of South African iris or gladiolus relatives to come into cultivation.

Wandflower makes clumps of very long, lax, grassy leaves with thin but strong stems up to 6 feet high in early summer. These stems branch at the top, and the weight of the opening flowers, like a shower of stars from an exploding rocket, cause the tips to arch elegantly. The bell-shaped flowers, each in a silver, papery base, bloom in soft shades ranging from white through pink to deep purple. Surprisingly, the flowers open at the ends of stems first and work back. To take the visual analogy further, angels-fishing-rods look particularly lovely when hanging over a pool, where they bend and sway with every passing breeze.

Unfortunately, the evergreen wandflower survives only in warm coastal gardens where it enjoys full sun and a well-drained but never dry soil. It is easily raised from seed (find a friend who grows the plant to get it really fresh). Sow 3 or 4 seeds in pots and carefully plant the resulting seedlings.

Digitalis purpurea

Digitalis purpurea

Digitalis species

Foxglove

Of the perhaps twenty distinct species of wild foxglove—the common foxglove and the perennial foxglove—strewn around Europe and central Asia, only two are commonly seen in North American gardens. But what a valuable and distinct pair they are!

Common foxglove, *Digitalis purpurea,* has two claims to fame. It is a source of the cardiac medicine that has saved innumerable human lives since it was isolated in the 1750s. The plant is also one of the visual pleasures of the late-June garden scene.

Foxglove is usually biennial and is best treated as such. From seed sown (or self-sown) in the late spring, leafy rosettes develop and overwinter to put up a great spike of flowers 4 to 6 feet high the following year. Each flower is like a big, downy, pink-purple or white thimble. The species' blossoms hang on only one side of the spike, but modern selections have blooms all around the spike like a delphinium (*Delphinium* cultivars). These are more spectacular and come in a wider range of colors, but they lack the grace of the wild plant.

Foxglove is a woodland-edge plant that takes deep shade in a moist, leafy soil. It survives to Zone 4 under winter snow. For a sunnier spot in a similar climatic range, there is the perennial foxglove, *D. grandiflora,* from southeastern Europe. It has a 3-foot-high clump of soft yellow bells that makes a long-lasting show from mid-June. If the blooms are cut down after flowering, later spikes often appear.

Disporum hookeri

Dimorphotheca sinuata

Dimorphotheca species

Cape-marigold

The genus *Dimorphotheca* has been carved up by botanists in recent years and the perennial species were moved to the genus *Osteospermum.* However, in some lists the perennial species still retain their old name.

Of the species that remain, *D. sinuata* is the most commonly available in the seed catalogs. It is yet another of those daisy relatives whose myriad colors turn a short South African spring into one of the floral wonders of the world. After seed germination in autumn, the plant develops to a foot high during the cool, moist winter to burst into flower five or six months later. Once seed is set, the plants die.

Since it responds to the Mediterranean climate pattern of mild, wet winters and warm, dry summers,

cape-marigold is suited to southwestern gardens that share similar conditions. In progressively colder zones, sow seeds directly in the ground in spring or start them indoors and plant outside when all danger of frost is over. The plant needs light soil and the sunniest spot possible, since the flowers open only when the sun shines, reflecting the brilliance in their bright orange-yellow petals.

D. pluvialis, white with a purple disk, is also well worth growing and needs similar cultivation.

Disporum species

Fairybells, fairy-lanterns

Various common names like fairy-lanterns and nodding-mandarin create strong images for this group of charming Solomon's-seal (*Polygonatum* species) relatives.

One of a dozen species, *Disporum hookeri*—fairybells—is the most frequently available, although it's still not very common. It is native to the coast ranges of California and British Columbia and across the Rockies in Alberta and Montana.

Fairybells needs a sheltered spot in partial shade, protected from the hot midday sun. In a cool soil rich in leaf mold, it makes a 2-foot-high clump of leafy stems with hanging, tubular flowers of creamy white that open in late May and June. The flowers are succeeded by translucent berries that look like tiny grapes hanging on hair-fine stems. The whole plant turns yellow in the

Dodecatheon meadia

Dodecatheon meadia

fall. This is not a spectacular plant but one of those quiet, graceful species that makes a woodland garden so subtle and attractive.

D. smithii, much larger, is well worth seeking out. Yellow or red berries follow creamy bells borne on 3-foot-high stems. This is known as fairy-lanterns and, indeed, with low evening sun shining on the dangling flowers it really seems to live up to its name.

A Japanese cousin is *D. sessile,* which has an especially desirable variegated form. The narrow leaves clothing the 2-foot-high stems are a striped green and white. The plant looks especially good with the smaller plantain-lilies (*Hosta* species), with which it shares a need for similar conditions.

Dodecatheon meadia

Shooting-star

This most distinctive member of North American native flora is a plant that, once seen, is never forgotten. *Dodecatheon meadia* is the best of the shooting-stars. Native to several eastern states from Pennsylvania south, it survives to Zone 4 under snow. Other species, including *D. clevelandii* and *D. jeffreyi,* are from the West Coast. It is best to grow each species where it naturally occurs. Since they are so alike, there is no point in looking for trouble.

A rosette of leaves resembling those of cowslip or primrose (*Primula* species)—a relative of shooting-star—puts up bare, 1-foot stems in late May with a cluster of buds at the tops. Then, just as you expect a conventional primrose display to appear, the individual little flower

stalks lengthen and hang down, and pink petals fold back around a pointed pink and yellow center. The whole head looks like an exploding fireworks rocket.

Shooting-star needs moist, peaty soil (although it takes some lime). Protection from the hot midday sun helps the plant remain in flower longer, but too much shade creates soft growth. Half a dozen shooting-stars planted a foot apart makes an eye-catching feature in the garden.

Doronicum cordatum

Doronicum species

Leopard's-bane

As there are no fearsome leopards in Europe or western Asia—where the thirty or so species of *Doronicum* originate—it can only be surmised that the bane is effective, and gardeners can enjoy leopard's-bane simply as attractive spring flowers.

One of the first perennials of the year (excluding bulbs), leopard's-bane continues the yellow of the declining daffodils into the end of May and early June. *D. cordatum* has clumps of heart-shaped leaves carrying 1- to 2-feet-high, hairy stems topped with wide yellow daisies that combine well with the soft purple spikes of honesty (*Lunaria annua*) and the spotted leaves of the lungworts (*Pulmonaria* species).

D. pardalianches is the great leopard's-bane, which reaches 3 feet high. It has become established in open woodland in areas of southern Scotland and could be used similarly, with spring wildflowers, in North America.

Leopard's-bane is hardy under a winter mulch to Zone 4 and probably beyond. It takes a well-drained soil and full sun when it flowers.

Because much of its growth is over by June, it is best placed under late-leafing deciduous trees. This works especially well in the South. In the mixed border it leaves a long summer gap, so a few small, late-flowering bulbs, such as tigerflower (*Tigridia* species) or harlequin-flower (*Sparaxis* species), should be added to carry the show when the leopard's-bane is gone. Although it is usually propagated by division, seed is an easy way to produce a large number of plants; these will not flower until the second year.

Echinops ritro

Echinacea purpurea

Echinacea purpurea

Purple coneflower

This plant native to the grasslands of the east-central United States from Ohio southward is one of the most spectacular of all the daisies. Stiff stems about 4 feet in height are clothed with dark green leaves. In midsummer, spherical black buds open and long purple-pink petals unfold and hang below the horizontal. The great central disk, is cone-shaped and an extraordinary orange-brown in color. The color combination is most unusual and the show often continues for two months. Even then, it's not over because the seed heads remain attractive, lasting into winter, when they shed their seeds and produce occasional seedlings nearby. These can be left alone or moved in spring, as soon as the purplish leaves emerge. It is usually wise to concentrate plantings for maximum effect.

There are several named cultivars with flowers that are closer to true pink and a white selection with a green disk. All are fine plants.

Purple coneflower is hardy under snow to Zone 4. The soil should not lie wet in spring. As with almost all daisies, full sun is essential. A couple of other species are sometimes available—although smaller and less dramatic, they are still worth a place in the garden.

Echinops species

Globethistle

Although there are almost a hundred species of globethistle native to Europe and western Asia, only a couple are widely used in North American gardens.

Echinops ritro is the one most often seen. Strong, 4-foot-high stems bear jagged leaves that are gray-white on the underside. This same color is more apparent on the flower stalks and makes the bright blue of the drumsticklike heads even more striking. The heads begin to take on color long before the individual flowers open. Thus, the display lasts from early July well into August. You can also cut the flower heads and dry them for winter decorations indoors. Do this before the flowers go to seed or they fall apart and make a mess. Named forms, which must be propagated by division, are the richly colored

Echinops ritro 'Taplow Blue'

Epimedium × *youngianum* 'Niveum'

'Veitch's Blue' and the tall 'Taplow Blue', which can reach over 5 feet in height. Both originated in English nurseries.

The great globethistle, *E. sphaerocephalus,* is a huge 6-footer with gray and green leaves and gray-white flowers. It is a statuesque plant for the back of the border. It reseeds itself, and unwanted plants should be removed before they become established. This and the other globethistles seem particularly attractive to night-flying moths.

Globethistle grows well in any good garden soil in full sun. It is hardy to Zone 4 and probably beyond.

Epimedium species

Epimedium

Considering the beauty of these little, mainly Asian woodlanders as well as their value as ground cover, it is remarkable that they are not commonly seen in gardens. Botanically related to the barberries (usually a shrubby family), epimedium looks like a tiny columbine (*Aquilegia* species) and has a similar charm. It grows in full shade in moist, leafy soil and increases slowly by shallow-growing rhizomes that can be divided in spring.

Some species have evergreen foliage and are good West Coast plants. The deciduous species, safe to Zone 4, have a seasonal growth pattern that is a delight to follow. Dry leaves overwinter and should be clipped as soon as new spring

growth is evident. Delicate flower stems begin to unfurl, gradually followed by leaves that make the plant look like an incipient maidenhair fern. Pink and purple at first, the foliage turns green later as the plant develops a wiry strength. Many species turn an attractive bronze in the fall.

The crimson-flowering 'Rose Queen' is the best-known variety of *Epimedium grandiflorum.* 'White

Epimedium × youngianum 'Niveum'

Eranthis hyemalis

Queen' is a variety with pure white flowers. Crossed with other epimediums, this species has produced the yellow *E. × versicolor* 'Sulphureum' and *E. × youngianum,* most lovely in its white form 'Niveum'. All are well worth growing and look especially good with the smaller spring bulbs.

From Algeria, the farthest west that any epimedium grows wild, comes *E. perralderanum,* the most striking of them all. The flowers are bright yellow and are borne on foot-high stems that stand above the glossy leaves.

Eranthis hyemalis

Winter aconite

The golden buttercuplike flowers of winter aconite, each surrounded by a choirboy's ruff of green bracts, are among the most heartening signs of early spring. Depending on the area and climate, this can be anytime from January to April. The plant, which bears flowers on 3-inch stems, is particularly lovely growing in masses with snowdrop (*Galanthus* species) through ivy or periwinkle under tall deciduous trees. It is impossible to have too much of winter aconite.

A native of southern Europe, the plant is naturalized in Great Britain and grows well in North America to Zone 4. In moist woodlands, in limey or lime-free soil, it carpets the ground and even seeds itself into a thin grass. Unfortunately, it resents disturbance and cultivation should be avoided after the plant goes to rest in early July.

Winter aconite is difficult to establish from the dry tubers usually sold. Try to beg a clump from a generous friend as the plant finishes flowering and set it out at once in a spot where it is likely to grow undisturbed. You can also gather seeds as soon as they are ripe (watch carefully from April on because they ripen quickly) and sow them at once.

Although much costlier to buy, the hybrid form *Eranthis × tubergenii* is well worth the expense. Developed in Holland, its profusion of 2-inch golden flowers is quite striking in early spring.

Eremurus stenophyllus

Erigeron × hybridus 'Most of All'

Eremurus stenophyllus

Foxtail-lily, king's-spear

There are around three dozen species of *Eremurus,* all native to Asia, where they grow on arid steppes, often with wonderful wild irises and tulips. This late-spring flush of flower is one of the most remarkable floral sights of the world. It is accentuated by the foxtail-lily, whose great flower spikes tower above the surrounding vegetation like church spires above a town. In some species, they exceed 10 feet in height.

E. stenophyllus is one of the smaller species, seldom above 3 feet high, but it has the typical shape and growth pattern. In well-drained soil in full sun, plant 3 or 5 dormant roots, which resemble dry starfish, a foot apart with the conical buds just below ground level.

A tussock of narrow, grassy leaves appears in spring and a central spike of starry yellow flowers shoots up (sometimes not until the second year after planting). By July it is over and the whole plant goes to rest. It is important to mark the spot so that a stray hoe does not chop off next year's buds. Foxtail-lily grows to Zone 4 under snow and a mulch of compost.

Snap up and try any other foxtail species or hybrids you find. All need similar conditions.

Erigeron species

Fleabane

The fleabanes make up a huge genus of about two hundred daisies, mostly native to North America. Many are weedy and not for garden cultivation, but several from the Rocky Mountain states have been interbred to produce extremely useful front-of-border perennials for early-summer display. Nomenclature is confused, but those listed as *Erigeron × hybridus* (or sometimes *E. speciosus*) are what you want.

With a few twigs around the edge to keep them together, the stems make a sphere of foliage 1 or 2 feet high (depending on the cultivar) that is entirely covered with wide, open daisies. Fleabane comes in a range of soft colors from white through pink to gentle lavender and

Erigeron × hybridus 'Walther'

Eryngium alpinum

purple. Fleabane is not for cold wet gardens. Grown in well-drained soil in full sun, it does well to Zone 5.

Very different is the *E. karvinskianus* from Mexico. It is a thin little foot-high plant with pink-tinged, ½-inch white daisies. Individually undistinguished, they create a floral carpet that is seldom out of bloom in Zone 7 and above. It seeds itself in the cracks of walls and paving. This fleabane has a definite charm and is well worth obtaining.

Eryngium species

Seaholly

It is difficult to accept that the highly distinctive seaholly is, in fact, related to celery and to Queen-Anne's-lace (*Daucus carota*). In seaholly, the typical flat flower heads of this group are transformed into domed heads surrounded by a ruff of bracts. There are some two hundred species of seaholly found around the world, varying greatly in form and size. Those especially prized in the garden share a strange metallic sheen. These species are mainly European in origin.

Seaholly grows best in full sun in any well-drained soil and even survives in poor, gravelly soil. Under winter snow, it succeeds to Zone 4 and perhaps beyond. All species flower in midsummer for a long period. The flower heads last until they shatter and spill their seeds. Seaholly is superb when dried for winter arrangements.

Eryngium alpinum has the biggest flowers of all. Above a clump of rounded leaves emerge 2-foot-high, shining blue stems, each carrying metallic blue flower heads. These are set in 3-inch collars of spiny bracts. Place this plant in the front of the border, where it does not have too much competition.

Close in size is *E. giganteum,* an extraordinary biennial species from the Caucasus mountains. It behaves in the typical biennial way: Seeds sown in spring flower 15 months later, while seeds self-sown from existing plants in autumn flower the second spring. After flowering, the plant dies. This pattern explains the other common name, Miss-Willmott's-ghost, which refers to the rather daunting English gardener who, it was said,

Eryngium giganteum

Eschscholzia californica

used to drop a few seeds in other people's gardens to flower two years after her visit. In the first year, the plant makes a clump of unexceptional green leaves. The second year a stout stem shoots up 4 feet or even taller. It has prickly leaves and even pricklier bracts around the flowers. Leaves, bracts, and flowers are all a shining, bluish silver.

E. bourgatii, native to the Pyrenees, is a 2-foot-high plant. The basal foliage is crisp, curly, and green with distinctive white veins. From this base come wiry stems with medium-sized, blue-green, thistly flower heads.

E. planum has 3-foot-high stems topped by a mass of small, steel-blue heads, each the size of a thimble. It is especially good as a cut flower, both fresh and dried.

All of the seahollies are distinctive plants and their garden positions and associates deserve to be well thought out.

Eschscholzia californica

California poppy

This is the state flower of California, and very suitably so, since it is one of the most spectacular of the state's wonderful array of wild plants. Here and in other Mediterranean climates, it behaves as a fall-germinating annual that flowers in early spring. Clipped over, plants may survive into a second year. They reseed themselves freely.

California poppy makes a 1-foot tussock of deeply divided leaves that are smooth and gray-green. Against this foliage the satiny flowers stand out remarkably well. The sepals are joined together to make a long, hoodlike cap that is pushed off intact when the bud bursts and the brilliant petals unfold. In the wild these flowers are usually confined to shades of yellow and orange, but selection and breeding has brought in cream close to white as well as pink and soft rose. All are lovely in full sun in well-drained spots.

In colder areas California poppy is grown as a typical summer annual, sown in place when the ground is warm. Where summers are short, sow seeds indoors directly in the pots from which they will be planted to avoid harming the brittle taproot.

Eucomis comosa

Euphorbia epithymoides

Eucomis comosa

Pineapple-lily

There are about ten species of these spectacular South African plants whose growth pattern really does live up to the common name. From a big hyacinthlike bulb comes a rosette of lax leaves, often lying on the ground. This untidiness is not noticed when the 2-foot-tall flower spike develops, first as a stout, foot-long, purple-spotted stalk, followed by a foot-long mass of outward-facing star-shaped flowers. At the top is a tuft of short leaves just like that on a pineapple.

The long-lasting flowers are creamy white with a purplish flush. The pattern of stem and pineapple tuft remains when the flowers are replaced by inflated seedpods later in the fall.

Pineapple-lily is for the warmest gardens in Zones 9 and 10, but it can be treated as a summer transient in northern areas. Start the bulbs indoors and plant outside after danger of frost has passed. Lift the bulbs again in the fall. A warm, well-drained soil in full sun is required.

Where pineapple-lily can be grown as a permanent plant it associates well with crinum-lily (*Crinum* × *powellii*), belladonna-lily (*Amaryllis belladonna*), and sun-lovers with dramatic foliage, such as yucca (*Yucca* species) and the smaller variegated forms of New Zealand-flax (*Phormium tenax*).

Snap up this and any other or something pineapple-lily (especially the amazing *Eucomis pole-evansii,* which can reach 6 feet tall) whenever you see them on a bulb list.

Euphorbia species

Spurge

Few plant genera contain more species than *Euphorbia,* which has around a thousand, and no other has such an extraordinary diversity of forms. Spurges range from little annual weeds to temperate perennials and subshrubs (including the Christmas poinsettia), as well as plants that, at first sight, are indistinguishable from cactus. All continents have wild spurges of one sort or another.

Closer examination shows the typical bracts that make most of the floral show. Typical, too, is the white latex exuded by any wound. It is

Euphorbia characias

poisonous and can cause a rash on sensitive skin, especially in sunny weather.

There are a number of valuable garden plants in this strange group. *E. cyparissias* is the cypress spurge from Europe, now often naturalized in North America on roadsides. Its roots run underground, producing a mass of foot-high stems with narrow leaves topped with the greenish yellow flower heads typical of hardy spurges. These start to develop their color by late June and last for many weeks. In fall the foliage turns clear yellow. Cypress spurge makes an effective ground cover in any well-drained spot with at least three-quarters sun. It survives to Zone 4 and probably even colder areas under winter snow. A word of warning: It can become a weed.

The eastern European *E. epithy-moides* (*E. polychroma* is the same plant) is much more likely to keep to itself. It makes a tidy plant 1½ feet high and wide, becoming a bright greenish yellow dome in May and June. In fall the leaves turn pink before they drop. Hardy to Zone 4, this spurge takes partial shade but prefers sun. Plant in any soil but the wettest.

E. myrsinites is an evergreen plant of hot, rocky slopes around the Mediterranean, yet it succeeds to at least Zone 5 under winter snow. In Zone 6, without a snow cover, the foliage burns badly.

It makes a low, floppy plant of fleshy, blue-gray, overlapping leaves with yellow flowers in June and July. This is a plant for the front of the well-drained border or rock garden. Explosive seedpods distribute the plant effectively.

Other marvelous evergreen Mediterraneans are *E. characias* and *E. wulfenii* (this may be a form of *E. characias*). In Zone 8 and above, these make 6- to 8-foot-high bushes. Stems of lush, narrow, blue-green leaves carry long heads of yellowish green flowers in spring. The stems die and are replaced from the base to provide a sort of biennial sequence. One of the most spectacular plants for warm, sunny spots, this spurge combines well with yucca (*Yucca* species) and bear's-breech (*Acanthus mollis*).

Eustoma grandiflorum

Eustoma grandiflorum

Eustoma grandiflorum

Prairie-gentian

Often listed as *Lisianthus,* the prairie-gentian is an eye-catching annual or biennial, occasionally cultivated in botanic gardens and only recently available to the general public. Because of its remarkable flowers, it has quickly caught on and new colors are appearing every year.

Prairie-gentian is a native of Nebraska and Colorado south to New Mexico. It reaches 3 feet in the wild, but garden selections are usually about half this size. Smooth, stiff stems with blue-gray leaves are topped by flowers in shades of purple, pink, and cream. Their shape is reminiscent of California poppy (*Eschscholzia californica*).

While the flowers and leaves are extremely beautiful up close, from a distance they give the impression of being made of silk and wire and shoved into the ground by an insensitive gardener. Indoors in a vase they look less improbable.

In most areas, sow prairie-gentian indoors along with the usual tender summer annuals and plant it outside in full sun in well-drained soil. In the warmest zones seeds can be sown outdoors, either in fall or spring, to flower where they germinate. Thin seedlings to at least 6 inches apart.

Felicia amelloides

Felicia amelloides

Felicia amelloides

Blue-marguerite

One of the reasons for coveting a garden in Zones 9 and 10 is the certain knowledge that there will be some flowers blooming in the garden every day of the year. The blue-marguerite is one of those that continues the show throughout the winter.

This is not a particularly prepossessing plant. It makes a 2-foot, sloppy subshrub if not continually pinched to maintain a compact shape. The leaves, too, have little to commend them, but there is always a charming flower or two to catch the eye. The long-stalked daisies, which measure 1½ inches across, are a clear, clean blue with a contrasting yellow central disk.

As a South African native the blue-marguerite is a permanent plant only in the warmest gardens, but it has a time-honored place in subtropical bedding schemes in colder areas. Root cuttings in fall and overwinter them in small pots kept in a frost-free location and exposed to bright light. Plant in full sun only when all frosts are over. Because of its natural tumbling habit, blue-marguerite also makes an excellent container plant for terraces or decks.

There is also a shrubby chrysanthemum (*Chrysanthemum frutescens*) known as a marguerite. The traditional form has white flowers, although there are also yellow and pale pink varieties.

Filipendula rubra

Filipendula species

Meadowsweet, dropwort,
queen-of-the-prairie

This is a group of valuable perennials that used to be included in the
shrubby genus *Spiraea,* and it still
falls into this category on some
nursery lists. Except for their flat-
topped heads of minuscule flowers,
these perennials also resemble
astilbe (*Astilbe* species).

Filipendula palmata is from the
westernmost part of Siberia, where
a maritime influence moderates the
predictably fierce climate. It makes
strong 4-foot-high growth with
pale-backed, jagged leaves topped
in July by flat heads of pale pink.

F. rubra is North America's version, bigger and brighter and one of
the most spectacular herbaceous
perennials grown. From Michigan
and Iowa south to Georgia, it grows
in rich, moist soil and half shade,
towering 6 feet above its compan-
ions. Queen-of-the-prairie is an apt
name. Deeply divided leaves grow
up the robust stems to foot-wide
flower heads that put on a brilliant
pink show in midsummer. 'Venus-
ta', which is a richer, deeper pink
form, should be sought out.

F. ulmaria is meadowsweet, sometimes called queen-of-the-meadow.

This is a European plant from wet
fields and riversides, where it grows
with loosestrife (*Lythrum* species).
Usually no more than 4 feet high, it
can reach 6 feet under good growing conditions and become invasive.
Creamy white flower heads have an
inverted cone shape. If the central
flower is removed as soon as it is
spent, the display continues on side
branches from June throughout
July. Also worth seeking is a fine
golden-leaved form (whose flower
spikes should be cut out since they
offer little to the scene) and also a
double-flowered form with fluffy
flower heads.

These three species all need moist,
rich soil. In dry spots they become
prey to powdery mildew and look

Filipendula vulgaris

Foeniculum vulgare

miserable. Give them full sun or half shade down to Zone 4 (*F. ulmaria* is a bit hardier still).

F. vulgaris, dropwort, is native to dry limestone uplands of northern Europe and must be similarly accommodated in the garden. It has crisp, ferny, basal foliage and 2-foot-high stems of cream flowers in June. The double-flowered cultivar 'Flore Pleno' is sturdier and therefore preferable.

Foeniculum vulgare

Fennel

The aromatic salad vegetable finocchio, anise, or Florence fennel—whatever name is used—is a wonderful addition to a greengrocer's shelves in winter and early spring. This is a form of *Foeniculum vulgare* selected for its ability to develop a bulblike aggregation of stem bases. Common garden fennel is the same plant without the bulb.

Usually a short-lived perennial, garden fennel is a native of southern Europe that has naturalized farther north and in parts of North America. It makes a 4- to 6-foot-high clump of strong, hollow stems and ferny leaves divided again and again into hair-thin segments.

Stems are topped by typical greenish yellow umbel heads, not spectacular but pleasantly attractive. All parts retain the aromatic quality of finocchio and have a number of culinary uses. Fennel is traditionally used with fish.

Fennel grows in poor, dry soil in full sun to Zone 4. Better conditions will result in a cloud of fine foliage but may shorten the life of the plant—no matter, because it reseeds itself. A bronze-leaved form is even more beautiful and acts as a splendid foil to scarlet or orange flowers in a sunny spot.

Fritillaria meleagris

Fritillaria imperialis

Fritillaria species

Fritillary, crown-imperial,
snakeshead

There are about a hundred *Fritillaria* species found in the Northern
Hemisphere, although they are absent from eastern North America.
They vary from dwarf plants only a
couple of inches high (often with
disproportionately large flower
bells) to robust 4-footers.

F. imperialis, crown-imperial, must
be among the most spectacular of
all hardy bulbs. Native to Iran and
northern India, it has been cherished in gardens since the sixteenth
century and is depicted in innumerable Dutch and Flemish flower
paintings.

Spring growth is prodigious. As
soon as the soil begins to warm, a
bullet-shaped shoot appears, elongating by the day and unfolding its

shining leaves as it goes. After 18
inches or so, the leaves stop, but the
stem continues for almost the same
length, ending in a circle of 2-inch
bells topped by a pineapplelike tuft
of leaves. It makes a pattern like no
other plant. The typical form has
orange bells held on a purple stem
and a yellow form has green stems.
In both, the hanging bells have five
teardrops inside, held against all
gravitational odds.

Although crown-imperial is visually incomparable, its scent, whiffs
of which occur as soon as the leaves
break the ground, is pure skunk.
Three or five bulbs planted 6 inches
deep, downwind, make a fine
clump. Full sun and a well-drained
soil are needed. All traces of the
plant disappear by early July.

F. persica, also from Iran, likes
similar conditions and in its somber
way is almost as eye-catching.
Gray-green leaves extend right up
the 2½-foot-high stems. As they get

smaller toward the top, a purple-
black bell covered with a grapelike
bloom hangs from each leaf joint.

F. meleagris is the snakeshead, a
classic wild plant of water meadows
in Oxfordshire, England. Now very
rare in that area, its range extends
through Europe to the Caucasus
mountains. At the top of foot-tall,
wire-thin stems bearing a few
narrow leaves appear one or two
strangely checkered, large purple
bells. A creamy white form is
equally attractive. Snakeshead likes
moist soil. Plant it under a deciduous shrub so that it may enjoy both
the early-season sun and later
protection.

All fritillaries are hardy, under
winter snow, to Zone 4 or beyond.

Fuchsia 'Gartenmeister Bonstedt'

Fuchsia 'Tom Thumb'

Fuchsia species

Lady's-eardrops, fuchsia

This extensive genus of shrubs or even small trees is spread throughout South America, and a few species can be found in Tahiti and New Zealand.

As a cultivated ornamental, fuchsia is grown in two ways: in most zones as an almost ever-blooming pot or greenhouse shrub that is sometimes planted outside in summer, and in Zones 8 and above as a more or less hardy subshrub. All forms have charming, pendulous flowers like giant jewelled earrings in colors ranging from white through pink to crimson and dusky purple. The buds droop from long flower stalks, and they open (or are popped—an almost irresistible temptation if you are passing at the right time) as four sepals fold back from the skirt of petals and long, extended stamens.

The most frost-resistant species, such as *Fuchsia magellanica,* come from far southern Patagonia and manage to overwinter with some wood intact to Zone 8. If the winter is severe enough to cut it back to the ground, the plant puts up new growth from the base in spring and can reach 6 feet within a season. From August on, the plant is hung with narrow crimson flowers. A white-flowered form has correspondingly pale foliage. These types make useful hedges in cool, mild areas such as Oregon. Most valuable in the garden is the white-edged variegated form, as well as a lovely cultivar called 'Versicolor', whose leaves are dusky purple-gray, similar to those of *Rosa glauca.*

The big-flowered hybrids are apt to lack the charm and elegant arching growth of *F. magellanica,* but the flowers, in all of their diversity of color, never fail to please. Usually the sepals and petals, which resemble a ballet tutu, are in contrasting colors.

Although there are dwarf cultivars, such as the relatively hardy 'Tom Thumb', which seldom exceeds 1½ feet in height, most forms double or quadruple this height as the climate permits. It is also possible to train a single woody stem into a standard form with a ball of foliage and flowers at the top.

All forms of fuchsia take half shade but prefer sun in the northern limit of their range. In hot gardens midday shade and a soil that does not dry out are essential. The plants burn easily. In the warmer zones the fuchsia mite can become a serious pest.

Where it cannot be left outside, treat fuchsia like bedding geranium (*Pelargonium* species). Lift the plant in autumn and cut back to a foot of stem. Pot each plant individually or pack several into boxes of peat and keep them dormant in a frost-free (but not warm) greenhouse until the following March.

Gaillardia pulchella var. *picta*

Galanthus nivalis

Gaillardia × *grandiflora* 'Monarch'

Gaillardia species

Blanketflower

This wide, flat daisy is among the most flamboyant sights of the perennial border. Originating mainly in the southern United States, perennial species of blanketflower are not suited to cold, wet gardens. However, a Zone 5 garden with perfect soil drainage and full sun is entirely acceptable.

Gaillardia pulchella is an annual, so cold weather is not a problem. Sow outdoors in areas with a long summer and indoors farther north. The plant makes a clump of soft downy leaves (the "blanket" in the common name) above which bright daisies are held on 2-foot-high stems. Red petals with yellow tips, or the opposite, are usual.

This species has been interbred with the fully perennial *G. aristata* to create a wide range of brilliant summer daisies. Aptly called *G.* × *grandiflora,* they are so successful that they have gone wild in some areas. Red, yellow, orange, and multicolored flowers bloom in late June and July with occasional flowers into fall. Some support is helpful, but they are best planted in the front of the border and allowed to flop forward.

Galanthus species

Snowdrop

For many people, snowdrop is the first heartening sign of the turning year. This can be January in the South or April in the North, but the message is the same: Spring is on the way.

There are about a dozen species of *Galanthus,* mainly from southeastern Europe and Asia Minor and, although distinct to the specialist, they are close enough to be just snowdrops to the home gardener. The pattern is fairly constant: A pair of narrow leaves spears the ground and by the time they unfold, the flower bud is already almost as high. The stem reaches a few inches in height and the flower becomes nodding, its three white petals spreading back like wings. As it swings on its hair-thin stalk in the slightest wind, nothing could be more charming.

Galanthus nivalis 'Balintargart'

Galega officinalis

G. nivalis is the common snowdrop, easy to naturalize under shrubs or in open woodland in both its single- and double-flowered forms. *G. elwesii* is larger—to eight inches high—and has grayish leaves. It is just as easy to grow.

Most gardeners plant dry bulbs 3 inches deep in fall and the plants take a couple of years to get established. It is much better to obtain a growing clump and divide it into individual bulbs. This is a good way to increase your stock, since there can never be enough of this plant in the spring.

Galega officinalis

Goatsrue

This is one of a half-dozen species of *Galega* native to Europe and western Asia. The specific epithet *officinalis* indicates its official or medicinal use in times past, when goatsrue was used to increase the flow of milk in nursing mothers. Goatsrue is also used as fodder.

In the garden it is a fine upstanding perennial for the midsummer border. At the beginning of this century several selections were made; a few are sometimes still available. These include 'Duchess of Bedford' and 'Carnea', which are pink and dark rose respectively. 'Candida' is a fine white form that dates from the eighteenth century. These are obviously candidates for heritage gardens. The original species has 4- to 5-foot-high clumps of pinnate leaves and carries masses of pointed spikes of tiny pea flowers in pink or white.

As long as it is given some support before reaching its full height (unsupported, the clump will fall apart), goatsrue earns its place in any sunny spot. A well-drained soil is necessary. Under winter snow and a leafy mulch, the plant is hardy to Zone 4.

Galtonia candicans

Galium odoratum

Galium odoratum

Sweet woodruff

This is a huge genus of over three hundred species scattered around the world. Some forms have bristly, scrambling stems that catch the passerby and cling to clothes. Others make little hummocks of tiny leaves and miniscule flowers. They are variously known as cleavers or bedstraws. Although few offer much to the ornamental garden, lady's-bedstraw and a couple of others have herbal applications.

Sweet woodruff, sometimes listed as *Asperula odorata,* is by far the most delightful of the bunch. It has a wide natural distribution in Mediterranean Europe. In Africa and Asia Minor it spreads into carpets of fresh, green leaves in deciduous woodlands. This pattern makes it a wonderful ground cover in the garden under trees or shrubs or around plantain-lily (*Hosta* species) in a shady border. Small plants, well-watered, soon build up a continuous carpet. It is easy to increase plants by rooting cuttings in pots of peaty compost or chopping whole spadefuls out of established clumps.

In warm areas it is virtually evergreen. In the North, spring provokes a sudden flush of 6-inch stems with whorls of narrow leaves. Tiny white flowers bloom at the top and the whole is sweetly scented like newly mowed hay. At this stage sweet woodruff is traditionally used to flavor white wine for an early-summer picnic.

Galtonia candicans

Summer-hyacinth

This is one of the easiest and most useful of summer-flowering bulbs. In spite of its South African origin, it is surprisingly hardy, surviving most years in Zone 6. In colder areas it is easy to lift the bulbs before the soil freezes and store them in a cool, frost-free place until the next spring. In warmer zones summer-hyacinth is entirely safe.

Planted in May, the bulbs soon begin to grow. From the center of a vertical spear of leaves emerges a strong, smooth stem with a head of flower buds rather like a fleshy ear of wheat. In August, when the plant is 3 or 4 feet high, the buds open to make a spike of pure white pendulous bells. Secondary spikes

Gaura lindheimeri

often continue the show into October. The seedpods are quite attractive and decorative if cut for drying before the flat, black seeds are shed.

Sadly, summer-hyacinth's reputation for fragrance is overestimated, but the plant is worth growing solely on its visual merits. A good garden soil and adequate moisture during the growing season ensure fine stems with plenty of flowers. The plant combines well with late-flowering shrubs such as butterflybush (*Buddleia* species) and bluebeard (*Caryopteris* species).

Gaura lindheimeri

Gaura

There are a dozen and a half of these evening-primrose relatives, but *Gaura lindheimeri,* native to Louisiana, Texas, and adjacent areas of Mexico, is the only one in general cultivation, and even it is not common. It has a real use as a long-flowering perennial, especially in the southeastern United States, where high summer temperatures quickly exhaust many of the usual border perennials. Gaura manages to keep going, as long as some irrigation is provided right into fall.

The plant makes a thin, domed bush, 3 or even 4 feet high and wide. Wiry stems and narrow leaves are covered from late June onward with a cloud of little pink and white flowers, like hovering insects suddenly stilled. It is safe to Zone 6 and beyond if planted in a warm, well-drained spot. Plant gaura when small and leave it alone, like peony (*Paeonia* species) and false-indigo (*Baptisia australis*), to develop its woody base undisturbed.

This is a good plant for the front of the border, where its height varies the pattern without hiding plants behind it. It also gives interest, with spring bulbs underneath, to foundation plantings.

Gentiana asclepiadea

Gazania rigens 'Ministar Orange'

Gazania rigens

Treasure flower, gazania

Here is yet another wonderful daisy
from South Africa that is a valuable ground-covering perennial in
Zones 9 and 10. It is well worth
growing as an annual in colder
climates.

Whether used as an annual or perennial, gazania needs a sunny spot
and well-drained soil. Above its
narrow leaves that grow almost flat
on the ground is a wide-spreading
display of 3-inch daisies. Once
bloom begins in July, it continues
for months. In the warmest areas,
the plant is seldom without a flower
or two.

The species has brilliant orange
petals with a dark eye accentuated
by a white spot. In combination
with the silvery leaves of some
forms, this presents a dramatic

show. It must be propagated by division, which is difficult, or by cuttings, also not easy, and overwintered
indoors in cold areas.

There is also a wide range of modern hybrids, bigger and variable in
color but often coarse in habit.
Many of these can be grown from
seed. Some of these react less to
light than the species (which closes
its flowers at night and on dull
days). Some hybrids keep their
flowers open even in rainy weather.

Gentiana species

Gentian

To most gardeners the word *gentian* means blue. Indeed, some of
the species have a quality of rich,
clear blue that is unexcelled by any
other flower. There are over three
hundred species of these mainly
mountain plants spread around the
temperate world or in the high
mountains of the tropics. In cultivation they make good plants for
the rock garden or for the very
front of less specialized borders.
Although those from the Alps and
Himalayas are the most dramatic
when in flower, the two described
here are more easily grown.

Gentiana asclepiadea is the aptly
named willow gentian. Native to
Greece and east into Asia Minor, it
makes a clump of outward-arching
leafy stems with upward-facing

Gentiana septemfida

Geranium endressii

tubular flowers of true-blue. Flowering in late summer, it is lovely with ivy-leaved cyclamen (*Cyclamen hederifolium)* and takes the same conditions of moist, leafy soil in half shade. It can be grown to Zone 6 or even 5.

Similar conditions suit *G. septemfida,* the fringed gentian. The common name refers to the little beard inside the petals. This foot-high plant produces blue flowers in midsummer. A few short twigs pushed into the ground around the base of the plant help to keep the clump together.

Geranium species

Cranesbill

A dozen or so species of cranesbill (of the three hundred scattered around the temperate world) are among the most valuable garden perennials. They are hardy plants—those listed here survive to Zone 4 under winter snow—and should not be confused with the summer bedding geraniums (*Pelargonium* species).

Cranesbill takes sun or half shade, but the hotter the garden the greater the need for shade. Ideally it grows in a moist, leafy soil, but any normal garden soil suffices. The elegant combination of foliage and flower continues for months.

From the Pyrenees, *Geranium endressii* is one of those invaluable plants that is evergreen and always in flower in mild areas. Where winters are fierce, it opens its first clear, pink flowers above a flush of

new leaves in June and continues until hard frosts intervene. A fine 18-inch ground cover, this geranium is lovely with purple bearded iris (*Iris* species) while it is in flower, and it extends the interest in the garden for months after the iris is gone.

G. himalayense (also listed as *G. grandiflorum*) makes an elegant, foot-high plant. Its wide, open flowers are intensely violet-blue with distinct veins. This is an early summer bloomer, excellent under old-fashioned roses (as are all cranesbills). Its foliage turns an attractive yellow in the fall.

G. ibericum, despite its name, is from southwestern Asia and southeastern Europe. A bigger plant than *G. himalayense,* its leaves are

Geranium macrorrhizum

Geranium sanguineum 'Album'

Gerbera jamesonii 'Happipot'

rounded and its flowers, which
tend more to violet, are held on
sticky flower stems. A cross between the two is *G. × magnificum,*
a lovely purplish violet and well
worth seeking out.

G. macrorrhizum, a native of southern Europe, has been cultivated
since the sixteenth century as an
ornamental and an herb (grown for
the aromatic oil of geranium). It
makes a tight dome about a foot
high and spreads outward. To add
to the interest, the semi-evergreen
leaves turn colorful shades in autumn. 'Ingwersen's Variety', the
best cultivar, has flowers that are
red to soft rose-pink.

Huge 4-foot-high clumps of fingered leaves are typical of *G. psi-
lostemon.* Its mass of black-centered

magenta flowers is dramatic in half
shade with Welsh-poppy (*Meconopsis cambrica*) or orange lily
(*Lilium tigrinum*).

G. sanguineum is the bloody
cranesbill. The dark magenta flowers on this foot-tall plant bloom
over a long season starting in late
June. A white variant is taller and
flops over, but both are lovely
plants that close the year with
autumn tints.

Gerbera jamesonii

Transvaal daisy

This South African perennial daisy
(the only commonly cultivated of
some seventy species within the genus) is for the warmest zones only.
Long-lived clumps of hairy leaves,
sometimes white-backed, are more
or less evergreen. The older, outer
leaves lie flat on the ground and are
apt to get mud-spattered in freshly
disturbed soil. The plant needs full
sun in rich, well-drained soil.

From late spring until the fall a
long succession of wonderful daisies
bloom up to 4 inches across on foot-
high stems. Narrow petals, each
separate from the next, gradually
curve back. The glowing, orange-
red blossoms are perfect in form
and extremely long-lasting as cut
flowers.

This is a plant that the breeders
should have left alone. In the
search for an increased color range

Gerbera jamesonii

Geum 'Mrs. Bradshaw'

(now spanning white, yellow, pink, red, and orange) and ever bigger flowers, the original elegance has been lost. The double-flowered and dwarf types have even less to commend them.

Transvaal daisy is now offered in quick-maturing forms that are grown as tender annuals in colder zones. Their flowers are not as lovely and the plants are not easily recommended.

Geum species

Avens

Of the fifty or so species of these temperate-world rose relations, less than a half dozen appear in the garden and the nomenclature of these is confused. They provide good clumps of leaves, rather parsleylike, with hairy stems topped by bright flowers early in the season. The woody clumps need regular dividing and replanting in fresh soil. The plant needs full sun or half shade and it survives to Zone 4 under snow or a leafy mulch.

Geum chiloense is from Chile; *G. coccineum* may be the same thing. Probably neither true species is in garden cultivation, but they have produced several common yet highly desirable offspring with double flowers. 'Mrs. Bradshaw' is

a fiery orange-red, and 'Lady Stratheden' is yellow (both of these grow true from seed). 'Fire Opal' hovers between them in color. All are about 2 feet in height, flowering through May and June.

G. × *borisii* is a smaller plant that makes a good leafy ground cover with foot-high stems bearing clear, orange, single flowers 1½ inches across. All these bright flowers combine well with the greenish yellows of spurge (*Euphorbia* species) and carry the floral season into summer with the late-blooming tulips (*Tulipa* species and hybrids) and daffodils (*Narcissus* hybrids).

Gladiolus byzantinus

Gypsophila paniculata 'Bristol Fairy'

Gladiolus species

Gladiolus, cornflag, sword-lily

As a cut flower, with its 4-foot spire of lilylike flowers opening in sequence up the spike, gladiolus is extremely popular. In the garden the big hybrids begin by looking magnificent with swordlike leaves and lower flowers in bloom, but can end up rather messy. For border decoration the smaller *Gladiolus primulinus* and its cultivars are often a better bet. Full sun and good soil help ensure a good show.

The genus is an enormous one of almost three hundred species with a north-south distribution from England to South Africa. The garden types can be grouped under the name *G.* × *hortulanus.* Varying in height from 2 to 5 feet, they bloom in almost every color but true-blue. Often the lower petals have attractive contrasting flashes of color on the throat.

Although gladiolus is hardy in Zones 9 and 10 (and may survive below this), it is usually grown from corms every year. For a succession of flowering, plant corms 5 inches deep every week or two in April or May when the ground is warm. From planting to flowering takes about three months. Lift the corms before hard frost and store them over winter.

In mild areas try any of the wild species obtainable. The charming purple *G. byzantinus,* an elegant June-flowering plant from southern Europe, is probably safe to Zone 7. It can be difficult to confine in light, warm soil.

Gypsophila species

Baby's-breath

Of the hundred and twenty-five or so species of *Gypsophila,* three are commonly cultivated in the garden. The one that best deserves the baby's-breath description is a wonderful perennial, *G. paniculata,* which comes from Eastern Europe to central Asia.

G. paniculata produces a great cloud of tiny gray-white stars in July from a 4-foot-high dome of tangled stems. Its thin, little leaves are almost unnoticeable. Planted behind oriental poppy (*Papaver orientale*), which leaves such an early gap when it goes to rest in July, baby's-breath fills the space beautifully. It needs good drainage and full sun (it grows well in the thin limestone soils of the Niagara escarpment) and survives to at least

Gypsophila elegans 'Covent Garden'

Helenium autumnale

Zone 4. Double- and pink-flowered forms are also available. The taller cultivars need support.

G. repens is a wide-spreading plant for the front of the border or rock garden. It grows to only 9 inches and covers itself in a midsummer show of pink or white. Native to the mountains of Europe, it thrives under conditions similar to those enjoyed by its relative *G. elegans*.

An annual from the Caucasus mountains, *G. elegans* is easily grown, either sown in the garden as the ground starts to warm up in spring or planted out from trays. In California it can be treated as a winter annual. Typically a foot or so in height, this baby's-breath has pink and purplish forms, but none is quite as attractive and showy as the original white.

Helenium autumnale

Sneezeweed

As a common native occurring throughout much of North America, this lovely plant is apt to be considered less of a garden plant on this side of the Atlantic than in Europe. However, if prejudice against a local son (with pejorative hints of hay fever) can be disregarded, then sneezeweed has a lot to offer.

It makes thickets of 5-foot-high stems and great sprays of distinctive daisies in late summer and fall. Each flower has a spherical central knob of velvety texture and slightly reflexed petals. The color range epitomizes autumn: yellow, mahogany, brown, and bronze. Some forms have contrasting eyes.

Sneezeweed needs to be kept away from the purples and pinks of phlox (*Phlox* species), but it associates well at the back of the border with plumepoppy (*Macleaya* species) and bugbane (*Cimicifuga* species).

The cream flowers of bugbane and milk white leaves of plumepoppy are perfect foils in the shrub border or mixed border, as are variegated dogwoods such as *Cornus alba* 'Elegantissima Variegata'. Or encourage warm tones by planting purple canna (*Canna* × *generalis*) in back and use the strong, low-growing leaves of winter-begonia (*Bergenia* species) to hide the base of sneezeweed.

There are a number of cultivars, some dating back to the last century. 'Riverton Beauty' and 'Riverton Gem', two of the best-known varieties, are yellow and mahogany respectively.

Sneezeweed is one of the easiest perennials to grow in a sunny spot in any soil but the wettest. It is hardy to Zone 3. The robust clumps need regular dividing about every three years to keep the growth constant.

Helichrysum petiolatum

Helianthus × multiflorus

Helianthus species

Sunflower

There are about one hundred and fifty species of *Helianthus,* all native to the New World. They include the tuberous Jerusalem artichoke (*H. tuberosus*), although much more important as a food source for humans is the common sunflower (*H. annuus*). Native from the southern part of Canada into Mexico, it is the most astounding of all annual plants, reaching 10 feet in height and in late summer carrying a great flaming yellow sun of a flower measuring up to a foot across.

In the garden, smaller versions are a better bet for decoration. There are selections with more and longer-lasting flowers on each plant, as well as a choice of flower color, including wine red and mahogany. Sow seeds in place when the soil warms up, or in areas with a short summer set out plants in a spot in full sun. Four frost-free months are essential for growing sunflower.

Crossed with *H. decapetalus,* a perennial from the central United States, the common sunflower has produced *H. × multiflorus.* There are a number of cultivars, all of them good perennials hardy to Zone 3. They grow to 6 feet tall and bear late-summer sprays of single or double daisies in various shades of yellow. The popular 'Loddon Gold' has strong, deep yellow blooms. 'Capenoch Star' is a softer shade that is easier to combine with other plants. Both are useful in any sunny spot.

Native sunflowers such as *H. scaberrimus* and *H. tomentosus* are well worth introducing into a wildflower garden in a location where the plants' running roots are acceptable.

Helichrysum species

Strawflower, everlasting

There are several hundred species of *Helichrysum* from the Old World and Australia, representing annuals, herbaceous perennials, and woody shrubs. Some of the subshrubs are valuable in the warmest zones; in these areas their aromatic leaves give them the name curryplant. The shrubby perennial *H. petiolatum* is a lovely widespreading, gray-leaved plant for summer bedding anywhere.

But the one species that everyone knows is *H. bracteatum,* the strawflower. In its Australian home it is a good perennial and it behaves similarly in California. It is more commonly cultivated as an annual sown indoors and planted outside when all frosts have passed. It needs a good, light soil and as sunny a place as can be found. A row in the vegetable garden is sensible when it is grown as a cut flower.

Modern selections are a couple of feet high or more, the stiff stems

Helichrysum bracteatum

Heliopsis helianthoides

carrying strange, cup-shaped daisy flowers that consist of rigid, glossy petals. The colors range from cream through yellow and bronze to dusky pink and purple. The flowers are truly everlasting but their stems are not. Florists mount the heads on wires for indoor dried decorations.

Heliopsis helianthoides

Oxeye

The oxeye-daisy of British gardening books is a small, white, yellow-eyed chrysanthemum. This oxeye is a very different plant more closely resembling a sunflower. It is a great, robust 5-footer with wide-spreading heads of yellow daisies.

The North American oxeye is native to a relatively narrow band through the central United States from Illinois and Missouri south to Texas and Louisiana. It was introduced into cultivation in Europe around 1714. Several good selections have since been returned to the United States.

The plant ranges in height from 4 to nearly 6 feet when grown in rich soil. Strong stems branch into wide heads of 2½-inch daisies that are orange-yellow with a darker disk. The garden selections are single

or semidouble and vary in color from orange-yellow to pale yellow. August is their month of glory, but the sepals whiten after the flowers fade, and still look attractive.

Oxeye grows to Zone 4, under mulch, in any good garden soil exposed to full sun.

Helleborus orientalis

Heliotropium arborescens

Heliotropium arborescens

Heliotrope, cherry-pie

Of the approximately two hundred and fifty species strewn around all the continents, this heliotrope is the only one in general cultivation. A favorite container plant grown for its scent in Victorian times, it is still cultivated in Europe as a commercial source of perfume.

Native to Peru, heliotrope is hardy in Zone 10 and sometimes 9. Elsewhere it is a houseplant or summer annual. Propagate either by cuttings or grow annually from seeds and plant outside when all chance of frost is over.

Heliotrope is a borage relative and shares the rather rough, bristly leaves of so many of the family. Flat flower heads of small, fragrant flowers are usually a rich purple

(white forms are much less effective). The purple flowers combine well with dusty-miller and other plants with gray foliage.

Plants can be lifted in the fall (instead of being left to die of cold) and maintained over the winter in a greenhouse. You can develop a woody framework on the plant or train it as a standard on a single stem to obtain a large plant for season-long display. It makes a good patio plant combined with fuchsia (*Fuchsia* species).

Helleborus species

Christmas-rose, lenten-rose, hellebore

Despite the common names, these are not roses at all, but buttercup relatives. With their wide-petaled cups and gold and green centers, they are attractive plants for shaded borders. Plant them under shrubs and at woodland edges in any leafy soil except the driest and wettest. Hellebore prefers lime but tolerates acid soil.

The Christmas-rose, *Helleborus niger,* is an exquisite plant that does not often live up to its name. Even in warm areas flowering seldom occurs before February. In the North it is more likely to happen at Easter.

Christmas-rose comes from rocky woodlands of Central Europe. It makes a low clump of leathery, fingered, evergreen leaves that develop hard, round flower buds at

Helleborus corsicus

Helleborus orientalis

their base at the start of winter. The 3- or 4-inch-wide blossoms, like pure white chalices on 8-inch stalks, are very dependent on weather: The colder the climate, the later they bloom. Zone 5 is probably its limit, but a good snow cover will take it farther. When snow cover is doubtful, even in Zone 6, a mulch of dry leaves held in place with net or pine boughs will protect the plant. It is a good idea to apply slug bait before mulching.

H. orientalis is the lenten-rose from Asia Minor. It is a lighter, less stocky plant with fingered leaves on foot-high stems. Each stem grows from the ground and is topped by nodding flowers in a range of colors from creamy white through soft pink to dusky plum purple. Most are exquisitely spotted, too. As the flower stems extend anytime from February to May, depending on climate, the previous year's leaf stems start to lean outward. The flowers are standing alone by the time they open. As the blooms fade, the weight of developing seed capsules causes them to tip over and a crown of new leaves takes over.

There are a number of other herbaceous species that can be lumped under the name lenten-rose. All are beautiful and should be tried. Their cultivation and zone recommendation is the same as for the Christmas-rose.

H. corsicus (also listed as *H. lividus corsicus*) is a subshrub from the Mediterranean. It has the same growth pattern as the lenten-rose, but its 2-foot-high, woody stems carry toothed leaves and are topped by heads of pale green flowers. Depending on the strain of plant and the site, flowering occurs for several weeks sometime between November and May. This is a dramatic plant for a well-drained, semishaded spot in Zone 7, although it will survive to Zone 5 with protection.

Hemerocallis 'Wine Cooler'

Hemerocallis 'Bitsie'

Hemerocallis species

Daylily

There are fifteen-odd *Hemerocallis,* all clump-forming plants with long, arching, narrow leaves. Native to the Far East, some have been cultivated there for two or three thousand years for both food and aesthetic effect. They are exquisitely depicted on Chinese and Japanese screens.

The breeding and selection that began in the East has reached extraordinary lengths in the West with thousands of cultivars already named and more appearing every year. These can be chosen from an up-to-date catalog or by visiting a nursery to see the variations possible.

Selections vary from little plants not much above a foot in height (for example, the charming, deep

yellow 'Stella de Oro') to great 4-footers. Some begin to flower in late May; others start later but continue through September. Although the pattern of elegant lily-like blooms held on leafless stalks above the foliage remains constant, the flower color ranges from palest citron yellow through deep orange to pink and dusky red. Both single and double forms are available. Some varieties defy the common name, as each flower blooms longer than one day. Most, however, produce a new flush of flowers every day.

The following three species encapsulate the range. *H. lilioasphodelus,* the lemon daylily, is one of the first to flower. Usually about 2½ feet high, it has clusters of deliciously fragrant, clear yellow flowers with elegant reflexed petals. It looks lovely with the first lupines (*Lupinus* species) of the year and spreads easily without being invasive.

H. middendorffii is only 1½ feet in height. Its compact clusters of rich, orange-yellow, lilylike flowers open in June.

H. fulva is the old tawny daylily, which has gone wild on so many roadsides in North America, and its 4-foot-high stems of rusty orange flowers are a familiar sight in July. A form with double flowers is equally robust. It makes one of the best ground covers on a large, sunny bank in an informal garden.

Daylily is a superb plant for the garden. Long before the flowers open, the bright yellow-green spears of foliage present an interesting display. Often at the end of the season the plant turns golden. All species enjoy moist soil, even heavy clay, and tend to flower freely in full sun. They grow to Zone 4 under winter snow, and perhaps beyond.

Heuchera sanguinea 'Huntsman'

Hesperis matronalis

Hesperis matronalis

Sweet-rocket, dame's-violet

Native to central and southern Europe, sweet rocket is a favorite cottage-garden plant that came to North America with the early European settlers and is now naturalized in many areas.

As a short-lived perennial, sweet-rocket makes a clump of 4-foot-high stems with narrow leaves. The top halves of the stems are crowded with four-petaled flowers. Opening from mid-May and continuing throughout June, they gradually bloom up the spike. If dead-headed at once, side shoots often extend the show. If not, seed production is prodigious and may give more self-sown seedlings than you want, although the plant is seldom a pest.

Typically the flowers are a soft purple, but any seedling population contains darker and paler forms as well as white. All are scented, a feature that is especially noticeable in the evening. There are double-flowered forms that must be propagated by division or cuttings, but these are not easy to keep going.

Sweet-rocket needs a moist soil. It flowers well in full sun or half shade, enjoying damp woodland-edge conditions down to Zone 4 or even beyond. Although common, it is still a worthwhile plant for the flower garden.

Heuchera species

Alumroot, coralbells, rock-geranium

There are almost fifty species of *Heuchera,* all from North America. They are saxifrage relatives with woody rootstocks spreading to build up wide, low clumps of rounded, hairy leaves and narrow spikes of tiny bell-shaped flowers. A couple have become favorite garden plants in North America and Europe.

H. americana, the rock-geranium, is native from Ontario south to Georgia. It is grown less for its spikes of greenish flowers than for its foliage. The great English gardener Gertrude Jekyll called it satin-leaf, which admirably recalls the strangely attractive marbled sheen of the young leaves. The

Heuchera sanguinea 'Alba'

Hibiscus moscheutos

plant needs to be kept well-fed and watered to encourage its continual production. It is hardy to Zone 3.

H. sanguinea has a natural distribution in Arizona and New Mexico, yet its garden forms seem quite safe in Zone 5, if not beyond, under the requisite mulch. Known as coralbells, the species has foot-high spikes of scarlet bells in June. There are selections that grow to 2 feet high and bloom in colors ranging from white through pink to brilliant red. All have strong basal foliage.

All species need moist, loose soil and do well in sun or half shade. The time to divide or transplant clumps is in late summer.

Hibiscus species

Rose-mallow, hibiscus

The most common perception of hibiscus is that of a tropical shrub grown indoors for its brilliant flowers. In fact, among the two hundred and fifty–odd species scattered around the world are annuals and perennials as well as hardy shrubs and tall tropical trees.

Rose-mallow is one of the most amazing herbaceous perennials grown. The woody rootstock is dormant until mid-June, when a few wispy shoots appear. Increasing temperatures infuse them with strength and in a month they are 4 to 6 feet high with wide, soft leaves and developing buds at the tips. These soon open, one at a time, to vast saucer-shaped blooms up to 9 inches across. The bloom continues into September.

Hibiscus moscheutos, the common rose-mallow, is native to marshy areas from Michigan south to

Georgia. It is hardy to Zone 6 with good winter protection. Full sun and some care are required. *H. coccineus* is similar and continues southward into the coastal swamps of Florida. It is not a plant for the north, but there is a hybrid group including the popular 'Southern Belle' that combines the features of both species. Flower color varies from white, often with a dark eye, through pink to dark red.

Plant spring bulbs around rose-mallow to decorate the space in the early part of the year. The bulbs then rest as the mallow grows.

Hippeastrum hybrid

Hosta fortunei 'Albopicta'

Hippeastrum cultivars

Amaryllis, Barbados-lily

Hybrid species of *Hippeastrum* are well known as indoor container plants. Soon after they are planted, the huge bulbs put up drumstick-like flower stems with the flowers initially enclosed in a green sheath. At about 18 inches the sheath splits and the great trumpet flowers, commonly two or four in number, unfold. Each can be 6 inches long and wide and the group looks much like an old-fashioned public-address system. Brilliant scarlet is the most common color, but pink, white, and striped cultivars are also offered. The long, strap-shaped leaves follow the flowers and usually, but not always, go to rest before the next season's flower stem appears.

Amaryllis is grown as a permanent plant outdoors only in Zones 9 and 10. It needs a rich, leafy soil with ample moisture during the growing season. Although a sunny spot is preferred, the plant tolerates part shade. In the North it is possible, if somewhat extravagant, to plant bulbs in June for summer display. The bulbs must be lifted before the first frost.

Where the bulbs can be left undisturbed to build up a clump, the flowers become smaller and better balanced with the stem height. Some smaller-flowered cultivars are becoming available and are strongly recommended both for warm gardens and for pots.

Hosta species

Plantain-lily

An effective garden without plantain-lily is almost inconceivable. In all its diversity, this perennial is among the most valuable for shaded sites. The broad, lustrous leaves provide a marvelous contrast with other shade-lovers, like ferns, and are also invaluable as cut greenery for indoors. Leaf color includes many shades of green and some that are nearly blue, and many have spectacular variegated patterns. Flower spikes, which can approach 5 feet in height, carry small lilylike trumpets in shades of purple and soft lavender paling to white.

Many of the dozen or so species from the Far East, in addition to an ever-increasing number of garden cultivars, are grown in North America. Plantain-lily has been a

Hosta undulata 'Univittata'

part of the Japanese garden scene for centuries and it was from those gardens that the original nineteenth century introductions came. This explains the unusual situation of variegated forms having full species names.

Plantain-lily enjoys deep, moist soil in full or part shade and will even succeed under trees if the soil is not too dry, but in such spots avoid cultivars with puckered leaves (aptly known as seersucker plantain-lily) because they tend to collect fallen debris in the crevices of the leaves.

Plantain-lily is one of the easiest plants to grow and to increase. In spring simply cut up pieces of established clumps in the same manner that you would slice a cake. Transplant each slice and fill its hole with good compost. Seeds can be sown to provide enough plants

for mass ground cover. The seeds take three years to develop and will probably be extremely variable. Plantain-lily is hardy, under winter snow and a leafy mulch, to Zone 4 or beyond.

It is convenient to describe plantain-lily according to size and to recommend just a few of the best. In the smaller group (1½ feet high and 1½ feet across), *Hosta sieboldii* has glossy, oval leaves with a white edge and spikes of purple flowers. 'Louisa' is a dainty version with white flowers. *H. lancifolia* is good for late-season flowers. *H. undulata* has twisted leaves with a white central flash. 'Blue Cadet' and 'Blue Boy' have lilac flowers above bluish foliage. 'Gold Edger' is self-descriptive.

In the 2-foot-by-2-foot class, *H. crispula* has wavy white-edged leaves. There are several good cultivars of *H. fortunei*: 'Albopicta' has yellow-green leaves that gradually darken, 'Wayside Blue' with bluish leaves increases well, as does the golden-leaved 'Gold Standard'.

H. plantaginea and its cultivars comprises another group of medium-sized plantain-lilies, about 2½ feet tall and wide. These plants, which prefer at least half sun, bear flowers in August with a delicious fragrance that is especially strong in the evening. 'Honeybells' and 'Royal Standard' are two particularly good cultivars.

The big plantain-lilies can have leaves a foot across, making clumps up to 3 feet wide. *H. sieboldiana* 'Elegans' is gray-blue and 'Frances Williams' adds a variegated edge to this. Both have flower spikes that

Hosta 'Thomas Hogg'

Hyacinthus orientalis 'Delft Blue'

stand just above the leaves. 'Krossa Regal', also blue-leaved, has flower spikes up to 5 feet high.

Plantain-lily has only one disadvantage in the garden. Because it is so easy to grow, it can become invasive, pushing out other worthwhile plants. With care, however, it can become a vital part of the seasonal progression, especially when underplanted with small spring bulbs such as snowdrop (*Galanthus* species) and scilla (*Scilla* siberica). Eventually the plantain-lily itself becomes the underplanting to carefully selected shrubs.

Hyacinthus orientalis

Hyacinth

This is one of the most popular bulbs for indoor decoration in winter or spring: The fat spikes, tightly packed with intensely fragrant bell-shaped flowers, last for three weeks in a cool room.

The species grows wild from the eastern Mediterranean into Asia Minor, where it was first cultivated hundreds of years ago. In the seventeenth century it became one of the bulbs for which Holland became famous, and a vast diversity of color forms was selected. These include white, yellow, blue, purple, pink, and red. Double flowers are now seldom seen and even the cultivar range is reduced. Nevertheless, hyacinth retains a valuable place in the garden.

Plant bulbs 6 inches deep and 6 inches apart no later than September or early October. Good drainage and spring sun are needed. In

Zone 5 and colder regions, a winter mulch is wise. Depending on the area, flowering takes place sometime between early April and late May. Afterward, do not cut off the leaves until they turn yellow. Unless the hyacinth is planted as part of a formal bedding scheme, there is no need to lift the bulbs and overwinter them. In subsequent years the bulbs increase and produce more flower spikes, but these are thinner and better suited to the open garden.

Hydrangea arborescens 'Grandiflora'

Hydrangea quercifolia

Hydrangea species

Hydrangea, hills-of-snow,
hortensia

There are about twenty species of
Hydrangea, with a strange natural
distribution in parts of the eastern
United States and the Far East.
They are free-standing shrubs or
climbers valued for their summer
flowers, although they remain interesting into the fall and beyond.
They associate well with herbaceous plants and some even behave
as such.

Two native species are particularly
good and, although common, deserve
a place in the garden. *H. arborescens* (sometimes called hills-of-
snow) comes from the lower part of
New York state and southward,
with subspecies inhabiting the
mountains of the southeastern
United States. In the garden it
makes a thicket of 4-foot-high stems
with downy leaves and terminal
flower heads. These have a

wonderful progression in their
development. By late June developing flower heads cover the shrub
with lime green. Gradually expanding, the flowers turn cream and
then white. In late August, now
fully grown, they revert to green.
With frosts and leaf fall, the heads
become papery and hold their buff
color until spring.

Because this hydrangea flowers on
new wood, it can be treated as an
herbaceous plant and many experts
recommend that it be pruned hard
in the spring. In a good garden soil
this is a mistake, as it encourages
huge flower heads up to 9 inches
across. These are flattened by the
first summer storm and spend the
rest of the season on the ground. It

is better to thin out the shoots and
cut back only the dead foliage.
Hills-of-snow, which is hardy to
Zone 5 and perhaps 4, takes shade
or sun.

H. quercifolia is the oak-leaved
hydrangea. From the southeastern
United States, it is hardy to Zone
5. It makes a stoutly branched
shrub up to 6 feet tall, slowly suck-
ering outward. The lobed leaves are
hairy and turn warm russet-red in
fall, setting off the broadly triangular green flower heads. These also
turn cream to white in summer. A
statuesque plant, this hydrangea is
best in half shade. It looks lovely
with the perennial bellflower *Campanula lactiflora,* especially when
underplanted with spring bulbs.

The florist's hydrangea or hortensia
is *H. macrophylla.* Native to Japan,
this plant grows to 8 feet tall and
flowers mainly on the previous

Hydrangea macrophylla

Iberis umbellata 'Fairy Mix'

Iberis sempervirens

year's wood. It is a plant for the mild and moist West Coast, although it survives to Zone 6. The flower heads are dome-shaped and white, pink, or purple. When grown in acid soil the flowers are a brilliant blue; in alkaline soil they are pink or reddish. You can make acid soil more alkaline, and hence change the color of the hydrangea blossoms, by adding lime or superphosphate. Closer to the wild species are the lace-cap forms with flat flowers heads. This pattern is repeated in *H. aspera,* a lovely 8-foot Himalayan native with velvety leaves that is hardy to Zone 7.

All hydrangeas enjoy partial shade in moist, leafy soil.

Iberis species

Candytuft

Iberis sempervirens, perennial candytuft, is a Mediterranean subshrub whose species name translates as "ever living." Forming a wide, foot-high clump of narrow, dark green leaves, it is frequently employed as an edging plant or a permanent part of a rock garden. It makes a good foliage backdrop for small spring bulbs; as they go to rest, it starts to put on its own floral display. In May perennial candytuft becomes covered with little flat heads of four-petaled white flowers. There are usually a few still on the plant well into autumn.

Cultivars such as 'Little Gem' and 'Compacta' are self-descriptive. Although the species can be grown from seed, the cultivars must be propagated by cuttings or division.

Perennial candytuft is hardy to Zone 5, but without decent snow cover it is apt to look very ragged by the end of winter. It will need to be clipped over, losing much of its evergreen effect. Any good garden soil in full sun is suitable.

I. umbellata, the annual candytuft found in old cottage gardens, is an easy, showy plant that can be used as a winter annual in California and southern Florida and as a summer annual elsewhere. Around a foot high, selections are available in white, pink, rose, crimson, and lilac.

Impatiens balsamina

Incarvillea delavayi

Impatiens species

Balsam, busy-lizzie, patient-lucy, touch-me-not

The last of these common names (and there are several others) is the most descriptive, as anyone who tries to gather balsam seeds will agree. When ripe and swollen, the little seedpods burst at the slightest touch, throwing out their contents in all directions. This is a common denominator of most of the five hundred–odd impatiens species native to the warmer regions of the Old World.

I. balsamina is a Chinese species often called rose-balsam. In a sunny spot in good soil, it makes a stout, 2-foot-high plant. In the joints of its narrow leaves the frequently double flowers are carried throughout summer. As an annual it can be sown indoors or directly in the ground, but it will take no frost at either end of the season.

I. wallerana, the old busy-lizzie, in its modern forms has completely changed the summer garden. Originally a perennial from tropical East Africa, it is now available in annual strains that flower in pink, scarlet, magenta, or white or in combinations of these colors. Shade-loving plants, they vary from 6 inches to over a foot in height and spread. If planted as soon as the soil has warmed up, they produce sheets of color as long as they are well watered. The first breath of frost spells immediate death. Cuttings taken before this can be easily overwintered indoors on warm windowsills. They will flower indefinitely.

Incarvillea species

Incarvillea

This small genus of Asian perennials with only a dozen or so species includes some of the most surprising hardy plants grown. They are unlikely relatives of the native Indian bean tree (*Catalpa* species) but look like a cape primrose (*Streptocarpus* species) that has strayed into the open garden and decided to stay regardless of the weather.

Incarvillea delavayi forms a clump of dark green, divided leaves (rather slow to develop in spring) that puts up stout stems up to 2 feet high. Each carries three or four trumpet-shaped flowers, deep rose in color and up to 3 inches across, with broad rounded petals. They last well, usually throughout June,

Indigofera gerardiana

Indigofera gerardiana

but when the petals eventually fade a strikingly long seedpod develops to continue the interest.

While *I. delavayi* spread from Western China into Tibet, *I. mairei* remained in China proper. It has equally sumptuous flowers, great trumpets up to 4 inches across. A similar rose color paling to white or yellow in the tube, they are carried only 6 or 9 inches above the leaves. 'Bees Pink' is a good selected form.

Incarvillea needs a deep, rich soil in a sunny spot. It must not be allowed to dry out as growth develops. In Zone 5 it is wise to provide a leafy mulch. With this and a snow cover it is probably safe in colder zones.

Indigofera species

Indigo

Members of this huge genus of around seven hundred species have for centuries provided the indigo of commerce. They are from the old, mainly subtropical world, but a couple are hardy shrubs that combine well with other woody plants and with herbaceous perennials.

Related to the pea and bean, indigo has elegant leaves on arching stems that carry spikes of typically pea-shaped flowers in summer. The subsequent pods, at first purplish and then darkening with age, can remain dry and ornamental well into winter.

The Himalayan *Indigofera gerardiana* is the most attractive of the species suitable for North America. It is safe to Zone 7, where it behaves herbaceously, putting up a thicket

of stems 4 feet high and dying back each winter. Its rose-purple flowers appear for many weeks in late summer. In warmer areas it can reach 10 feet in height and begins to flower earlier in the season. Full sun and any good garden soil are required.

Two other species, *I. kirilowii* from Korea and *I. potaninii* from China, seem to be hardier still and are gradually becoming more available. They are valuable summer subshrubs and should be sought out.

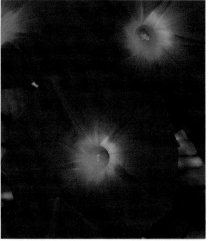

Ipomoea tricolor

Inula ensifolia

Inula species

Inula

There are over a hundred species
of these mostly perennial daisies
spread around temperate and subtropical regions of the Old World.
One of them is *Inula helenium,* or
elecampane, once a well-known
herb whose root was used to treat
bronchitic conditions and skin af-
flictions. It was grown in the New
World in the Shaker herb fields
and has become naturalized in
some areas.

Although elecampane and its close
cousin *I. magnifica* are worthwhile
garden plants, they grow to a robust 6 feet tall and cannot fit into
every garden. A more accommo-
dating species is *I. ensifolia,* a valuable front-of-the-border plant. It
makes a tidy clump of 1½-foot-high

stems thickly furnished with narrow
leaves and topped with a mass of
bright yellow daisies in July. Each is
held singly on its own wiry stalk.

Coming from eastern Europe and
the Caucasus, *I. ensifolia* is hardy
to Zone 4 under snow cover in any
good, well-drained garden soil. It is
a plant that shows off its brilliance
in full sun. In half shade the clumps
thin out, stems flop, and the whole
essence of the plant is lost.

Ipomoea species

Morning glory

There are not many climbers that
make a really good show within a
few months of spring sowing.
Morning glory is a valuable plant
in this respect. It is especially good
for new gardens, where it provides
height, privacy, and an almost in-
stant show. It climbs easily to 15
feet before the frosts of autumn put
a stop to its rampant colonialism.

Common morning glory, *Ipomoea
purpurea,* is an annual twiner from
tropical America that, seeding itself from year to year, has become
naturalized in parts of the southern
United States. It can be sown
either indoors and planted outside
after frost is gone or sown in place
in the garden. Where the growing
season is long it twines rapidly over
any support provided, living or
dead, making a mass of heart-
shaped, hairy leaves and covering

Iris 'Stepping Out'

Ipomoea tricolor 'Heavenly Blue'

itself from late July onward with velvety trumpets that are pink, white, or purple. Good soil, moisture, and full sun are required.

More elegant is *I. tricolor,* a perennial in its South American home but treated exactly as *I. purpurea* in North America. It has smooth, pale green leaves and variably colored flowers. The best by far is the exquisite form called 'Heavenly Blue', in a clear sky blue fading to white in the throat. It is one of the joys of the late summer garden, opening at dawn and closing by midafternoon. As the weather cools, the flower remains open all day, reconciling the gardener to the approach of autumn.

Iris species

Iris

All two hundred–odd *Iris* species are lovely plants, some more spectacular than others. The flower shape may seem to vary, but they all share the highly distinctive fleur-de-lis pattern. All parts of the iris flower are grouped in threes: three outspread petals (the falls), three upright petals (the standards), three stamens, and three stigmas (the female part of the flower that receives the pollen) hidden among fringed or bearded outgrowths. The falls are invariably veined, spotted, or otherwise marked by the pollen guides evolved as signposts for the bees.

Most irises are native to the northern temperate parts of the world and thus are hardy in the majority of North American gardens. They are all good perennials in their natural habitats but do not necessarily behave this way in cultivation. Most, however, are easy to grow.

Many people associate the word *iris* with the tall bearded types common to *I.* × *germanica.* This species, itself a hybrid of unknown origin, is seen in the wild growing on dry banks and field edges throughout the Mediterranean. With other related species and intense selection, it has produced thousands of named cultivars.

In spring, sheaves of flat leaves extend from overwintering buds on the fleshy rhizomes. Each leaf puts up a stout stem carrying up to half a dozen fragrant flowers that open in succession over two weeks or so during late May or early June. Every color and combination of color except scarlet is possible, and often the falls are exquisitely veined in contrasting shades. These bearded

Iris spuria 'Lark Song'

Iris pallida 'Variegata Aurea'

irises are hardy to Zone 5 or even 4 with a good mulch of green branches and snow on top (unnecessary in Zone 6).

The rhizomes should be divided every three years as soon as it is convenient after flowering. A well-drained soil and full sun are required. In windy gardens, where many of the big modern hybrids are easily knocked down, avoid the nuisance of staking by planting the intermediate (2-feet-tall) or dwarf (1½-feet-tall) bearded irises, both of which flower earlier in the season. They require the same conditions as the larger form.

Another fine, tall bearded iris is the exquisite *I. pallida* from the South Tyrol in the Alps. The leaves are grayish and the lavender flowers stand 3 feet tall. There are two lovely variegated forms—one cream and the other white-striped—that deserve special care. Give them adequate room because they do poorly when crowded by other plants. The *I. spuria* types are valued for their

vertical swordlike foliage—up to 4 feet high—above which stiff stems of yellow, blue, or bronze flowers bloom in mid-June. Both of these Europeans take any soil in a sunny spot and are hardy to Zone 5.

Flowering at about the same time as the bearded types are the Siberian irises, an extensive group based on *I. sibirica* from Eastern Europe and the Soviet Union. Although the 3-foot-high stems of 3-inch-wide flowers last no longer than the bearded types, the clumps of arching, grassy foliage remain effective throughout the season (as with *I. pallida*) and hence make superior landscape plants. Colors range from white through blue to deep burgundy. Hardy to Zone 5, they succeed best in full sun in moist soil.

A North American native from the Southeast is *I. cristata,* the little

crested iris. Only 6 or 8 inches high, it makes wide-spreading clumps that flower in April and May. Flower color ranges from white to several shades of blue. All color forms are lovely with early spring bulbs. Best grown in shade, the crested iris likes a leafy soil. It is safe to Zone 5 and perhaps beyond with winter protection.

I. reticulata is the favorite of the group of beautiful, dwarf, bulbous irises native to southeastern Europe and Asia Minor. From bulbs planted 3 inches deep in October, a few narrow, stiff leaves appear in early spring bearing two or three exquisite, violet-scented flowers. Deep or pale blue or wine purple, each has a gold marking on the falls. This and the dwarf *I. histrioides* are 9 inches high and make good perennials in well-drained spots to Zone 4. The little yellow *I. danfordiae* is easy to grow from newly bought bulbs, but it seldom bulks up to make a permanent clump.

Iris foetidissima

Iris pseudacorus

Bigger bulbous species are concentrated in the wild in southwestern Europe and cross into northern Africa. *I. xiphium* has produced the so-called Dutch and Spanish irises, well known as cut flowers in florists' shops. In the garden, in Zone 7 and warmer areas, they need a sunny spot in well-drained soil. They can be treated as annual, autumn-planted, late-spring-flowering bulbs disposed of yearly, or they can be allowed to remain and develop permanent clumps. *I. xiphioides* seems to be a better perennial. Known as English iris (although it comes from Spain), it is a stocky 2-footer making clumps of stiff leaves. In late June it produces beautiful wide flowers in shades of blue, violet, and white. English iris, which prefers moister soil than other bulbous species, succeeds to Zone 6.

For milder areas there are several irises with evergreen leaves that make them valuable additions to the year-round landscape. Particularly fine is *I. confusa* from western China. Good in shade or sun, it produces bamboolike, 3-foot stems in spring. From the top of these stems hang outward-facing fans of leaves that develop sprays of blue and white orchidlike flowers the following spring. Cut the spent flowers immediately to renew the clump. This is a lovely plant for Zones 9 and 10.

A hardier, evergreen iris is the northern European *I. foetidissima,* the gladdon or gladwyn, which survives to Zone 8. The summer flowers are not exciting (although the cultivar 'Lulza' is good), but they develop seedpods that split to reveal brilliant orange seeds. These remain on display throughout winter above the dark, arching evergreen leaves. Gladdon takes deep shade in moist soil.

Hardy to Zone 7 with protection is a wonderful evergreen group clustered around *I. douglasiana.*

Known as California or Pacific Coast hybrids, these irises are native from Oregon to southern California. They make low arching clumps of grassy leaves and for several weeks from early May bear fringed flowers in a range of soft colors. They are lovely in a rock garden or the front of a border in full sun and well-drained soil.

A final group of irises (although there are many more worth investigating for most gardens) prefers wet soil. These are suitable for waterside planting. They include the native North American violet-flowering purple flag, *I. versicolor,* and the European *I. pseudacorus,* whose 4-foot clumps of long, narrow leaves are topped with even taller stems of yellow flowers in June and July. It also has a golden variegated form that makes a brilliant accent early in the year.

Kniphofia uvaria 'Ada'

Ixia maculata

Ixia species

Cornlily

The name cornlily is also applied to some of the smaller, wild *Gladiolus* species to which *Ixia* is closely related. Along with crocus and freesia, cornlily belongs to the side of the huge iris family that has tubular flowers.

Cornlily is an elegant South African plant that grows from corms. In the wild, growth begins in autumn and the wispy leaves, initially as thin as the grasses through which they grow, develop over winter. Wiry stems up to 2 feet tall carry wide, starlike flowers that bloom in a range of surprising colors.

Ixia maculata is the most common species, with flowers in cream, yellow, orange, red, or pink. All have contrasting dark centers.

With bright blue-green petals and a black throat, *I. viridiflora* is one of the most striking cornlilies. It should always be massed for the greatest effect.

To succeed as a perennial, cornlily must be grown in Zone 9 or 10. In colder areas the corms should be lifted in fall, kept in cold storage over winter, and replanted in spring for summer flowering. Well-drained soil and full sun are essential wherever the plant is grown.

Kniphofia species

Red-hot-poker, torch-lily

There are seventy-odd species of *Kniphofia* native to tropical and subtropical Africa south of the equator. Although those grown in North America are from South Africa, the coolest part of the range, they are on the edge of hardiness for most gardens here.

Although different forms vary greatly in size—flower spikes may be from 2 to 6 feet tall—they share the same growth pattern. Naked stems rise from a clump of narrow leaves in late summer. The top of the stem is packed tight with narrow, tubular flowers that are either red or white.

Hybrids of *K. uvaria* are those most likely to survive in the North, but even in Zone 6 they need a good winter mulch or the clump will die

Kochia scoparia

back each year. You can lift the plant in late fall and overwinter it indoors, but the plant is not worth it. In warmer areas there are better species. *K. galpinii* is one of the smaller types, only 3 feet high with tidy leaves and orange-red spikes, lovely with summer-hyacinth (*Galtonia candicans*).

K. caulescens is a magnificent evergreen species for Zones 9 and 10. Fat rhizomes resembling an elephant's trunk lie on the ground, clothed with beautiful gray-green leaves. Chubby red pokers are tipped with yellow.

All torch-lilies need good drainage, adequate summer moisture, and full sun.

Kochia scoparia

Summer-cypress, burning-bush

The eighty or so members of this genus are closely related to such vegetables as beet and spinach and to such weeds as fat-hen. Only one species is grown as an ornamental—summer-cypress. As its name suggests, it is an annual foliage plant of value. Native from southern Europe eastward to Japan, the plant has naturalized in many other parts of the temperate world.

Although in warmer zones seeds can be sown directly in the ground and fully grown plants will develop by the end of the season, it is still usual to start seeds indoors. In northern areas plant them outside only when the soil has warmed up.

By September the plant is 3 or 4 feet in height and makes an almost perfect sphere (taller than wide) of wiry stems and narrow leaves. The foliage is bright green in the early months and turns brilliant purple-red at the onset of colder weather.

As a specimen plant in bedding schemes or as a temporary hedge, few plants are more distinctive than burning-bush. Its uniformity makes it especially useful in formal settings. Plant it in any good garden soil in a sunny spot.

Lamium maculatum

Lamiastrum galeobdolon 'Herman's Pride'

Lamiastrum galeobdolon

Yellow-archangel

This is a genus with only one species, yet it has had a confusing time botanically. It is still sometimes included as *Lamium* in nursery lists. A native of European woodlands, it is one of the most valuable ground-cover plants for shady sites. It succeeds even in the difficult conditions under evergreen trees, as long as summer moisture is adequate.

Yellow-archangel is an evergreen perennial that behaves like a rambunctious strawberry. Clumps with hairy, oval leaves, green with grayish marbling, put out long, leafy stolons or horizontal stems that root at every node. The popular cultivar 'Variegatum' has a distinct marbled pattern and is marginally

less vigorous than the species. However, both can scramble up and over low shrubs. From established clumps, foot-high stems of yellow flowers appear in spring and make a fine foil for the bigger spring bulbs.

Yellow-archangel is suited to any leafy soil that doesn't dry out. The plant is safe to Zone 4 with a good snow mulch. In warm areas it will take over if not held in check.

Lamium maculatum

Spotted deadnettle

Although none of the forty or so species of *Lamium* is native to North America, all are found in gardens here, either as ornamentals or weeds. Of the ornamentals, spotted deadnettle is seen most often. It is a useful little plant as an unaggressive ground cover with the typical square stems and opposite leaves of the mint family.

The soft, downy foliage does not look as if it could survive northern winters. In fact, it is evergreen and remains so under snow, certainly to Zone 4. It creeps by short runners, rooting at the nodes as it goes. Some stems remain leafy while others, seldom above 6 inches high,

Lamium maculatum 'Aureum'

Lathyrus latifolius

produce soft pink or white, hooded flowers in the leaf joints during the late spring.

It is not the bloom but the foliage that earns the plant its place in the garden. The species has green leaves marbled with gray. 'Beacon Hill' has silvery gray foliage, and 'Aureum' features green leaves with yellow blotches along the midrib. All grow well in soil that does not dry out completely in summer, and they will even take full shade. Spotted deadnettle is a good ground cover to obscure the declining foliage of spring bulbs and give summer interest to a spot.

Lathyrus species

Sweet pea

Lathyrus latifolius is the everlasting pea. In this case *everlasting* refers not to flowers that retain their color and form when dried, but to the fact that this European native is a perennial sweet pea.

It is a robust herbaceous climber, scrambling up fences or other supports by means of tendrils to a height of 8 feet or more. The distinctively winged stems carry sea-green pinnate leaves and, from July onward, pink to magenta flowers. A lovely white-flowered form is easier to associate with other plants, and seedlings from it may produce a range of softer pinks.

Although plants are slow to develop from seed, once established they go on for many years. Any soil but the wettest or driest is acceptable. The plant is hardy to Zone 3.

Although everlasting pea is a visual joy, it has none of the fragrance of its annual sweet pea cousin *L. odoratus*. This is still a wonderful, old-fashioned plant for northern summers. It can also be grown as a winter annual in mild climates. However, annual sweet pea cannot take excess summer heat in the Southeast.

Lavandula angustifolia

Lavatera trimestris

Lavandula angustifolia

English lavender

It is not clear why in North America this is called English lavender when in England it is known simply as lavender. Perhaps it is because the plant on this side of the Atlantic evokes English cottage gardens.

Few plants are better known or more loved. The 1½- to 3-foot-high shrubby dome of grayish, narrow, evergreen foliage bears spikes of tiny, tightly packed flowers in June and July. These are scented with the aromatic oil of lavender, which takes its unrivalled place in so many soaps and sachets. The typical flower color is, of course, lavender, but selected forms are available with white, pale pink, true blue, and deep purple blooms. All are well worth growing and they associate wonderfully with pinks (*Dianthus* species) and old-fashioned roses.

English lavender is native to hot, dry hillsides of the Mediterranean, and as such is surprisingly hardy as long as its requirements of perfect drainage and full sun are met. With the help of some pine branches or other open mulch in winter, it appears safe in most years to Zone 5. In warmer areas it can be used as a low hedge.

For warm gardens, others of the twenty-five or so *Lavandula* species are possible, but they lack the charm of English lavender.

Lavatera species

Treemallow

The name treemallow is a direct translation of *Lavatera arborea,* a coarse plant of little garden use. *L. olbia,* on the other hand, is a delightful subshrub from the Mediterranean. It is suitable for warm gardens, probably no colder than Zone 8 although some may want to try it in a protected, well-drained, sunny corner in colder climates.

L. olbia makes a soft-stemmed shrub of downy gray-green, up to 8 feet tall, with maple-shaped leaves. From June to late fall, long, wandlike stems carry clear, rose-pink mallow flowers in the leaf joints. This is a wonderful, nonstop display, lovely with species roses, the perennial bellflower *Campanula lactiflora,* and lily-of-the-Nile

Leucojum vernum

Leucojum aestivum

(*Agapanthus* species). The best form of this treemallow is 'Rosea', possibly a hybrid and best increased by cuttings.

L. trimestris is another Mediterranean. As an annual, it is suitable for colder areas as long as there are at least four frost-free months. It reaches 3 feet in height and bears typical mallow flowers, the rose-red petals enclosing a center of yellow stamens. It may be started indoors and planted outside later or sown directly in the garden in areas with a warm spring.

Leucojum species

Snowflake

Of the nine or so species of *Leucojum,* all Europeans, a couple are useful additions to the range of more familiar bulbous plants. They are related both to snowdrop (*Galanthus* species) and daffodil (*Narcissus* species) and indeed the bulbs can easily be confused with those of daffodils if dug up by mistake in the garden.

In bloom, snowflake can be distinguished from other, similar nodding white flowers by the fact that it has six petals of equal length that do not open outward very far, thus creating a bell shape.

L. vernum, the spring snowflake, develops its leaves and flower stems at the same time in earliest spring. The leaves are wider and brighter green than snowdrop leaves. The flowers open, one or two to a 6-inch stem, from February to April, depending on the climate. Petals are yellow-tipped. This is a plant for leafy soil under deciduous trees and shrubs. Spring snowflake goes to rest during summer.

L. aestivum is the so-called summer snowflake, but it is usually blooming in May, and much earlier in mild climates. Spears of lush, narrow green leaves precede the 18-inch flower stems, each with a nodding cluster of white bells. The petals are green-tipped. A plant of moist meadows and woodland edges, it should be planted in a spot that mimics those conditions.

Both species should be planted in early autumn. They naturalize easily and are hardy to at least Zone 4.

Libertia formosa

Liatris spicata

Liatris species

Gayfeather, blazing-star

This is a splendid genus of about forty species, all of them native to North America. Although botanically they are daisies, neither foliage nor flower is daisylike. Narrow, grassy leaves appear from little clumps of hairy corms. Stiff stems clothed with similar leaves push up in late June. The top half of the stem is packed with buds. In direct opposition to most plants, the spike starts to open from the top. As it gradually opens downward, it resembles a fireworks sparkler. The effect is a bottle brush of mauve so brilliant it can be seen from far across the garden.

Liatris spicata, a plant of moist areas, is native from Michigan to Long Island and southward. Seldom above 2 feet tall, it needs an uncrowded spot in the front of the border. Smaller still is the cultivar known as 'Kobold' or 'Gnome'. *L. pycnostachya* has a more southern distribution. It is the monster of the genus, reaching 5 feet on occasion. It prefers a well-drained soil.

Both need full sun and, with a winter mulch, are hardy to Zone 4. Where the brilliance of the species would be too much, fine white cultivars can be used. Gayfeather is best not cut down in fall but left to mark clearly where the corms lie.

Libertia species

Libertia

To lighten the effect of broad-leaved plants, which are predominant in most gardens, the narrow leaves of a monocot, springing grasslike from its clump, are always desirable. When the plant is evergreen and also offers a good flower and subsequent seed display, as libertia does, it is invaluable.

There are about twenty species of these iris relations. All are Southern Hemisphere plants, and so unfortunately are suitable only for the warmer gardens of Zone 8 and above.

The Chilean *Libertia formosa* makes a 2-foot-high foliage clump. In summer another foot is added to this by the flower spikes, which carry sprays of flat, pure white

Ligularia przewalskii 'The Rocket'

Ligularia dentata

flowers with bright yellow stamens. Orange, marble-size seedpods follow in autumn and often remain well into winter.

A very similar species is *L. ixioides,* differing only in that it seldom exceeds 2 feet in height. This is a New Zealander (Chile and New Zealand share a number of plants) whose leaves take on a color in winter that is almost as bright as the seedpods. Propagation from seed of both species gives flowering plants in the second year.

Libertia needs well-drained soil and adequate moisture in a location that is not too hot. Half to three-quarters shade is ideal.

Ligularia species

Ligularia

These dramatic daisies for a late-summer display need plenty of moisture. Waterside or even boggy conditions are good, but a well-fed and well-watered border works also.

Ligularia dentata (sometimes listed as *L. clivorum*) is from China and Japan. It makes clumps of distinctive foliage with 2-foot-high stalks holding almost circular leaves up to 9 inches across. From these, stout stems rise 4 feet high in July and open in August to great branching heads of orange daisies. Although the species and the selection 'Orange Queen' have dark green leaves, two smaller forms, 'Othello' and 'Desdemona', have purple-flushed stems and lower leaf surfaces

It is a color that associates wonderfully with cardinal flower (*Lobelia cardinalis*).

Giving a very different silhouette is *L. przewalskii* from northern China. Its best form is 'The Rocket', a name that describes it well. Above fingered leaves, black, 6-foot stems shoot up to burst into a narrow spike of bright, little yellow daisies.

These ligularias are easy to grow to Zone 4. Full sun, with a little shade in the heat of the day, is ideal. The foliage is irresistible to slugs.

Lilium martagon

Lilium auratum

Lilium species

Lily

The word *lily* suggests beauty, purity, and perfection. These qualities are fully exemplified by the eighty or so species of *Lilium* spread around the Northern Hemisphere and the many hundreds of hybrids derived from them.

Must true lilies grow from bulbs whose scales are not enclosed in any outside sheath, making them look like small globe artichokes. With fleshy roots still attached and lacking sheaths, they dry out very easily and do not have the shelf life of other bulbs like daffodils and tulips. Lilies should be bought as soon as they appear (or better yet, ordered from a specialist supplier who will ensure they arrive in good condition) and then planted at once. For most species this is in early fall. In cold areas or when delivery has been delayed, bulbs should be stored in barely moist peat and sand or potted, kept cool,

and planted in spring. Species that develop feeding roots on their growing stems need deep planting (up to 6 inches deep for the big *L. auratum*).

Any soil—acid or lime, heavy clay or light sand—can support fine lilies, as long as drainage is good. Although most lilies accept some shade (a little in the heat of the day helps the flowers last a bit longer), they are really sun-lovers. In the wild they grow in open, often rocky terrain.

Most commonly available lilies are hardy to Zone 4 or even 3 under winter snow and a leafy mulch. Many become good perennials, building up ever-bigger clumps. When seen to decline, they should be lifted in early September and the largest bulbs replanted a foot apart in another well-prepared site. Regular insecticide spray will deter aphids, which spread the virus diseases to which lilies are prone.

Associates of lilies should be carefully considered. Three of the innumerable possibilities include planting them with peonies (*Paeonia* species), among wide-spaced plantain-lily (*Hosta* species) and in front of rhododendrons (*Rhododendron* species). (The early-flowering orange lilies clash with peonies, however.) If varieties are carefully chosen, bloom can continue from early June through October.

Flower shape varies from the classical outward-facing trumpets of the madonna lily (*L. candidum*) to the flatter, upward-facing flowers of the orange lily (*L. bulbiferum*) to the reflex-petaled turk's-cap types (*L. martagon* and others). The now highly diverse hybrid strains both repeat and combine these shapes in every color but blue. Almost all are highly scented.

L. auratum is the golden-rayed lily of Japan and one of the most exotic looking of all bulbs grown. On

Lilium regale

Lilium 'Achilles'

stems up to 8 feet high and clothed from top to bottom with narrow leaves, a cluster of great flowers begins to open in August. Each can be 10 inches across, of flat turk's-cap form and outward-facing. Each glistening white petal has a central gold band and the whole flower is spotted with scarlet. As if this were not enough, the flowers are deliciously perfumed. A site out of the wind is essential or staking will become a problem.

L. speciosum is known as the showy lily. Another late-flowering Japanese species, it is a smaller (but still to 5 or 6 feet high) and more elegant species that is easier to use in the garden. Turk's-cap flowers can be pure white, white and pink, or carmine and variously spotted, all held in a leafy spike. These Asian lilies prefer an acid, organic soil with plenty of summer moisture. If this is difficult to provide, the showy lily makes a fine container plant if given plenty of fertilizer.

Also from Japan is *L. longiflorum.* It is only a couple of feet in height, with a leafy stem that produces up to a half-dozen narrow, green-flushed, white trumpet flowers. This is known as the Easter lily or the Bermuda lily (where it almost became naturalized).

The gardens at Kingwood Center in Ohio have great beds of this lovely lily built up from planting the Easter greenhouse display over the years. There, it flowers in July in dappled shade. It is not a plant for the coldest areas, however.

Much easier for general garden use is the regal lily from western China. *L. regale* will flower in two years from seed but it takes many more years (and rich living) to build up to 6-foot stems, each bearing a dozen flowers. Opening in late June, the trumpet-shaped flowers are white with a yellow throat

and purple outside. It grows easily in any well-drained soil to Zone 4 and perhaps beyond.

L. martagon is typical of a great range of turk's-caps. Straight stems up to 5 feet tall carry a pyramidal spike of as many as 25 wide-spaced flowers in dusky purple or white. Unfortunately, its scent is disagreeable. This lily from Europe and Asia takes woodland conditions as well as full sun.

A cultivational exception to all of the above lilies is *L. candidum,* the exquisite madonna lily. From limestone uplands of northern Greece, it is very hardy; certainly to Zone 4 and even to Zone 3 with some care. It matures in late summer, overwintering as a ground-level tussock of leaves from which the strong 4- or 5-foot stems of pure white trumpets shoot up the following June. It goes to rest almost immediately and this is the time to plant it, placing the bulbs only just below ground.

Limonium latifolium

Limonium sinuatum

Linum narbonense

Limonium species

Sea-lavender, marsh-rosemary, statice

There are around one hundred and fifty of these rather strange plants strewn across all five continents. Most are adapted to arid areas or salt marshes, where much of the water is unusable by plants. All species require full sun.

The thick, leathery, dark green leaf rosette of *Limonium latifolium,* an eastern European, is typical of the group adapted to salt marshes. It arises from an extremely woody rootstock above which grows a 2-foot dome of wiry stems, divided and divided again and ending in a cloud of tiny lavender-blue flowers, each held in a pale, papery base. The effect lasts for many weeks beginning in late July. Even when it ends, the flowers maintain their shape into winter. This is a plant for the front of the border. It is hardy to Zone 5.

Although this and many other perennial species of *Limonium* are used in winter bouquets, the best species for this job is *L. sinuatum,* also known as statice. It is usually grown as an annual. Native to Mediterranean seashores, it has wavy leaves and in summer 2-foot winged stems that carry flat-topped heads of small flowers. These papery, horn-shaped blooms come in a wide range of dusty colors: off-white, straw yellow, mist blue, and rose. Like any other half-hardy annual, it should be planted in well-drained soil when frosts are over.

Linum species

Flax

There are probably few field crops as beautiful as flax. This source of linen and linseed oil turns the landscape as blue as the sky for a brief week or two each year. For garden decoration the annual flaxes are too fleeting to be of much use (although *Linum grandiflorum* is a good red one). You have to turn to *L. perenne* to get the same silky, funnel-shaped flowers on a reliably perennial plant. This species is widely distributed throughout Europe. The American prairie flax is a subspecies that is worth growing in the West, if seeds can be obtained.

The best of all is a Mediterranean, *L. narbonense,* a more compact plant with bigger flowers. It makes a twiggy clump of stems to 18 inches high with small, narrow leaves and a summer-long display of azure blue flowers paling to

Linum perenne

Liriope spicata

white in the throat. It needs a warm, well-drained soil in full sun probably not much beyond Zone 6. A protected spot and good mulch may take it farther. Certainly it is a plant worth cherishing. It looks especially good with gray-foliaged plants like *Artemisia schmidtiana.*

Liriope species

Lilyturf

The name *lilyturf* is entirely apt: All of the five or so species of *Liriope* (pronounced le-RYE-oh-pee) are indeed lily relatives and the smallest, *L. spicata,* makes a tight, lawnlike ground cover that needs no mowing. It cannot take the constant trampling of true turf, but it makes a fine weed inhibitor around shrubs in either sun or shade.

The species known as big lilyturf, *L. muscari,* is a much more valuable plant since it combines ground-cover effectiveness with a fine fall-flowering display. Individual plants rise from a tuberous rootstock, rather like daylily, and make clumps of arching, grassy leaves about a foot high. Stiff 18-inch spikes push up in late August. The top 6 inches of each spike are closely packed with beadlike flowers that are deep violet. Bluer and

white varieties are available, as are variegated types. They associate beautifully with nerine (*Nerine* species) and belladonna-lily (*Amaryllis belladonna*).

All lilyturf species are Asian. As evergreens, they succeed best in warmer climates, overwintering poorly, with seared leaves, in Zone 6. Adequate summer moisture gives the best growth.

Lobelia × gerardii

Lobelia cardinalis 'Cherry Pie'

Lobelia species

Lobelia, cardinal-flower

Combined with scarlet sage (*Salvia splendens*) and sweet-alyssum (*Lobularia maritima*), the little edging lobelia (*Lobelia erinus*) contributes the blue in patriotic red, white, and blue annual bedding schemes. A 6-inch plant, the lobelia provides sheets of true-blue, pale or dark depending on the cultivar. A South African native, it is generally sown in spring and planted outside after frosts are over. In California the show continues to Christmas and a few plants may overwinter. If clipped back, the plant regrows for another season.

Lobelia has other, more unusual faces among its approximately three hundred and seventy-five species. There are huge herbaceous

plants from the mountains of tropical Africa. South America also offers species for warm-weather gardens. *L. laxiflora* from Mexico is a long-flowering subshrub and the Chilean *L. tupa* is a magnificent, 5-foot-high herbaceous plant that is well worth searching out.

L. cardinalis, cardinal-flower, is another surprise, especially when found flowering in the wet woodlands of Quebec or Vermont. (Although native along the entire eastern side of the continent, it seems exotically out of place in the north.) Three-foot-high spikes of glowing scarlet make cardinal-flower one of the most spectacular plants, but it is not always easy to grow in the garden. It needs summer moisture, acid soil, and half shade. The plant, which is pollinated by hummingbirds, looks wonderful towering above smaller garden plants.

Cardinal-flower has been crossed with the Mexican *L. splendens* and other species. The old 'Queen Victoria', with scarlet flowers above purple foliage, is one such hybrid, but none is a reliable perennial in the North. Safer is *L. × gerardii* ('Queen Victoria' is one parent and the blue *L. siphilitica* is the other), which is effective in Zone 6. It grows up to 2 feet high with spikes of rich purple flowers in late summer. It looks superb with *Ligularia dentata* 'Othello' and enjoys similar conditions—plenty of moisture and full sun with a little shade during the heat of the day.

L. siphilitica, which is native to Ontario southward, is also well worth growing. It tolerates the moist lime soil in which cardinal-flower does so poorly. Two-foot-high spikes of blue flowers bloom in July and August. The plant is hardy to Zone 4.

Lunaria annua 'Variegata'

Lobularia maritima

Lobularia maritima

Sweet-alyssum

This is a plant often used in carpet bedding schemes in which a sheet of white is required, or in which bands of white are arranged to interweave with other colors. It is a seaside plant of the Mediterranean growing on sand and in rock crevices. A wispy plant with loose, spreading, foot-long stems, sweet-alyssum bears a profusion of fragrant, four-petaled flowers that bloom in early summer.

Its potential for selection must have been seen early, because the tight, mounding plant that we grow now was a part of European gardens in the last century.

Although it is a short-lived perennial in the wild and may carry over in the mild West and South, it is usually grown as an annual. Only as an annual can it maintain the compact formality required by well-planned bedding schemes.

Sweet-alyssum is now available in a range of soft pink and purple shades, still charmingly scented, under names such as 'Royal Carpet' and 'Midnight'. Selected for dwarf habit and abundant flowers, these forms of sweet-alyssum are ideal for carpet bedding, for filling unexpected gaps at the front of the border, and for adding summer interest to the nonspecialist rock garden.

As its native habitat suggests, sweet-alyssum is a plant for full sun, perfect drainage, and lime soil. It seeds itself and reappears the following year in paving cracks. In the hot, humid summers of the Southeast it may not survive the season.

Lunaria annua

Honesty, silver-dollar, moonwort

The genus name translates as "moonwort," although "silver-dollar" is more descriptive, and the old common name, honesty, is still used most often. Regardless of its name, this is an invaluable, old-fashioned European biennial (not annual, as the specific name implies) that is decorative for several seasons of the year.

It is best to sow honesty seeds indoors in spring and plant the seedlings outside in a semishaded spot in May. Any soil seems acceptable. By the onset of winter each plant makes a clump of rather coarse, heart-shaped leaves that survives to Zone 5 and beyond under snow. The following May a strong, leafy stem shoots up and by the end of the month resembles a 2-foot-high purple stock (*Matthiola incana*)

Lunaria annua

Lupinus Russell hybrids

that it is perfect with late orange tulips (*Tulipa* species). As the four-petaled flowers drop, flat, almost circular seedpods that give the plant the name silver-dollar develop. They change from purplish to green and finally silvery white by late July.

When the pods are mature, the whole plant can be cut for dried arrangements indoors. Left in the garden, it looks good until shattered by wind during the winter. Subsequent self-sown seedlings make honesty a near-permanent plant. The volunteers can be transplanted in fall wherever they will fit in the garden scheme. White-flowered and variegated-leaf forms are worth searching out.

Lupinus species

Lupine

There are around two hundred species of these often highly ornamental legumes. *Lupinelike,* an adjective given to many plants, immediately evokes images of true lupines: spikes of brightly colored pea flowers above fingered leaves.

Lupinus arboreus, tree lupine, is from California. Suited to the West Coast, it grows north to British Columbia. A quick-growing, rather short-lived shrub about 6 feet high, in spring it is covered with stubby spikes of sulfur yellow, white, or lavender flowers. Reduce seed formation and keep the plant tidy by clipping it back after it flowers. Full sun and perfect drainage are essential.

Although the blue *L. polyphyllus* is also a Californian, it is herbaceous and can overwinter in colder zones.

The 5-foot-high species and the dwarf forms are worth growing whenever seed can be obtained. Much more available, and one of the joys of June, are the Russell hybrids, derived in part from *L. polyphyllus.* Seedlings planted in late spring produce just a few spikes in the first year, but bloom increases in the next and subsequent years. There are cultivars in almost every color spectrum and in heights ranging from 2 to 4 feet.

These lupines require good drainage and full sun up to half shade. They are hardy to Zone 4 if given a winter mulch.

Lychnis coronaria

Lychnis chalcedonica

Lychnis species

Campion, catchfly

There are about three dozen species of *Lychnis,* all herbaceous plants of mainly northern, even arctic, distribution. *L. chalcedonica* is perhaps the tallest. The stems reach 4 feet and are topped with flat heads of brilliant vermilion flowers in July. The common names Maltese-cross or Jerusalem-cross describe the flower shape. This species is from the eastern part of the Soviet Union. It is hardy to Zone 3, possibly 2, but it does not tolerate the humid southeastern United States very well. It needs good soil in full sun. The plant looks wonderful with the purple leaves of canna (*Canna* × *generalis*), but it is not a color that is generally easy to use.

Nor is the color of *L. coronaria* simple to combine with other flowers. Its furry gray leaves (hence the common name dusty-miller) have a softening effect on the bright purplish red flowers, though. This is a plant for dry soil in full sun, and it is not suited to the crowded conditions of herbaceous borders.

From Africa, Asia, and Europe, it survives to Zone 5 as long as it has perfect drainage. The white-flowered form is easier to use and needs the same conditions.

Less choosy is the European *L. viscaria,* the German catchfly. It makes clumps of narrow leaves that produce a summer-long display of vivid pink-purple flowers on 2-foot-high stems. Paler pink and white varieties are sometimes offered. All are easy plants for a front-of-the-border location in any ordinary garden soil to Zone 4. Plants often reseed under good conditions.

Lycoris squamigera

Lysimachia punctata

Lycoris squamigera

Magic-lily, resurrection-lily

Following the same pattern typical of species of *Amaryllis* and *Hippeastrum,* magic-lily forms a clump of strap-shaped leaves that goes to rest in late summer. Then suddenly a great head of flowers appears out of the ground. This is not uncommon in southern gardens, where many South African bulbs behave like this—but it is a great surprise to see it happen farther north, especially if you don't know the plant is in the garden. Magic-lily is one of very few hardy plants to behave in this manner. It is safe to Zone 5 as long as a good mulch, helped by snow, is provided.

Plant the big daffodil-like bulbs during the short time they are dormant in summer, or pot them in winter and plant them outside in late spring. Blue-green leaves develop quickly, followed in September by smooth 2- to 3-foot-high

stems, each with its head of deliciously scented, rose-pink, lilylike trumpets.

Magic-lily is not cheap to buy and is often slow to increase. Give it good soil and full sun in a special place, such as a courtyard bed, where it can be enjoyed up close. It associates well with autumn-crocus (*Colchicum* species), which flowers at the same time, and with winter-begonia (*Bergenia* species), which gives a strong foliage base that the magic-lily lacks when blooming.

Lysimachia species

Loosestrife

Of the more than one hundred and fifty *Lysimachia* species strewn around the subtropical and temperate regions of the world, a half-dozen are useful garden perennials.

L. ciliata is a North American native. In Ontario, Canada, it is a plant of moist meadows and woodland edges, at its best in heavy clay soil. Stems of soft, downy leaves can reach 4 feet, but 3 feet is more usual. In July the upper leaves have a solitary, nodding, pale yellow bell in each leaf joint. A purple-leaved form is worth seeking out.

The plant has become naturalized in parts of Europe, and in exchange the European *L. punctata* has gone wild in North America. This is a much more aggressive plant both in habit and in its rather brassy yellow color. Known as garden loosestrife, it likes

Lysimachia clethroides

Lythrum virgatum 'Morden Gleam'

conditions similar to those enjoyed by *L. ciliata*. It will take three-quarters shade—even under black walnuts—if the soil stays moist. Both species are hardy to at least Zone 4.

The gooseneck loosestrife, *L. clethroides,* from Japan is a more desirable plant, if less hardy. Its 3-foot-high stems end in elegantly arching tips crowded with little white flowers. It is an invaluable plant for a late show in the border, a fine contrast in shape and texture to Korean hybrid chrysanthemums (*Chrysanthemum* hybrids).

Lythrum species

Purple loosestrife

Although this group of plants shares a common name with the previous genus, the two are not close botanically. *Lysimachia* is related to primroses and *Lythrum* is in the loosestrife family.

Of the thirty-odd *Lythrum* species, two are widely grown. In the case of *L. salicaria* this is often involuntary. Brought over from the Old World, in North America it has become a common plant of roadsides and railroad tracks. Wherever the soil stays wet it makes great swaths of brilliant magenta from early August into September, growing up to 6 feet high. Later, as the flower spikes turn into brown seeds, the foliage offers bright autumn colors. Although attractive, it has invaded marshlands and many states have banned it. The Research Station

Arboretum at Morden, Manitoba, has developed some sterile selections, Morden cultivars, that are allowed. These cultivars include a fine range of plants with gentler colors, including pink, rose, and purple. In the garden these are not necessarily as aggressive, but a moisture-retentive soil or heavy irrigation will lead to the same type of rampant growth.

The smaller *L. virgatum* from Asia Minor is closely related. Its leaves and flower spikes are more slender, making it a preferable species for most gardens. Good growing conditions are essential, but it does not need as much moisture.

All species of *Lythrum* are hardy to Zone 3 and look lovely with species of *Miscanthus* grass.

Malva moschata 'Alba'

Macleaya cordata

Macleaya cordata

Plumepoppy

At first sight, no plant could be less poppylike, but in fact this is a poppy relation from Japan and China. Because it is pollinated by wind, it does not need the flaunting, insect-attracting petals common to poppies (*Papaver* species).

Regardless of its family tree, plumepoppy has a presence like no other plant and is one of the most valuable perennials in the garden. From fleshy roots (bright orange if accidentally chopped into with a spade) great hollow stems arise. They are slow to start in spring but soon gather speed, often reaching 8 feet high by midsummer. Once established they spread quickly by rhizomes. They also self-sow.

The leaves are beautiful—up to a foot across, rounded and lobed, grayish green above and milk white beneath. This is especially notice-able as they move in the wind. The stems are topped in late July

by foot-high spires of tiny, buff-pink flowers, the color made up entirely by the stamens.

Plumepoppy combines well with shrubs or with other herbaceous plants. Although its height indi-cates a back-of-the-border loca-tion, it deserves prominence so that the entire mass of foliage, from the ground up, can be seen.

Provide a fertile, well-drained soil in a sunny spot that is protected from late-spring and early-fall frosts. Zone 5 under mulch, and probably beyond, is acceptable.

Malva species

Muskmallow

Of the thirty or so species of *Malva* scattered mainly around the Mediterranean, only two are recommended for cultivation.

M. moschata is a useful and easy plant with a natural distribution in southern Europe and North Africa. Cultivation has taken it north and west, so that from Britain to the northeastern United States it has gone wild. This is not to suggest that the plant is aggressive, merely that it grows easily in well-drained soil in sun or half shade.

On leafy stems up to 3 feet tall, clusters of flowers bloom in the up-per leaf joints from July until Sep-tember, and sometimes even later. The flowers are typically hibiscus-like: a bowl of satiny petals with a center of stamens. The typical color

Matthiola incana

Matthiola incana 'Annua'

is a clear pink, but the white variety with paler green foliage is even more desirable—and it grows true from seed. The pallor of the blooms is enhanced by the pink-tipped stamens.

M. alcea is similar to *M. moschata* and requires the same kind of conditions. Its early nineteenth century form 'Fastigiata' has upright stems, sometimes 4 feet high, covered with the pink bowl-shaped flowers typical of the genus. It makes a good heritage-garden plant.

Both muskmallows are short-lived, so self-sown seedlings should be carefully moved during spring, when still small, into permanent spots in the garden. A deep taproot makes moving old plants a hazardous operation—they invariably die. Under snow or a winter mulch, muskmallow grows to Zone 4.

Matthiola incana

Stock

This plant, one of several bearing the old name gillyflower, has been held in great esteem for centuries. It is native to Mediterranean seashores, growing old and woody in rock crevices bathed in full sun. It has become naturalized in similar spots in California, where it is almost a subshrub in the garden, with a hummock of narrow gray leaves and spikes of four-petaled flowers throughout the winter and into spring.

In any other climate, however, annual strains should be grown. Although usually described as ten-week stock, the plant does not necessarily fit this name. Sow seeds indoors as you do for other annuals and plant outside when the soil begins to warm up. Since stock is not tropical like impatiens or begonia, a little late frost is not a problem if the plant has been hardened off first.

Fine spikes of wonderfully scented flowers, single and double in all soft shades except blue, are produced in July. The plant cannot take high humidity in summer.

Brompton stock is an invaluable biennial strain. Sown in May, it overwinters and flowers the following spring. Unfortunately, this stock is for mild Zones 8, 9, and 10 only.

Meconopsis betonicifolia

Meconopsis cambrica

Mertensia virginica

Meconopsis species

Blue-poppy, Himalayan-poppy, Welsh-poppy

Among the forty-five or so species of these mainly Asian poppy relatives are some of the most beautiful and tantalizing plants that can be grown in the temperate world.

Conditions must be just right. A woodland glade at the Botanical Garden, University of British Columbia, Vancouver, produces perfect perennial stands of blue-poppy, *Meconopsis betonicifolia.* The acid, humus-rich soil along with cool, moist summers, mild winters, and a seaside location protected from wind provide ideal conditions. In June the 6-foot-high stems hold the most exquisite flowers imaginable—5-inch-wide bowls of rich sky blue with a center of golden stamens.

In less favored areas, although gardeners continue to fight every inch of the way, the plant is apt to be biennial, with smaller blooms and the blue color diminishing to mauve. It survives to Zone 5 as long as the rest of its needs are met.

The little Welsh-poppy, *M. cambrica,* is much easier to grow (it self-sows readily), although it requires similar conditions. Above clumps of smooth, blue-green leaves, thin stems produce fleeting flowers, orange or yellow, throughout summer. It seeds itself in cool corners without ever becoming a pest. A rather ragged double cultivar, 'Flore Pleno', is also available.

Mertensia virginica

Virginia bluebell, Virginia cowslip

There are at least four dozen species of these borage relatives spread around the Northern Hemisphere, with representatives even in the Arctic. But this lovely East Coast woodlander, wild from New York to Alabama, is the only species commonly seen in gardens. It fully deserves its place, combining with wakerobin (*Trillium* species) and the later spring bulbs to produce one of the loveliest displays of the gardening year.

Borage usually has hard, bristly leaves that are unpleasant to touch, but those of Virginia bluebell are soft and as smooth as silk. Spring growth is rapid. By mid-May the arching stems are 2 feet high, each hung with a curving spray of blue, bell-shaped flowers. In little more than a month everything turns yellow and the plant goes to rest

Mimulus cardinalis

Mimulus × hybridus 'Quick Step'

again, its season complete. Pink and white varieties are equally beautiful.

Hardy to at least Zone 4, Virginia bluebell needs the conditions for which it is perfectly adapted: a leafy soil in full sun or half shade with plenty of moisture during the brief growing season. The location should be marked so it is not accidentally hoed in summer.

Mimulus species

Monkeyflower, monkeymusk

The drifts of bright yellow seen along Scottish streams and Devonshire ditches turn out, on examination, to be *Mimulus guttatus,* the common monkeyflower native from Alaska southward to Mexico. This North American genus is still a useful, if overly exuberant, plant in the West. It needs wet soil in full sun. *M. moschatus,* which has a similar distribution, puts on a show of pale yellow, brown-spotted flowers throughout summer.

The scarlet monkeyflower, *M. cardinalis,* is more garden-worthy and, at up to 4 feet, twice as tall. Its stems are clothed with sticky leaves and scarlet or orange-red flowers blooming in the leaf joints from late June on. The blossoms are typical of all monkeyflowers in their shape—two-lipped like snapdragon (*Antirrhinum majus*).

Native from southern Oregon to Arizona, the plant needs moist soil that does not freeze too deep; this makes it suitable for Zone 7 and warmer areas only.

In recent years these and others among the one hundred and fifty or so *Mimulus* species have been used to produce hybrid strains that are useful additions to the small number of shade-tolerant summer annuals available. Usually called *Mimulus × hybridus,* these are dwarf, spreading plants with bright, open-faced flowers spotted with contrasting colors. Moist soil is essential.

Moluccella laevis

Mirabilis jalapa

Mirabilis jalapa

Marvel-of-Peru, four-o'clock

As the name four-o'clock suggests, this is an ideal plant to place by a deck or patio where you spend time in the evening. During the day it is a 2- to 3-foot dome of pleasant but unexciting foliage with heads of promising buds. In late afternoon dozens of these buds open into long-tubed flowers similar to, and almost as fragrant as, tobacco-flower (*Nicotiana* species). The color range is unusual: pink, yellow, or white and often striped and marked with one of the other colors. The flowers remain open all night and are withered by the next day's hot sun. The display lasts from July to frost and the blooms stay open until noon as fall approaches.

Mirabilis jalapa, which has a wide distribution in tropical South America, was first collected in Peru in the sixteenth century—hence the plant's common name. None of its sixty or so relatives are in cultivation beyond the confines of botanic gardens.

Marvel-of-Peru is a good perennial in the warmest gardens. It forms enormous round black tubers that can be lifted and stored like dahlias (*Dahlia* cultivars) in cold areas. Gardeners without the benefit of a cellar can plant newly raised seedlings in full sun after frosts have passed. They rapidly increase in size.

Moluccella laevis

Bells-of-Ireland, shellflower

This is an extraordinary annual from Asia Minor and the only species of this small genus worth growing. It is particularly valuable in dried winter arrangements indoors.

In the far North or Northeast, where summers are very short, sow seeds indoors in spring and plant outside when frosts are over. Elsewhere you can grow a stand of bells-of-Ireland from seeds sown directly in the ground. It grows quickly in good soil in a sunny spot (a row in the vegetable garden works well). However, it is essential that seedlings be carefully thinned, initially to 3 inches and then to 6 inches apart, to attain tall spikes. Soon the plant looks like a lush, smooth-leaved nettle.

You have to search for the flowers, and the effort is hardly worthwhile. They are hidden in the foliage,

Monarda didyma 'Donnerwokbe'

right against the stem. Each small, pale purplish or white flower sits in a lime green shell-like base. Although none of this makes a great show in the garden, the flowering stems are excellent when cut and dried. Bells-of-Ireland is therefore is a good plant for the cutting garden. Depending on when the stems are cut, the shell-like base of each flower remains palest green or turns a warm straw color. Cut too soon, the flowers wither miserably.

Monarda species

Monarda, beebalm, oswego-tea

This is one of the plants collected in Virginia by John Tradescant (of *Tradescantia* fame) for the gardens of King Charles I in the early seventeenth century. William Curtis depicted it in one of the earliest plates of his *Botanical Magazine.* It has kept its garden popularity for some three hundred and fifty years, and for good reason.

One of a dozen *Monarda* species, all native to North America, *M. didyma,* beebalm, has the most to commend it. Growing to 4 feet tall, the plant is a typical member of the mint family, with square stems and leaves in pairs, each at right angles to the one below. They are wonderfully aromatic and have been used in herbal teas.

In July and into August, whorls of hooded red flowers erupt at the tops of the stems. Varieties such as 'Cambridge Scarlet', 'Croftway

Pink', and 'Snow Queen' extend the color range. Beebalm must have a rich, moist soil in at least three-quarters sun.

A closely related species is *M. fistulosa.* Also about 4 feet tall, this plant has smaller flowers in a range of softer colors. It is easier to combine with the brilliance of purple phlox (*Phlox* species) or purple loosestrife (*Lythrum* species). It also tolerates drier soils than its cousin.

Muscari armeniacum

Morina longifolia

Morina species

Whorlflower

There are two useful representatives of this small, mainly Himalayan genus—and both deserve greater use. Hardy certainly to Zone 5 and probably beyond with the help of snow and a mulch, these are plants for the front of the border. Once established, they are long-lived.

Morina longiflora gives the impression, early in the season, of a thistle missed by last autumn's hoe. But the leaves are pleasantly aromatic and soon a clump of foliage builds up with strong, 2- to 3-foot-high stems. At this stage it could be mistaken for bear's-breech (*Acanthus* species), although in Zone 5 these are not common.

Beginning in midsummer the flowers start to open in successive whorls up the stem. Long-tubed and hooded, they start out white, age to pink, and after pollination turn deep rose. The display can be extended by cutting the flower stems and using them as a dried winter decoration. Be careful of the spines protecting the flower whorls.

Another species, *M. persica,* is sometimes offered. It is pricklier and has a narrower flower spike, but is also a very worthwhile plant. Good, well-drained soil and full sun are essential for both species.

Muscari armeniacum

Grape hyacinth

The name grape hyacinth refers to the flower spikes of this small relative of the true hyacinth (*Hyacinthus orientalis*). Just before the flowers open, the spikes consist of tight little blue or violet buds resembling miniature, upright bunches of grapes.

There are over three dozen species of *Muscari* native to the Mediterranean into Asia Minor. They are an important part of the wonderful spring flush of flowers that is so typical of the area. They are equally valuable in North American gardens in most climatic zones.

Unlike most spring-flowering bulbs, which remain below ground until winter is past, clumps of grape hyacinth begin to push up foliage in September. In mild areas this continues throughout winter, and by April the plant has formed an untidy, grassy tussock with foot-long,

Myosotis sylvatica

Myosotis sylvatica 'Alba'

narrow, strap-shaped leaves. From this arise several bare flower stems, 9 inches tall, each with deep violet bells at the top.

In cold climates, Zone 5 and below, the overwintering foliage becomes battered. In these areas grape hyacinth should be grown among other plants or in thin grass to hide the mess. Fortunately, flowering is not affected by the condition of the foliage.

Plant grape hyacinth bulbs in early fall in any soil but the wettest in full sun or part shade. The bulbs should be placed 2 inches deep, in groups of six or more.

Myosotis sylvatica

Forget-me-not

There are annual, biennial, and fully perennial species of *Myosotis* strewn around the cooler parts of every continent. Some species are no more than an inch tall, others reach a couple of feet in height, but most are only of botanical interest.

M. sylvatica is a common European plant brought into cultivation centuries ago and bred for its tight domes of brilliant blue blossoms. It is a common feature of spring bedding schemes in mild areas, grown under tulips (*Tulipa* species) or hyacinths (*Hyacinthus orientalis*).

For this use, the best method is to sow seeds in May with other spring-flowering biennials such as Brompton stock (*Matthiola* hybrids) and wallflower (*Cheiranthus cheiri*). Grow seedlings and plant them out in October. The first flowers open sometime between February and March, depending on

climate, and last many weeks. The highly selected types most often used need overwintering in frames in colder areas.

However, certainly to Zone 5 and beyond under a reliable snow cover, seeds scattered among and under shrubs in late spring produce plants that overwinter and flower in April and May. These reseed themselves and overlapping generations develop, ensuring that no spring is without forget-me-nots. Pink and white varieties cannot compare with the blue.

Narcissus 'February Gold'

Myrrhis odorata

Myrrhis odorata

Sweet-cecily

This is a splendid relative of Queen-Anne's-lace (*Daucus carota*). Although traditionally an inhabitant of the herb garden, it fully deserves a place in shady borders and among shrubs—both for its foliage and its flowers. (Any catalog of hardy herbs that offers myrrh is referring to sweet-cecily. It has no connection at all with biblical myrrh.)

Sweet-cecily is European and can be found in Scottish hedgerows growing with meadow cranesbill (*Geranium* species) and the perennial bellflower *Campanula latifolia,* an association well worth repeating in any garden. The first warm days of spring encourage a flush of fernlike leaves, and by June 3-foot-high leafy stems spring up. Each stem is topped with the flat head of tiny flowers typical of the family. Both flowers and leaves are strongly anise-scented.

The display is short and leaves you with two choices: Either let the big black ornamental seeds develop, or cut the whole thing to the ground and with a bit of watering encourage another batch of fresh green leaves to develop.

Sweet-cecily is very hardy, probably to Zone 2 or 3, and it does well in almost any soil in sun or shade. Although it is pleasant to discover self-sown seedlings, it is wise to move them to a desired location when they are small: The rootstock of established plants is enormous and impossible to move.

Narcissus species

Daffodil, narcissus, jonquil

Spring is almost inconceivable without daffodils and narcissus. (The names are interchangeable—those with long trumpets are more apt to be called daffodils and the small-cupped types with numerous flower heads are usually called narcissus.) The two dozen or so wild species, concentrated in southwestern Europe, are beautiful, bulbous plants belonging to the same family as *Amaryllis* species.

Particularly fine forms have been collected since early times and over the last two centuries immense numbers of cultivars have been bred and selected for every possible use. There are tall and short types with both single and double blossoms in every shade of yellow, from palest cream to bright orange. Now there is even a range of soft pinks.

In mild areas such as California that correspond climatically with their native habitat, daffodils can

Narcissus 'Actea'

Nemesia strumosa

be in flower from December ('Paper White' and 'Grand Soleil d'Or') to May (*Narcissus poeticus*), and all are good perennials. Elsewhere, daffodil time arrives whenever spring arrives.

Daffodils need a long growing season and they should be treated as permanent plants, not as annuals to be lifted after flowering. Plant bulbs at least 6 inches deep no later than October (even the small, rock garden species should go 4 inches down). Plant in a location that gets full sun until late May (for example, under deciduous trees) and in any soil but the wettest. Daffodils are ideal for naturalizing. It is impossible to have too many, but give some thought to color associations with other spring-flowering plants.

After flowering, the foliage must be allowed to yellow naturally before being cut off. This is to build up next year's flower buds within the resting bulbs.

Nemesia species

Nemesia

Orange is a color that is not easy to use well. It is apt to shout in the garden, as anyone who has grown marigolds (*Tagetes* species) knows. Although this same color is dominant in the hybrids of *Nemesia strumosa,* there is an unusual softness about it, especially when it is toned down by the shades of cream often present.

There are about fifty species of *Nemesia,* relatives of foxglove (*Digitalis* species) mainly from South Africa. The wild *N. strumosa,* which reaches 18 inches in height, has spikes of wide-mouthed flowers opening over a long period. Modern selections have tended to emphasize a compact form or dwarfness. Although admirable for carpet bedding, larger plants with an open habit are much more desirable for general use.

Nemesia is available in seed packets of mixed colors, as well as in solid shades: yellow, orange, scarlet, or flame gold. 'Blue Gem', a cultivar of the species *N. versicolor,* has blue forget-me-not flowers with a white center.

Nemesia should be sown indoors with other summer annuals and planted outside in full sun when all danger of frost has passed. If cut back after the first flush of flowers and given water and fertilizer, it will regrow and continue to flower into the fall.

Nepeta × faassenii

Nerine bowdenii

Nepeta × faassenii

Catmint

Nepeta is a huge genus of some two hundred and fifty species. Often aromatic and distributed mainly in dry areas of the Old World, they are related to lavender (*Lavandula* species), mint (*Mentha* species), and sage (*Salvia* species). Several of the species are used as herbs.

Catmint is an extremely valuable garden plant wherever it will grow. This is easily to Zone 4, and beyond under certain snow. It needs full sun and perfect drainage to ensure that it remains perennial. Growing to 2 feet high and wide, the plants are covered with small, gray, scented leaves and innumerable sprays of little lavender-colored flowers.

The display begins in June and lasts for six weeks, making a perfect accompaniment to pinks (*Dianthus* species) or old-fashioned roses. Catmint also combines well with peonies (*Paeonia* species). As the first flush of blooms begins to fade, clip the plant, reducing it by half. With a bit of irrigation and some fertilizer, it will repeat its show with flowers that continue to open well into fall.

In areas where lavender is not hardy enough, catmint makes a fine alternative as a low summer hedge or border edging. Plant snowdrop (*Galanthus* species) and crocus (*Crocus* species) with catmint. These bloom early and then the growing catmint hides their declining foliage.

Nerine species

Nerine

The twenty or so species of *Nerine* (pronounced nee-RYE-nee) are lovely autumn-flowering bulbs from South Africa. Related to *Amaryllis* and *Narcissus* species, they are suitable only for the warmest climates because they grow throughout winter.

As with belladonna-lily (*Amaryllis belladonna*), nerine bulbs are planted in August when they're dormant. Placed just below the soil surface, slender flower stems emerge from the bare ground almost at once. When the stem reaches about 18 inches high, the bract splits, and up to a dozen delicate, lilylike flowers open. In *Nerine bowdenii* these are a clear, true pink and last for a surprising length of time, often well into October.

This is the easiest and hardiest species, surviving to Zone 8 in the shelter of a sunny wall. The green

Nicotiana alata

Nicotiana alata 'Domino Crimson'

leaves need protection in unusually cold snaps and the plant must have perfect drainage. Nerine goes to rest by May, so other plants are needed to fill the spot after it is out of sight. Dusty-miller (*Senecio cineraria*) or lamb's-ears (*Stachys byzantina*) provide a fine silver foil. Creeping rosemary (*Rosmarinus officinalis*) also combines well with nerine.

The wavy petals of *N. bowdenii* and its excellent cultivar 'Fenwick's Variety' are accentuated in other species such as *N. flexuosa* and *N. undulata*. These and the rest of the twenty or more species are extremely desirable plants for the warmest gardens.

Nicotiana species

Flowering-tobacco

This plant deserves a spot in the garden where wafts of its languorous scent can be appreciated. Plant it near patio furniture or a window or sliding glass door that can be opened in the evening.

The seventy-odd species of *Nicotiana* are native to South America, the South Pacific, and Australia. Commercial tobacco and the valuable insecticide nicotine are found in this genus.

Ornamental flowering-tobacco, also called jasmine-tobacco, originates with the South American *N. alata*. This is a rather coarse, sticky-leaved 4-footer with sprays of long-tubed, greenish white flowers. The flowers look half dead and limp during the day, but they respond to pollinating night-flying moths by opening their petals at dusk and pouring out their perfume. The blooms appear ghost white across the darkening garden.

Modern hybrids extend the color range into dusky pinks and reds. There are also compact varieties whose flowers open during the day. These innovations all come at the expense of scent. When selecting a plant, you must decide whether appearance or fragrance is more important. Fortunately the huge *N. sylvestris,* a 5-foot-tall plant with foot-long leaves and long-tubed, intensely scented white flowers, looks and smells good both day and night.

Flowering-tobacco is a tender perennial treated as an annual, sown inside and planted outdoors in a sunny spot when frosts are over. It is perennial in the warm-winter climates.

Nigella damascena

Nierembergia hippomanica
'Purple Rose'

Nierembergia hippomanica

Cupflower

The thirty or so species of *Nierembergia,* all of them potato relatives, are native to the cooler parts of South America. The Argentinian *N. hippomanica* is a spreading, foot-high plant with narrow leaves and a summer-long display of upward-facing, bell-shaped, blue flowers with a yellow throat. The plant looks like a nontrailing morning glory (*Ipomoea* species).

Taller and with a more striking show of bigger, violet-colored flowers is the wild variant known as *N. hippomanica* var. *violacea.* It is the cupflower usually offered in nursery catalogs. Given full sun and a well-drained soil, it is a marginally dependable perennial to Zone 7. Elsewhere it is grown as an annual. Sow seed indoors in early

March and then pot each seedling individually in a small container. Young plants should be large enough to plant outside when frosts are over. At the end of the season clip the plants back and hope for the best. They sometimes survive the winter, even in areas where they are not expected to do so.

Plant cupflower at the front of a border, where it associates perfectly with gray-leaved dusty-miller (*Senecio* species).

Nigella damascena

Love-in-a-mist, fennelflower

Both common names are descriptive: Love-in-a-mist refers to the powder blue petals almost lost in a haze of hair-thin bracts, and the fennel reference recalls the finely divided, filigreed leaves of the well-known herb.

Nigella damascena is the best-known of twenty-odd species, all annuals native to the Mediterranean region and all effective overwintering annuals in warm-winter gardens. Seeds scattered in place in September or October germinate during the first fall rains. They grow slowly, flower in April, and set seed soon after. In the wild the seeds remain dormant during the heat of summer, but with normal garden irrigation a second generation germinates almost at once and flowers by July.

It is this summer generation that cold-climate gardeners must enjoy. Sow seeds in a sunny spot as soon

Ocimum basilicum

Ocimum basilicum

as the ground is workable—no need to wait until frosts are over. Almost any soil will do. Thin the seedlings to 6 inches apart to produce the best plants: The flowers will be bigger and so will the inflated seedpods, which are worth keeping for dried winter arrangements. Before picking the pods, be sure to shake out some seeds for next year.

Ocimum basilicum

Basil

Several herbs are included in this book because they are ornamental in addition to being useful in the kitchen. The purple-leaved forms of basil, especially the crimped and twisted leaves of 'Purple Ruffles', are especially decorative.

However, the truth is that common basil is nothing much to look at. It is a typical mint relative with square stems and, by late summer, smallish spikes of pale purple flowers. The small-leaved bush basil is a tidy little plant, but with most basils beauty is in the nose—not the eye—of the beholder. No garden plant has quite so wonderfully aromatic a scent; it is reminiscent of freshly ground pepper with hints of tropical fruit and rare spices.

Originating in the Old World tropics, basil does not tolerate cold. Seedlings raised indoors should be planted outside in a sunny spot in rich soil when the soil has warmed up and frosts are long over. With plenty of water, plants will grow rapidly to 18 inches high. The first crop of leaves can be dried for winter use; the plant soon renews them.

Of the other approximately one hundred and fifty species, a few are sometimes available commercially, but they aren't nearly as desirable as *Ocimum basilicum*.

Omphalodes cappadocica

Oenothera missourensis

Oenothera species

Sundrops, evening-primrose

The common names separate the eighty-odd species of *Oenothera* into those that flower during the day and those that open in the evening but close early the next morning.

The best of the sundrops is *O. fruticosa.* (The virtually interchangeable *O. tetragona* is frequently listed in nursery catalogs.) The plant forms a 12- to 18-inch-high bush with narrow foliage that turns bronze in the fall. It carries heads of bright, shiny yellow, cup-shaped flowers in late June and July. The plant looks splendid in front of metallic blue seaholly (*Eryngium* species). Enhance the effect further with a clump or two of stonecrop (*Sedum* 'Autumn Joy'), whose salmon-bronze flowers late in the season almost echo the fall foliage color of sundrops. A native of the eastern

United States, it is hardy to Zone 3 and perhaps beyond in any soil but the wettest. The plant grows best in full sun.

O. missourensis is one of the most beautiful evening-primroses. Its spreading stems, which lie flat on the ground, bear huge, pale yellow flowers with reddish sepals throughout summer and early autumn. A front-row plant, it thrives in full sun and well-drained soil to Zone 5.

Omphalodes species

Navelwort

Of the two dozen or so species of *Omphalodes,* which are native to Europe, Asia, and Mexico, only two or three are commonly seen in gardens. These are useful spring-flowering plants, rather like the tidy perennial forget-me-not (*Myosotis* species) to which the navelwort is closely related. The common name refers to the circular seeds, which were thought to resemble the navel of Venus.

O. cappadocica, from Asia Minor, is less than a foot high, with gray-green, heart-shaped leaves. It produces sprays of bright blue, white-eyed flowers in May and early June. A splendid, gentle colonizer, it spreads by rhizomes (underground stems) without ever becoming a nuisance. Friends and

Onopordum acanthium

Omphalodes luciliae

neighbors are always grateful to receive any extra plants. *O. verna* is a half-sized version.

From Greece eastward into Asia Minor comes *O. luciliae*. Usually around 6 inches high, it has narrower leaves than the other species and a tufted habit. Although the buds are pink, the half-inch flowers bloom a clear, lovely blue.

Navelwort is a useful associate of the earliest spring bulbs, whose declining leaves they help to mask. Moist, leafy soil in half-shade is ideal. Plants are hardy to Zone 4.

Onopordum acanthium

Silver-thistle

Considering its natural distribution from southern Europe eastward into Asia, alternative common names such as Scotch-thistle and Argentine-thistle seem farfetched. However, this useful and dramatic plant may well be seen in gardens there and elsewhere in the temperate world.

A biennial, silver-thistle is one of the most dramatic and statuesque of plants. Sow seeds directly in the ground in late spring or start them indoors and plant them outside in a permanent spot later. By the end of summer each plant has an 18-inch-wide rosette of silver, felted leaves, fiercely armed on the edges. The next year, as temperatures increase, a single, winged, leafy stem—as

silvery as last year's leaves—shoots up and soon a broad spray of purple thistle flowers appears. Finally the whole plant dies, shedding its seeds.

In most gardens, self-sown seedlings appear late the next spring, often in the most unexpected places. The plants seem to pop up just where their striking appearance gives the best effect. If a plant comes up in an unacceptable spot, however, move it while it's young. Grown in a sunny spot in any good soil, silver-thistle survives to Zone 4 with a leafy winter mulch.

Ophiopogon planiscapus 'Ebony Knight'

Origanum vulgare

Ophiopogon species

Mondo-grass, lilyturf

It is not surprising that the most common species of *Ophiopogon* shares the name lilyturf with *Liriope*. The two are very alike and easily confused. Since they also share similar needs and uses, their differences hardly matter, except to specialists.

O. jaburan, also known as jaburan-lily, comes from Japan. It makes a tufted plant of half-inch-wide grassy leaves up to 2 feet long. Appearing in fall are spikes of small white flowers, rather like elongated heads of grape hyacinth (*Muscari armeni-acum*). The variegated forms, with their brilliant white or yellow-striped leaves, are especially orna-mental. Since jaburan-lily is evergreen, it is effective only in the warmer zones. Although it survives to Zone 6, winter burn ruins the plant and it must grow a new set of leaves in spring.

O. japonicus is a smaller plant and an excellent turf-maker. It bears distinctive blue fruit in fall follow-ing the rather unexciting flowers. Even more striking is *O. planiscapus* 'Arabicus', whose leaves mature to the color of black grapes. As a focal point in a grouping of small plants, it always catches the eye.

Mondo-grass does well in sun or shade, although it needs adequate summer moisture to remain lush.

Origanum species

Marjoram

Of the dozen and a half species—all more or less aromatic—from Europe and Asia, several marjo-rams are grown by keen herb gardeners for culinary and even medicinal virtues.

In its native home, Crete dittany (*Origanum dictamnus*) is prized for herbal tea, but it is also worth growing in a rock garden for its woolly white leaves. Beyond Zone 7 it is not reliably hardy, and the same is true of *O. majorana,* sweet marjoram. However, they can be sown indoors in spring and then planted outside. Gather their pun-gent, downy leaves in late summer and dry them for winter use. Full sun is essential for developing the aroma of these two species.

O. vulgare, common marjoram, is a much easier plant to grow—and a more ornamental one. Native to

Origanum vulgare

Ornithogalum umbellatum

much of Europe and a typical plant of the limestone Cotswold hills in England, it makes hummocks of dark leaves and develops spreading stems with flower heads that bloom in early summer. The effect is somewhat like a pink catmint (*Nepeta* species). The plant is hardy to Zone 3 or even beyond in almost any soil, and it will even take dry shade. A golden-leaved cultivar 'Aureum' makes a tidy 8-inch dome of flowers but seldom blooms. It needs good soil in half-shade.

Ornithogalum species

Star-of-Bethlehem

The best-known of the hundred-plus species of *Ornithogalum* is chincherinchee (*O. thyrsoides*), the splendid, long-lasting cut flower from South Africa. Unfortunately, it is rather uninteresting as a garden plant.

By contrast, the flowering show of *O. nutans* is sadly fleeting, giving no more than two weeks of bloom, but these are two weeks of gentle beauty. Bulbs planted in autumn produce grassy leaves in spring, and they flower after the main season of daffodils (*Narcissus* species), to which they make good additions naturalized in grass. Flower spikes up to 18 inches high carry a number of wide bell-shaped blooms, silvery green on the inside and green and white on the reverse. Nothing is lovelier in detail, but their short season can easily be missed. Plant

bulbs at least 4 inches deep in any soil but the wettest. Sun or shade is equally acceptable.

The same conditions are needed to grow the little *O. umbellatum,* but the spot must be sunny for the flowers to open. Under the proper conditions, heads of milk white stars appear just above ground level in spring. You can plant them under deciduous trees, since they bloom early in the season before the trees leaf out.

These two European species are hardy to Zone 3. Since they are apt to self-sow vigorously, gardeners in warm climates should beware.

Paeonia lactiflora 'Lotus Queen'

Paeonia 'Bowl of Beauty'

Paeonia species

Peony

There is no grander old-fashioned flower than the double, red form of *Paeonia officinalis,* which has been cultivated in Europe since the sixteenth century. Its huge blood red globes open in May.

The tuberous roots, flowers, and seeds of *Paeonia* species were once prescribed for epilepsy and other illnesses—dangerous recommendations since peonies are poisonous. Nevertheless, the Chinese peony, *P. lactiflora,* and the Chinese moutan or tree-peony, *P. suffruticosa,* are still listed in Chinese medical texts for reducing fever and dispelling blood clots.

Medicinal uses aside, peonies have been treasured both in the East and West for centuries. In their season, they are still among the most beautiful flowering plants.

P. lactiflora is an elegant plant, tall and slender compared with the old cottage-garden, double, red peony. In June the 3-foot-high plant bears large, white, bowl-shaped flowers with a gold center. The bronze stems and leaf stalks and the dark foliage set off the flowers perfectly. It was bred by the Chinese for a thousand years before it reached the West at the beginning of the nineteenth century. It has been a source for the amazing range of modern hybrid peonies. Hybrid flower color varies from white and yellow through all shades of pink to a startling red. The flowers may be single, double, or anything in between. There is a peony for every taste and style of garden.

Although peony breeders continue to busy themselves, they will never surpass the beauty of some wild peonies. One is the famed *P. mlokosewitschii,* which English gardeners call mollie-the-witch. Native to the Caucasus mountains, it is a 2-foot-high plant with exquisitely lobed leaves, pinkish and bronze as they unfold, encircling cup-shaped flowers of soft, creamy yellow. The flowers open in late March in the southern United States and two months later in the North. Although very hardy, it needs protection from wind.

Closely related to mollie-the-witch is the very desirable *P. wittmanniana.* Its shining leaves, pink-tinted as they unfold, provide a perfect foil for the nearly 6-inch, creamy yellow flowers. It is this species that has been used to bring yellow into the range of hybrid Chinese peonies.

Another fine wilding is *P. tenuifolia.* It has crimson flowers with leaves cut to the fineness of fennel, making it very distinctive.

Paeonia lutea var. *ludlowii*

Paeonia suffruticosa

Try this or any other of the thirty or so species, the hardiest from northern Europe and Asia, that you can obtain. If you grow the peony from seed, be aware that it is slow to germinate and will take at least three years to flower.

For warm-winter gardens there are two California species (*P. brownii* and *P. californica*) and several from the Mediterranean. *P. cambessedesii,* native to islands off the coast of Spain, is especially fine. It has rose-pink flowers and leaves that are deep green on top and purple underneath. Just over a foot in height, it needs a northern exposure at the base of a shrub.

Most herbaceous peonies are hardy to Zone 3. They enjoy any good garden soil and up to one-third shade in hot-summer areas. Once planted (with buds just at soil level), leave them alone. Specimens thirty years old are not uncommon.

Tree-peonies, deciduous shrubs that can also live for decades, flourish under similar conditions. *P. lutea* var. *ludlowii* is by far the most desirable of the group. Native to Tibet, it seems most at home in northwestern gardens, where it seeds itself with abandon. Quickly reaching 6 feet high or more, its strong stems bear fingered, pale green leaves. Nodding, clear yellow flowers bloom among the upper leaves in June.

For most people, tree-peony means *P. suffruticosa,* the Chinese moutan. Very slow-growing, it can

eventually reach 6 feet tall and even wider. In winter its gnarled branches are awkward, but as the elegant, fingered leaves develop, the plant assumes a quiet beauty. Spherical flower buds open into the most amazing blossoms, exceeding even the diversity of the herbaceous peonies. Blossoms can be 8 inches across. Hardy to Zone 5, this and other tree-peonies tolerate sun while flowering and accept shade later when the trees leaf out.

For three seasons of color, underplant herbaceous or tree-peonies with early spring bulbs and with gladiolus (*Gladiolus* species) or summer-hyacinth (*Galtonia candicans*). After the flowers have passed, species peonies have late-summer seedpods of brilliant scarlet.

Pelargonium capitatum 'Attar of Roses'

Papaver orientale

Papaver species

Poppy

No other hardy plant, not even peony, has flowers quite as blatantly gorgeous as oriental poppy (*Papaver orientale*). Native to southwest Asia, it requires a sunny spot in deep soil with perfect drainage. Under those conditions it is hardy to Zone 3. Growth begins early as a rapidly extending clump of hairy, divided leaves develops. In late May, 2- to 3-foot stems appear, each with a huge nodding bud. When the bud stands straight up, it is ready to open. The enclosing sepals split and fall. Crinkled, taffetalike petals tumble out, arranging themselves in a great bowl surrounding a large, black stigma (female part of the flower, receiving the pollen) and a mass of black stamens.

The flowers are a brilliant scarlet or vermilion accented with purple-black blotches. Pink and white, as well as double, varieties are also available. The whole plant goes to rest by July. The planting site should be marked and the gap planted with something else.

P. nudicaule, Iceland poppy, is a less certain perennial grown more commonly as a biennial. Young plants sown indoors are planted outside in spring (they are very hardy) for a summer display. Foot-high stems above a flat rosette of grayish leaves carry a lovely array of smooth, bowl-shaped flowers in cream, yellow, orange, or pink. These and all other poppies need full sun and good garden soil.

Pelargonium species

Geranium

Of all the wonderful plants that South Africa has given to the world, *Pelargonium* species is probably the most widely used. Bedding geraniums are grown by the thousands of acres, Martha Washington types fill greenhouses, and scented-leaf species have economic value.

There are over two hundred and fifty wild species including herbaceous perennials, but the majority are evergreen shrubs, some even succulents. They are hardy, permanent plants only in Zones 9 and 10. Elsewhere cuttings are rooted in autumn and overwintered in frost-free greenhouses or grown annually from seed and planted outside when frosts are over. In the garden they need full sun and a soil that does not stay wet. Overfeeding produces much foliage at the expense of the flowers.

The scented geraniums have been worked over by the breeders but

Pelargonium tomentosum

Pelargonium × domesticum

most are still very close to the original species. Although the flowers may be attractive, they do not make much of a show. The plants are grown for the texture and the aroma of their foliage. They are useful in herb gardens as a source of potpourri material. They are also valued as a foliage accent in summer bedding schemes and in patio containers. Here are just a few of the many species or near species (they are apt to interbreed) of scented geraniums available from specialist nurseries.

P. capitatum, the rose-scented geranium, has fragrant, long-stemmed, hairy leaves. The whole plant, which is seldom above 18 inches high, makes a rather lax hummock. 'Attar of Roses', with its pink-purple flower heads, is a good cultivar.

P. graveolens, the sweet-scented geranium (sometimes also referred to as the rose-scented geranium), is one of the sources of geranium oil. It is a difficult species to root from cuttings. Its almost triangular, deeply divided leaves give the plant a delicate appearance. As with other scented geraniums, its foliage is more important than its pink flowers. 'Lady Plymouth', which has white and gray-green variegated leaves, is one of the best cultivars.

P. quercifolium, the aromatic oak-leaved geranium, is a much bigger plant. Lush, green, divided leaves and small heads of pink flowers build up to a 5-foot-high shrub. In Zone 9, if surprised by a frost, it will usually spring up again from the rootstock.

P. tomentosum is a distinctive species with broad, velvety, peppermint-scented leaves. Seldom above 2 feet high, it has wide-spreading, fanlike branches. Planted with white summer-hyacinth (*Galtonia candicans*), it makes a fine late-summer picture even in the North.

Just as scented geraniums are valued for their aromatic foliage, the ivy-leaved geranium (*P. peltatum*) is prized for its form. It is a wonderful plant for covering banks, for tumbling over dry walls in frost-free areas, and for cascading over hanging baskets and window boxes. If kept fertilized and watered, it is never out of flower and its curtains of shining leaves always look bright and fresh. Single or double flowers come in every shade of pink and purple. Seeds of hybrid strains, which are usually propagated from cuttings, are becoming available.

The Martha Washington or regal geranium is botanically known as *P. × domesticum.* It is a complicated mix of species bred for flower size. Over crimped leaves, wonderful flower heads bloom in an range of colors: white through all the pinks to deep thundercloud purple. Often the wavy petals have a contrasting color blotch at the base. Although the regal geranium has

Penstemon gloxinioides 'King George'

Penstemon hartwegii 'Hewell's Pink'

been a traditional cool-greenhouse plant for over a century, it is also a valuable bedding plant in Zones 9 and 10. Because of its heavy flower heads, the plant needs a sheltered location and careful dead-heading to keep it from looking messy.

By comparison, the bedding or zonal geranium is much easier to grow as long as its basic requirements are met. The soft, rounded, aromatic leaves make an attractive base to the long-stemmed flower clusters—these are available in every shade from white through the pinks to brilliant scarlet. Derived from a number of species, the zonal geranium is known botanically as *P. × hortorum*. New cultivars that can be grown from seed are introduced each year. The old types, as well as those with variegated leaves, must be increased by cuttings.

Penstemon species

Beard-tongue

This wonderfully ornamental genus has about two hundred and fifty species, almost all of them native to the western edge of North America. They vary from low shrubs suitable for rock gardens (these are generally from the Rocky Mountains) to lush perennials. As foxglove relatives (*Digitalis* species) they all have spikes or clusters of tubular flowers in a dazzling array of colors from white through all the pinks to scarlet and deep purple. Many have fringed "beards"—hence the common name—in a contrasting color within the throat. They thrive in full sun and well-drained soil.

Penstemon barbatus, one of the hardiest species, does well with some protection to Zone 5. Its slender stems of narrow, paired leaves carry late-summer spires of scarlet flowers, which bloom for weeks. It is native from Utah into Mexico.

P. hartwegii, another Mexican species with fine scarlet spikes of 2-inch-long flowers, is only for warm-winter gardens. It and other species have been combined in *P. gloxinioides,* a valuable group of brightly colored, large-flowered perennials that are hardy only in the Southwest. They can be grown as annuals from seeds sown in spring, but they fail to make much of a show in the first year. Rooted cuttings, overwintered and planted the next year, perform well.

Perilla frutescens

Perovskia atriplicifolia

Perilla frutescens

Roast-beef-plant

This is the only commonly grown species of a small group of Asian annuals. A useful foliage plant in summer bedding schemes, roast-beef-plant resembles a robust coleus (*Coleus × hybridus*). Both have the square stems typical of plants in the mint family, but unlike coleus *Perilla frutescens* does not relish shade. Growing to 3 feet tall, it has spikes of purplish hooded flowers that bloom in late summer.

Related to basil, it was once included under the genus *Ocimum*. (It has no connection with *Iris foetidissima,* also referred to as roast-beef-plant.) Although it lacks the warm spiciness of true basil, it does add a distinct astringent flavor to certain dishes. In Japan the oily seeds and the leaves are used in a number of dishes. It was the plant's usefulness in cooking that gave it the common name roast-beef-plant in the West.

Both the green wavy-leaved and the purple forms are sown indoors and planted outside in full sun after all frosts are over. A few early-sown purple roast-beef-plants make good accents in bedding schemes, especially when placed behind green-leaved wax begonias (*Begonia × semperflorens-cultorum*) and edged with variegated spiderplant (*Chlorophytum elatum*). In areas where the summer is long enough for the production of ripe seeds, *P. frutescens* can sow itself and become somewhat weedy, although seldom to the point of being a pest.

Perovskia atriplicifolia

Perovskia

This is one of a small genus of subshrubs from the dry foothills of the western Himalayas. It has all the attributes necessary to plant it in the herb garden or any border where gray leaves and a misty cloud of tiny flowers are desired late in the season.

From a permanent woody base, 3-foot-high stems of gray-white, highly aromatic leaves gradually develop into elegant spikes of small blue flowers. This progression takes the whole season, with the flower display at its best in August and September. The skeleton remains attractive even when killed by frost.

Unlike the majority of gray-leaved plants, which are Mediterranean and almost always tight and compact, perovskia is open and airy. It looks superb as a backdrop for

Petunia × *hybrida* 'Summer Madness'

Petunia × *hybrida* 'Sheer Madness'

nerine (*Nerine* species) in warm-winter areas, and elsewhere it helps to lighten the bulk of late-flowering stonecrop (*Sedum* species).

Perovskia is hardy to at least Zone 5 in well-drained soil in a sunny spot. It is undaunted by scorching summer winds. 'Blue Spire', an especially good cultivar, has deeply cut leaves and lavender-blue flowers.

Petunia × *hybrida*

Petunia

It is difficult to imagine the summer garden without petunias. Although common (and therefore despised by some), the petunia is valuable in providing a nonstop display of flowers from June until the frosts of fall.

The garden petunia is the hybrid product of several of the showier wild species (there are about thirty, all from tropical and subtropical South America). The color range in both single and double flowers is now enormous—from white and yellow through blue and purple to scarlet, often with striped petals or contrasting eyes. They should be used with some care in a harmonious color scheme rather than just to achieve blaring brilliance.

Breeders have selected a diversity of plant habits from dwarf forms little more than 6 inches high to others three times that height. Flower size is another matter of choice; in general, the cultivars with smaller flowers provide a more continuous show. Pinch off the faded flowers of the big doubles to keep the plants blooming profusely. This is easiest to do when the plants are grown in containers.

Plant petunias only after all danger of frost has passed. They need at least three-quarters sun and good garden soil.

Phlox drummondii

Phlox divaricata 'Dirigo Ice'

Phlox species

Phlox

Almost all of the sixty-odd species of *Phlox* are native to North America. Only one grows wild elsewhere, on the eastern edge of Asia across from Alaska. Several species are valuable ornamentals in perennial and annual gardens.

P. drummondii, annual phlox, is a wildflower of south-central Texas. Even in nature it has a kaleidoscopic color range from white and buff through pink to scarlet and purple. With such genetic diversity it is not surprising that the plant breeders have had a field day with it. Colors have been extended throughout the spectrum and flowers often have a contrasting eye.

From a rather thin, 18-inch wildling, garden forms have been developed that are more compact and wide-spreading, ideal for annual bedding schemes or the front of mixed borders. Plant them after all

frosts are over in a sunny location in good garden soil. With regular fertilizing and watering, the brilliant show lasts all season long.

P. divaricata, wild sweet-william or blue phlox, is a woodlander of eastern North America. Seldom much above a foot high, it has running stems that fortunately are not at all aggressive. These root at the nodes and develop vertical flowering shoots that make a lovely show in May and early June. The inch-wide flowers are soft blue or violet with white and pink variants. This very desirable plant needs leafy, moist soil and half sun. It is hardy to at least Zone 3.

The most common of the perennial, big border phloxes is derived from *P. paniculata,* native to much of

the eastern United States. In the wild it is a robust 6-footer of rich, moist valleys. Although the flowers typically are a soft pinkish lavender, there are wild variants that are white and nearly red. Its willowy growth and undemanding nature make it a desirable plant worth searching out. However, the wonderful range of hybrids with their great rounded heads of musk-scented flowers in late summer are irresistible. The height varies between 3 to 5 feet, depending on the cultivar chosen and the conditions under which the plant is grown. All colors except yellow occur, and often flowers have a contrasting eye. Care must be taken in grouping plants, since some combinations are garish. There is also an excellent variegated-leaf cultivar called 'Harlequin'.

A second important group of perennial phlox is variously listed as *P. maculata, P. suffruticosa,* and *P. carolina.* The plants are native

Phlox paniculata 'Pastorale'

Physostegia virginiana 'Variegata'

to the central United States and they need conditions similar to those enjoyed by *P. paniculata:* good, moist garden soil and at least three-quarters sun to Zones 4 or possibly 3. This group has darker, more leathery foliage and earlier flowers borne on a much narrower spike. Colors are less strident; 'Miss Lingard', for example, has lovely white flowers.

If you remove the central flower head of tall perennial phlox the moment the majority of the flowers are spent, another show from secondary side shoots will often follow. Sadly, phlox is subject to a debilitating mildew that can cover the foliage. If not treated early enough, it can ruin the flower display as well.

Another delightful perennial species is *P. subulata,* moss-pink. As a 6-inch-high, mat-forming plant, it could hardly be more different from its tall, summer-flowering cousins. It provides brilliant color in the rock garden in May and early June, covering its clumps of narrow pinklike (*Dianthus* species) leaves with flat, upward-facing flowers. The color range includes white, purple, and all shades of pink from soft peach to nearly magenta. Native to higher elevations of the Northeast, moss-pink is hardy to Zone 3 under a protective snow cover. It thrives in well-drained soil in a sunny location.

Physostegia virginiana

Obedience plant, false-dragonhead

This valuable, late-summer flowering perennial is a relative of the mints and sages (*Salvia* species). Its claim to fame is that its flowers, which are on hinged stalks, remain in place when twisted. (It is ideal for flower arrangers who want all the flowers to face the same way.) Beyond its party trick, obedience plant earns its keep in the border.

The wild species, from New Brunswick, Canada, to South Carolina, has 3- to 4-foot-high square stems, pairs of narrow leaves, and foot-long spikes of pink tubular flowers in September. It is particularly attractive with Japanese anemone (*Anemone* × *hybrida*) and just as long-lasting.

'Summer Snow' is a white-flowered cultivar that is about half as tall and blooms in August. It is especially

Platycodon grandiflorus

fine as part of a white group fronting the earlier-flowering bugbane (*Cimicifuga racemosa*). They all relish slightly moist soil.

The bright pink 'Vivid', which also flowers in August, is about a foot high. It is a good companion for winter-begonia (*Bergenia* species).

Although obedience plant has running roots, it makes good clumps and does not become a pest. It needs full sun and any good soil that doesn't dry out. The smaller cultivars appreciate biennial lifting and soil rejuvenation to maintain vigor. Obedience plant is hardy to Zone 3 under the protection of an early snow cover.

Platycodon grandiflorus

Balloon-flower

This is a bellflower (*Campanula* species) relative that always attracts attention. Usually around 1½ feet tall, some forms are almost double this height. Still, it is a plant for the front of the border, since no one can resist trying to pop the inflated flower buds (although their pop is less satisfactory than that of *Fuchsia*). An accessible spot saves footmarks in the border.

Purplish stems arising late in the season are a sudden reminder of balloon-flower's presence. It is easy to forget that the tuberous rootstock is there and, seeing a gap in late May, plant something over the top. Leaving last year's stems until spring before cutting them down is an invaluable memory aid.

Once begun, growth is rapid, and a clump of smooth, blue-green leaves supports the balloon-shaped buds,

which open into wide bells. Blue, pink, or white flowers bloom over a long season from early August onward. There are double forms that last even longer, but they lack grace. Worthy cultivars include 'Mother of Pearl', which has soft pink flowers, and 'Mariesii', a fine, compact plant that begins to flower in July.

Balloon-flower is native to China and Japan, where it was a garden flower long before being introduced to Europe in the late eighteenth century. It does well in North America to Zone 4, or even 3, under a cover of mulch or snow. The plant thrives in a sunny location in good garden soil that drains quickly after the spring thaw.

Podophyllum peltatum

Polemonium caeruleum var. *album*

Podophyllum species

Mayapple

The native North American mayapple, *Podophyllum peltatum,* is one of the joys of deciduous woodlands from Quebec to Florida and Texas. In response to warm spring days, the first sign of growth is a cluster of what look like mushrooms pushing through the leaf-littered soil.

The stem quickly extends and the parasol-like top unfolds into one or two large, flat leaves, lobed and wavy, a foot above the ground. Nodding between the pairs of leaves is a single waxy flower resembling a small, creamy camellia (*Camellia* species). It is fleeting but of supreme beauty. In some years it is followed by a yellow plumlike fruit that ripens in September and is worth making into jam. Mayapple leaves remain ornamental throughout summer.

P. hexandrum is the Himalayan version. The leaf pairs are more deeply divided and marbled with bronze. The flowers stand erect between the leaves like sculptured, blush buttercups. The fruit, which follows more reliably that that of *P. peltatum,* is a rosy red plum and ripens earlier.

Both mayapples are wonderfully distinct plants. They gradually extend their clumps when grown in leafy soil in up to three-quarters shade. The North American native is hardy to at least Zone 3 and the Himalayan is not far behind; probably hardy to Zone 4.

Polemonium species

Jacob's-ladder

The two dozen or so species of *Polemonium* are spread mainly around the temperate Northern Hemisphere, with a concentration in the western United States. There are several good plants in the West not generally available from the nursery trade; they are worth searching out from specialist wildflower seed catalogs.

P. caeruleum is widespread in Europe and Asia. It gets the name Jacob's-ladder from the pairs of narrow leaflets climbing up the 3-foot-high stems. In early summer the top foot of the stems is crowded with little, cup-shaped, clear blue flowers with conspicuous yellow stamens. White and pinkish variants are not an improvement. Remove the stems as soon as the

Polemonium caeruleum

Polygonatum odoratum 'Variegatum'

flowers are finished to help the clump of basal leaves retain its spring green freshness.

A charming native of much of the eastern half of the United States is *P. reptans*. Seldom above a foot high, it spreads gently to provide a late-spring display of soft lavender-blue, bell-shaped flowers above the typical ladderlike leaves.

Jacob's-ladder, which is hardy to Zone 3, can take up to half shade in good garden soil.

Polygonatum species

Solomon's-seal

These invaluable plants for deciduous woodland in most cases maintain their fresh foliage and fine silhouette even in late summer. They help overcome the desiccated look so common in shady gardens devoted solely to the spring scene.

Polygonatum commutatum, native to New England and southward, is the largest Solomon's-seal. Stiff, arching, 5-foot-high stems carry a sequence of smooth leaves over the arch, all in the same horizontal plane. In late May clusters of narrow, white, creamy, bell-shaped flowers hang underneath. Superb towering above ferns and plantain-lily (*Hosta* species), it requires the same leafy soil of these plants. *P. multiflorum* is a European version, half the size and just as beautiful, spreading similarly from fleshy rhizomes (underground stems). The

flowers of both are sometimes followed by black berries. A highly desirable variegated form 'Variegatum' is well worth searching out. Less vigorous than the species, it has fat shoots that are pink-tinged as they emerge. The elegant leaves then unfold to display an attractive, clear white edge.

P. odoratum var. *thunbergii* is from Japan. Less obviously arched, it is noted especially for its scented, greenish flowers and lovely cream-variegated leaves.

All species need moist, leafy soil and are hardy to Zone 3. They are very adaptable to exposure, growing in anything from full sun to deep shade.

Portulaca grandiflora 'Afternoon Delight'

Polygonum bistorta 'Superbum'

Polygonum species

Knotweed

The second syllable of the common name aptly describes many of the one hundred and fifty–odd species of *Polygonum* that are wild (or have become so) around the world. Even some of the most beautiful species have colonial intentions.

P. cuspidatum is one such plant. Sometimes called Mexican-bamboo (although it is from Japan), it starts from a deep, woody rootstock with pink asparaguslike shoots that seem to grow by the minute as spring warms up. By July it is 6 or 8 feet high with stout, arching, hollow stems and large, heart-shaped leaves. In late August each stem is topped with a cloud of tiny white flowers. It does well in moist soil and full sun but will take almost any conditions. Although extremely beautiful, it is almost impossible to eradicate once established. *P. cuspidatum* var. *compactum* is half the

size A leathery-leaved plant with pink flowers, it is only marginally less aggressive.

P. bistorta is very different. In June a robust clump of broad leaves sends up many stems with bottle-brush heads of pink flowers. Occasional stems arise throughout summer as long as the soil does not dry out. The cultivar 'Superbum' is best.

P. affine is a Himalayan, useful as a front-of-the-border mat for a September effect. Rose-pink spikes make a good show a foot above the dark green leaves. This plant needs full sun.

All of these knotweeds are hardy to Zone 3 except *P. cuspidatum,* which dies back at the first breath of frost.

Portulaca grandiflora

Moss-rose, sunplant

Few gardeners fail to meet the flat-growing, fleshy-leaved purslane (*Portulaca oleracea*) as an annual weed. Some consolation may be found in the fact that it can be eaten in salads along with the lettuce it infests. Cultivated forms have bigger leaves, but this species has little to commend its appearance.

A close relative, the South American *P. grandiflora* is one of the most brilliant annual flowers available for a sunny spot. It also has little fleshy leaves on a nondescript plant a foot wide and slightly less high. In late June, however, the first buds suddenly burst open to flaunt their unlikely flowers. The double or semidouble blossoms are 1½ inches wide and have crimped petals. They come in a kaleidoscopic range of brilliant colors—all

Potentilla atrosanguinea 'Gibson's Scarlet'

but true-blue. Also called moss-rose or sunplant, *P. grandiflora* needs full sun and perfect drainage in a fertile garden soil. Under these conditions it will flower throughout the season. As a native of the tropics, it must be sown indoors and planted outside only when the soil is warm and all risk of frost has passed.

Potentilla species

Cinquefoil

The shrubby cinquefoil (meaning five-leaved) is a common low shrub that usually flowers in shades of yellow and is invaluable in cold areas. There are also many herbaceous cinquefoils among the five hundred or so species strewn around the temperate world.

A couple of European species sometimes offered should be treated with care: *Potentilla anserina,* silverweed, is beautiful but noxious in light soils; and *P. reptans* is an invasive weed in heavy soils.

P. atrosanguinea, however, combines beauty and a slight degree of difficulty to make it eminently desirable. Silvery, five-lobed leaves form a fine clump for the front of the border. From July onward the plant produces a succession of gorgeous blood-red flowers like those of the common strawberry, a close relative.

A Himalayan species that survives to Zone 4 in North America, it enjoys a sunny spot in good garden soil. Over the years gardeners have selected and bred a number of fine cultivars, all of which are worth searching out. 'Gibson's Scarlet' blooms in a dazzling shade of red. Other cultivars are available with single or double flowers in mahogany, orange, or yellow.

When dividing the rather woody rootstocks of these species, do it in late spring and water regularly until the clumps are established.

Primula veris

Primula japonica

Primula species

Primrose, polyanthus, cowslip

There are about four hundred species of *Primula* spanning the cooler regions of the Northern Hemisphere (with only a very few south of the equator). It is pleasant knowing that, however many you grow, there are always other beautiful types still to try.

Among the European species that have been cultivated for centuries is *P. vulgaris,* the well-loved English primrose. It forms a rosette of netted leaves and produces one pale, sulfur yellow flower per stem. These deliciously scented flowers bloom for several weeks in spring. There are also a number of

cultivars in soft pastel colors. In England primrose covers banks and floors of deciduous woodlands in the same way that wakerobin (*Trillium grandiflorum*) grows in the northeastern United States. In most of North America it needs cool and moist, but not soggy, soil with summer shade.

Another British species is the spring-flowering cowslip, *P. veris.* From a very similar leaf rosette, a 6- to 9-inch stem carries a head of nodding bell-shaped flowers with bright yellow petals and long, pale green sepals. Wonderfully scented,

cowslip prefers drier soil than English primrose and even seeds itself in paving cracks.

From the Maritime Alps comes *P. auricula.* It forms a rosette of wavy, leathery leaves and in spring produces a head of wide primrose flowers with thick petals. Colors in the wild are usually soft yellow or purple, and both leaves and flowers have a dusting of white that looks like meal. *P. auricula* has been a favorite flower since the eighteenth century, when vast numbers of varieties were bred and grown as container plants. A number of lovely old forms are still available in a range of unusual, dusky colors. Most enjoy well-drained soil with some summer shade.

Primula japonica

The popularity of *P. auricula* has switched to the polyanthus, a group of widely diverse strains of *Primula × polyantha*. These are the product of intense crossbreeding between primrose and cowslip, with oxlip (*P. elatior*) and probably others brought in. Typical primrose leaves and large flowers—around 2 inches across—are available in a range of dazzling colors. They are valuable cool-season plants for warm-winter gardens and for spring displays in the North. The bright reds and oranges are best kept to more formal parts of the garden. The soft blues and yellows associate wonderfully with naturalized spring bulbs. It is best to raise a new batch from May-sown seeds each year, since the modern hybrids are not always good perennials.

The Himalayas and other parts of Asia are home to an amazing diversity of *Primula* species. Many are high alpines, difficult to cultivate. Others are robust perennials that enjoy moist soil, even bog conditions, and some summer shade. *P. florindae* is one of the most spectacular. It forms a rosette of long-stemmed, heart-shaped leaves. Tall stems up to 4 feet high carry nodding primrose bells, dusted with white. It flowers for weeks, and on the West Coast, in Oregon and British Columbia, looks marvelous with the first of the blue-poppies (*Meconopsis* species).

Easier to grow in the East is *P. japonica,* which likes wet, organic soil. It is one of the many lovely candelabra primroses, a group with flowers in whorls. Big rosettes of leaves put up several flower stems. Arranged in separate whorls up the stem, the flowers are purple-red with the typical white dusting.

All species of *Primula* described here are hardy to Zone 3 under certain snow or a mulch applied in early fall. All species need moisture; none are for dry gardens.

Puschkinia scilloides var. *libanotica*

Pulmonaria saccharata 'Mrs. Moon'

Pulmonaria species

Lungwort

These dozen or so borage relatives have the typical bristliness of the family. All are useful ground covers in sun or up to three-quarters shade. They grow well under trees as long as summer moisture is maintained.

The leaves emerge slowly in early spring. Flower heads appear at once, with the first blooms opening only 1 or 2 inches above ground. The brick red *Pulmonaria montana* (also listed as *P. rubra*) blooms as early as the beginning of February in warm-winter gardens. In the North it flowers two months later. The flower stems extend so that the plant is 1 foot high and 2 feet across during the main show in late spring. The leaves are more or less spotted with gray—hence both

Latin and English names. The best forms are entirely silver-gray.

Although all are worth growing, *P. saccharata* is perhaps the best. In addition to fine foliage, the flowers have a charming progression beginning with pink buds peeping from purple sepals. The blossoms then open to bright pink before changing to blue.

Lungwort is a European woodland-edge plant that enjoys leafy soil and some summer shade. It is hardy to Zone 3 under snow.

Puschkinia scilloides

Puschkinia

Whenever *Puschkinia* species is featured in autumn bulb catalogs, gardeners are inspired to plan the following spring's show. As *scill-oides* indicates, it is like a scilla, another little spring-flowering bulb. (The *-oides* suffix, which appears often in botanical names, means "resembling.")

In autumn, plant the bulbs 3 inches deep among shrubs, under deciduous trees, or in rock garden pockets. Any garden soil but the wettest will do. Planting puschkinia or any other spring-flowering bulb in the shade of a deciduous plant is perfectly fine—as long as the tree or shrub leafs out after the bulb has finished flowering and the leaves have had a chance to manufacture food for the following year's flower display.

The April show is charming. From between the leaves appear two or three stems up to 6 inches high,

Rhododendron P.J.M.

Rhododendron yakusimanum

each carrying a half-dozen wide-open, bell-shaped, white flowers with porcelain blue stripes. As a plant from Asia Minor and the Caucasus Mountains, it thrives under winter snow to Zone 5. It looks lovely massed with dwarf hybrid daffodils (*Narcissus* species) such as 'Jack Snipe'. It enhances the snow whiteness of giant snowdrop (*Galanthus elwesii*) and the sky blue of Siberian squill (*Scilla sibirica*), when it is interspersed with the other two bulbs. Add substance to this early-spring grouping with the leathery overwintering leaves of winter-begonia (*Bergenia* species), whose pink flowers soon contribute further interest.

Rhododendron species

Rhododendron, azalea

One of the biggest of all woody plant genera, *Rhododendron* has over eight hundred species varying from trees reaching 60 feet high in the subtropical jungles of Burma and Nepal to 6-inch-high sub-shrubs from the Himalayas. They are found all around the Northern Hemisphere and even in tropical northern Australia. There are rhododendrons for almost every garden, as long as certain facts are accepted: The plants must have moist, acid soil and some shade. They should also relate to the design and style of the garden, since isolated rhododendron bushes look odd and seldom do well.

The mild, moist areas of Oregon and Washington states offer ideal conditions for the evergreen species and their innumerable hybrids. There, *R. sinograde* and other Himalayan-foothill species reach their full size: They grow to 30 feet high and have 2-foot-long leaves and football-sized flower heads in May. The blossoms may be white, yellow, pink, or scarlet, often with a contrasting flash of color in the throat. In this region it is possible to have rhododendrons in bloom for eight months of the year, beginning with the small, purple-flowered *R. × praecox* in January and ending with the large, white-blossomed *R. auriculatum* in August. The latter is one of many rhododendrons producing huge, lilylike, trumpet-shaped flowers with a rich fragrance that floats across the garden. Especially elegant are cultivars of *R. cinnabarinum*. Eventually a dozen feet high, they have small blue-green leaves and long bell-shaped flowers in a diversity of plum-purple and buff-yellow shades.

In the more extreme climate of the eastern United States, only a greatly reduced number of evergreen species, including those

Ricinus communis

Rhododendron Kurume azalea

known as ironclads, survive to Zone 5. Even in that climate only woodland-edge conditions and moist, leafy soil are likely to offer sites in which large species do well. Unless the foliage is lush and healthy, a big evergreen rhododendron is not worth growing. Two weeks of even spectacular flowers are no compensation for eleven months of lackluster leaves.

Fortunately, there are some smaller species that are easier to incorporate into a garden. An excellent, hardy, twiggy example is the P.J.M. hybrid. Its purple flowers held above dark, rounded leaves make a fine picture in May. In recent years the Japanese *R. yakusimanum* has been used as a base for some splendid, low-domed hybrids with fine rounded heads of pink or white flowers.

Often easier to place are the deciduous types usually known as azaleas and sometimes called swamp honeysuckle. There are a number of native North American species

requiring woodland conditions, as well as others from Asia Minor into the Far East. The old yellow azalea *R. luteum,* from the Caucasus Mountains, has a lovely fragrance. It also has a fine fall leaf color.

Consult a specialist nursery for information on the various hybrid groups of deciduous rhododendrons, such as Mollis and Exbury azaleas. The plants are available in a vast range of flower color, including cream, scarlet, orange, and flame. Also consider evergreen Kurume azaleas, which form wide, rounded bushes with brilliant flowers in shades of red, pink, or purple. If you are mixing azalea groups and flower colors, be sure to position the plants carefully so they don't clash. Use ground-cover plants such as plantain-lily (*Hosta* species), lily-of-the-valley (*Convallaria majalis*), Solomon's-seal (*Polygonatum* species), and ferns to cool the fiery colors.

Ricinus communis

Castor-bean, castor-oil-plant

The seeds of the castor-bean look exactly like scarab beetles and are the source of an oil with wide medicinal and other economic uses. The seeds are also poisonous. Their spots attract small children, so it is probably safest not to plant castor-bean if children are likely to be in the garden.

In the warmest zones the seeds, sown directly in the ground, quickly produce a woody plant that reaches the proportions of a shrub or even small tree. The huge, maplelike leaves and clusters of small white flowers are pleasing on young plants but become wind-torn and ratty when old. In mild-winter areas, where castor-bean survives the winter, prune the plant hard in spring or replace it with a young plant.

In the North, fall frosts ensure that the plant does not lose its looks; death comes first. In the preceding three or four months, however, it is

Rodgersia tabularis

one of the most spectacular of annual foliage plants. Sow seeds individually in small pots and plant the seedlings outside in a sunny spot when frosts are over and the soil has warmed up. Growth is prodigious—8 feet in a season is not uncommon, with flowering often occurring by September. Castorbean looks splendid with common garden canna *Canna* × *generalis.* Any garden soil will do.

The name castor-oil-plant is also sometimes applied to *Fatsia japonica,* more commonly known as Japanese aralia. A fine, evergreen ivy relative, its lustrous, green-lobed leaves are similar to those of *R. communis.* The latter is sun-loving, while *Fatsia* thrives in full shade.

Although *Ricinus* has only this one species, a number of forms with green, red, or variegated foliage are available, as are dwarf types for small gardens.

Rodgersia species

Rodgersia

Found in China, *Rodgersia* is a small genus of wonderful waterside plants. With their immense leaves and spires of fluffy flowers, the plants associate well with the bigger plantain-lilies (*Hosta* species) and astilbe (*Astilbe* species). Moist soil and up to half shade ensure that growth is as lush and uninhibited as it should be. Rodgersia is hardy to Zone 4 and perhaps beyond with a winter mulch. Unfortunately, as with so many good plants, it is difficult to locate and expensive when found.

R. aesculifolia is well named. Like *Aesculus* species, the horsechestnut, it has leaves that are shaped like a hand—although they are smaller than horsechestnut foliage. Each leaf, which unfolds its crinkled, bronze-tinted lobes until they are held horizontally, is carried on a 3-foot-high, furry stalk. The late-summer flower heads, held above the leaves, are cream-colored and flushed with pink.

R. pinnata 'Superba' is worth every effort to obtain. Its bronzy leaves are shaped differently, more like a feather than a hand, and above them stand 3-foot-high stems of bright pink flowers. It associates especially well with the gray-blue foliage of plantain-lily.

R. tabularis is just as dramatic. A 4- or 5-foot-high plant with white flowers, it has circular leaves up to 2 feet across. A stalk supports each leaf in the center like an umbrella.

Rodgersia is slow to build up a good rootstock, but once established it lives for many years and needs little attention.

Rosa foetida bicolor

Rosa hugonis

Rosa species

Rose

The word *rose,* like the word *lily,* is attached to a number of unrelated plants whose only connection is their popularity. True roses, perhaps the best-loved of all garden plants, are extraordinarily diverse. There are more than 20,000 kinds of roses, some dating back to classical times. There are free-standing shrubs growing over a dozen feet in height and scrambling types that can reach the top of mature trees. Most are armed with fierce thorns.

Although there are over a hundred wild species, mainly from temperate areas of the Northern Hemisphere, less than a quarter have contributed their genes to garden roses. However, a number of the species are themselves highly ornamental flowering shrubs. Some of these open the rose year as early as May, even in the North: *Rosa*

primula and *R. hugonis* (Father Hugo rose) make 6- or 8-foot-high bushes covered with 2-inch-wide, yellow flowers and elegant fernlike foliage. Blooming soon afterward is *R. foetida bicolor* (Austrian copper rose). The top of the petals is a brilliant flame color and the reverse yellow. Sadly, this rose suffers from blackspot disease in many regions.

Most species roses, like other flowering shrubs, have a single bloom period. Fortunately some species, such as the 15-foot-high Himalayan *Rosa,* produce bright hips (fruit) that remain attractive until Christmas or even later.

The Japanese *R. rugosa* flowers and fruits together for several months. A very hardy species, it

has naturalized in great thickets on the sea cliffs of Maine. It typically has wide, pink, fragrant flowers, but there are hybrids with double flowers in a range of pinks and white. Two such hybrids, 'Blanc Double de Coubert' and 'Frau Dagmar Hartopp' ('Frau Dagmar Hastrup'), make good hedges.

Another species, *R. glauca,* is invaluable as a foliage plant. It has gray-purple foliage, small pink flowers, and from July onward scarlet hips.

Most of the old-fashioned or heritage roses also have a single flowering period. Their intensely double blooms that open flat are the roses depicted in seventeenth- and eighteenth-century Dutch flower paintings. Of European origin, some of these roses date back to the Middle Ages. Divided into categories

Rosa 'American Pillar'

Rosa 'Blanc Double de Coubert'

called gallica, alba, centifolia, damask, and moss, these roses are wonderfully scented. Their soft colors combine well with foxglove (*Digitalis* species) and other cottage-garden flowers. A new group of English roses bred by David Austin maintains the old-fashioned shape, but the plants flower throughout the summer.

The introduction to Europe of the continuous-flowering China rose at the end of the eighteenth century began the era of modern roses. First came the hybrid perpetuals with great, lush, heavily scented flowers on big bushes. Although still worth growing, they have been superseded by the modern hybrid teas and floribundas. The genes they inherited from the China rose and tea rose, both native to the temperate Far East, make these modern roses susceptible to frost in the North.

The best way to choose a modern bedding rose is to visit an extensive local rose garden. While most of the wild shrub roses and their descendants are hardy to Zone 4, many big-flowered or cluster-flowered bedding roses need winter protection in Zone 6 and below. It is worth searching for the hardier types that do not need the laborsome chore of tying up and mulching each fall. Some of these, such as the pink 'Country Dancer', are intermediate between the hybrid teas and the shrub roses.

Climbing roses range from the tender, thornless *R. banksiae,* which bears pale yellow flowers in late spring and is suitable only for warm-winter gardens, to hardy ramblers such as the single pink 'American Pillar' and the soft blush 'New Dawn'. Climbing roses can be grown on pergolas, walls, or even trained to scramble through a tree. Many climbers will remain bushlike, however, in cold climates.

Miniature roses have become popular for small gardens or raised beds. Although the open flowers are often only slightly bigger than a quarter, they retain the form of perfect tea roses and are available in a full range of colors.

Hybrid garden roses can be grown in any ordinary soil, as long as they receive sufficient food and water to maintain flowering throughout the season. Full sun is essential. The species roses are easier to grow, since they accept the conditions shared by other flowering shrubs.

Rosmarinus officinalis

Rudbeckia hirta

Rosmarinus officinalis

Rosemary

A major disappointment for those living in Zone 7 or colder climates is that rosemary cannot grow outdoors year round. This means that a big, potted rosemary bush put out on the terrace, patio, or deck in summer has to be brought into a cool room for the winter.

Any extra effort is worthwhile, however. Rosemary is one of the classic shrubs of the Mediterranean, growing in Portugal and Spain right around the Mediterranean Sea on hot, rocky hillsides. Old, 6-foot-high plants have low, twisted trunks and a mass of twiggy growth clothed with narrow, inch-long leaves. In late winter or early spring the plant is covered with

small gray-blue flowers. All parts are intensely aromatic and are used medicinally, in cooking, and in making perfume.

A number of variants have been collected and are available from specialist nurseries. There are forms with prostrate or vertical habits and types with pale pink or more intensely blue flowers. All need conditions that approximate those of their native habitat: perfect drainage, full sun, and—in areas close to their limit—protection from winter winds. In warm gardens rosemary makes a delightful, fragrant low hedge.

Rudbeckia species

Coneflower, black-eyed-susan

Of the twenty-five or so species of *Rudbeckia,* all of them North American, two have become favorite garden plants invaluable for their late-summer flower display in mixed herbaceous borders and thin orchard grass. They are beautiful both individually and in masses.

The flower shape is distinctive: a hard cone of tiny, deep purple florets make up the eye, surrounded by drooping petals. These are typically a warm orange-yellow but selections, notably the gloriosa daisy strains of *R. hirta,* are banded with warm brown and bronze. The plants are usually about 2 feet high with strong, wiry stems standing above a rosette of hairy leaves. *R. hirta* can behave as an annual or biennial, but it is likely to remain

Rudbeckia hirta 'Rustic Colors'

Ruta graveolens

perennial in the garden if divided and replanted every other year. Gloriosa daisies can be started just as easily each year from seeds sown indoors.

R. fulgida is a more definite perennial. Its brilliant cultivar 'Goldsturm' is used with ornamental grasses along Independence Avenue in Washington, D.C.

Black-eyed-susan is hardy to Zone 3 in good garden soil in full sun or half shade.

Ruta graveolens

Rue

Although there are about forty wild species of *Ruta* around the Mediterranean into western Asia, only *R. graveolens* is commonly grown. It has been an inhabitant of herb gardens for centuries—known as the herb-of-grace or even the herb-of-grace-of-Sundays. These seem like overly complimentary names for a plant with an unpleasant, bitter scent and the ability to cause a rash on sensitive skin, especially in sunny weather.

As an ornamental, however, rue has much to offer. It makes a subshrub up to 3 feet tall with twiggy branches clothed in smooth, fernlike, blue-gray leaves. In summer, strange small yellow flowers glint in the sun. The subsequent seedheads are quite attractive.

Rue makes a good low hedge in its usual form. Somewhat dwarfer and seldom flowering—not much of a loss—is 'Jackman's Blue'. Its much bluer foliage looks lovely with pale yellow-flowering plants.

Perfect drainage and full sun enable rue to survive to Zone 6, but not much beyond.

Salvia farinacea 'White Porcelain'

Salvia officinalis 'Purpurascens Variegata'

Salvia species

Sage

This huge genus of some seven hundred species is concentrated in Central and South America, around the Mediterranean, and in the steppes of the Soviet Union. *Salvia* offers a remarkable diversity of fine species for gardeners in Zones 9 and 10, where the shrubby Mexican sages, which can only be grown as potted plants or summer annuals in colder climates, flourish outdoors year after year. As lavender (*Lavandula* species) and mint relatives, they are in most cases noticeably aromatic. Names like pineapple-sage and blackcurrant-sage give clues to their scents.

The most familiar sage is *S. officinalis,* a Mediterranean flavoring herb whose use dates back to classical times. A low, spreading shrub with persistent gray leaves, it has spikes of hooded, early-summer flowers. Although this herb garden plant is ornamental and hardy to Zone 5 with some protection, it has three foliage variants that are less hardy but should be tried wherever they can be grown. 'Purpurascens', which has marvelous soft purple leaves and a wide billowing habit, blooms prodigiously. 'Icterina', virtually nonflowering, is a golden-variegated type that is equally robust. The delicate 'Tricolor' has marbled leaves of pink, gray-green, and cream. None of these is for cold areas—they are marginal in

Zone 6. All need good garden soil and perfect drainage in full sun.

S. sclarea is the aromatic clary from southeastern Europe. Usually biennial, it forms a clump of wide, hairy leaves the first year. In its second summer it produces a 3-foot-high mass of pale blue, white-hooded flowers. Even if it doesn't survive a second summer, seedlings invariably appear. *S. sclarea* var. *turkestanica* is an even more spectacular plant.

S. argentea, silver sage, is similar in habit. It has a rosette of white, felt-like leaves below white flowers. Although a couple of feet high in flower, it deserves a front-row position so that the foliage can be enjoyed. Easier to use is *S. × superba,* a hybrid of European origin that produces a great heap of strong

Santolina chamaecyparissus

Salvia splendens

purple flowers in midsummer. It reaches 4 feet if held up with a circle of twigs; the stems push through this and eventually cover it.

These perennial sages all prefer conditions similar to those enjoyed by their shrubby relatives. Two more sages, although subshrubs, are usually grown as tender annuals. These are the mealy sage, *S. farinacea,* which has 2-foot-high, white stems topped with blue flowers, and the ubiquitous scarlet sage, *S. splendens.* The brilliance of the latter may be difficult to combine in the garden, but it is wonderfully eye-catching. Purple, pink, and off-white cultivars are no improvement.

Santolina chamaecyparissus

Lavender-cotton

There are a half-dozen species and a few cultivars of these invaluable silver-leaved shrublets. All are ideal for low hedges, for formalizing parterre patterns, or for tumbling over dry walls.

Lavender-cotton is a typical plant of Mediterranean hillsides. In the garden it thrives in full sun and in soil with perfect drainage. Cold, wet winter soil spells death.

The plants have finely divided, whitish gray leaves. Unpruned they reach a couple of feet high but flop outward to twice that, so the usual practice is to keep them tidy by occasional clipping. This is always necessary in the North, where frost-damaged tips or whole branches must be removed. When

grown as a formal hedge, it is wise to shear the plants—against all normal practice—just before flowering. The bright yellow, buttonlike daisies are not a great addition and their weight causes the bushes to flop outward.

In informal situations flowering can be desirable, especially in forms with cream-colored blossoms such as 'Bowles Variety'. In Zone 6 lavender-cotton is erratically hardy.

Saponaria ocymoides

Saxifraga umbrosa 'London Pride'

Saponaria species

Saponaria

The most common of the thirty or so species of these Old World plants is *Saponaria officinalis,* soapwort or bouncing-bet. It is a pleasant, pink-flowering 2-footer, rather like phlox (*Phlox* species). The plant's claim to fame is its soap-producing ability, and it is still used to clean especially delicate or historic fabrics. Unfortunately, bouncing-bet is a dreadful colonizer in the garden and needs careful watching.

A better garden plant is *S. ocymoides.* This southern European makes a wide, foot-high dome of narrow gray-green leaves that are completely hidden under a sheet of penny-sized flowers in June. The typical color is rose-pink, but paler and darker forms are also available.

Saponaria associates well with pinks and border carnations (*Dianthus* species) in front of old-fashioned roses (*Rosa* species). With a winter snow cover it is hardy to Zone 3.

Saxifraga umbrosa

Saxifrage, London-pride

It may be surprising that with some three hundred wild species of saxifrage strewn mainly around the Northern Hemisphere, only one is listed here. The reason is that so many of those worth cultivating are from the high mountain ranges of Europe and the Himalayas and therefore need very special alpine rock garden care.

By comparison *Saxifraga umbrosa* is an easy-to-please evergreen. As the name London-pride indicates, it is often seen in that city edging paths of little front-garden flower beds. Its 4-inch-wide rosettes of stiff, waved leaves cluster together into a foot-wide clump. In April or

Scabiosa caucasica 'David Wilkie'

Scabiosa caucasica 'Perfecta'

May each rosette puts up a foot-high pink stem that bursts into a cloud of tiny white pink-spotted flowers. Nothing could be more delicate.

As a mountainside plant of Europe, London-pride can take a lot of frost but does not tolerate drying winter winds. It is most successful in the Northwest in any soil that neither remains wet nor dries out completely. Some midday shade is helpful in hot areas.

Scabiosa species

Pincushion-flower, mourning-bride

Although some of the eighty or so species of *scabiosa* come from as far afield as Japan and South Africa, those in cultivation are native to the Mediterranean or Asia Minor. The common name refers to the mass of stamens that look like pins stuck in a dome-shaped cushion. The best-known, *S. caucasica,* is valuable as a cut flower and as a border plant. From clumps of pale green, fingered leaves, strong 2-foot stems arise carrying handsome 3-inch-wide flowers. The fringed petals are typically a clear sky blue, but lavender-blue and white forms are also available. The show begins in June and continues into September as long as the soil is kept moist but not wet. One of the longest-blooming perennials, pincushion-flower is hardy to Zone 5 and even beyond with the usual help of snow or mulch.

A close relative is the annual *S. atropurpurea,* also known as mourning-bride. The name refers to the dusky purple color. Lighter shades through most of the pinks to white also occur in mixed seed packets. Mourning-bride has become naturalized in California. Elsewhere, sow it indoors and plant it outside later, or sow seeds directly in the ground after the soil has warmed up in spring.

Scilla siberica

Schizanthus pinnatus

Schizanthus pinnatus

Butterfly-flower,
poor-man's-orchid

The first of the common names of
this lovely annual is pleasantly descriptive. The second is positively
insulting to a plant that is far more
beautiful than many true orchids.
It is also far easier to grow, given
suitable conditions.

One of ten or so species of *Schizanthus,* all of them native to Chile,
butterfly-flower needs cool but frost-
free conditions, so it is frequently
grown as a winter annual in the
warmest gardens. Sown in August
or September, the delicate seedlings
develop a mass of pale, fernlike
foliage ending in a spike crowded

with flat flowers resembling an
exotic butterfly sunning its wings.
Almost all colors (except true-blue
and clear yellow) occur in solid
shades or in marvelous combinations. In cold-winter climates
butterfly-flower can be treated,
although with less success, as
a summer annual.

Distinctive strains vary from 1 to
4 feet in height. Regular feeding
and tip-pinching result in huge
domed plants that flower for weeks
on end.

Scilla siberica

Siberian squill

Although there are other, more exotic representatives of the eighty or
so species of *Scilla* grown in warm
areas, none is more beautiful or
more useful than this bright little
spring beauty.

The bulbs, surprisingly large for so
small a plant, should be planted
as soon as they are available in autumn (this is seldom before the end
of September). Plant them 3 or
4 inches deep to fill pockets in a
rock garden or to naturalize under
shrubs or deciduous trees. As long
as competition is not great, they
will divide as well as reseed themselves until a complete carpet of
squill develops.

In March or April, the planting
looks like a layer of clear blue sky
laid on the ground. Three or four

Sedum spectabile

Sedum spectabile 'Autumn Joy'

nodding, wide-open, bell-shaped flowers are carried on each 4-inch-high stem. At its best, the memorable effect lasts only a couple of weeks before the rich green leaves take over as ground cover.

By the end of June, shaded out by the canopy above, the leaves yellow and die and the bulbs go to rest. White and pink cultivars cannot compare with the original blue-flowering plant from the steppes of the Soviet Union. It is hardy to Zone 2.

Sedum species

Stonecrop

Most of the six hundred or so species of *Sedum,* spread around the Northern Hemisphere and the mountains of the tropics, are fleshy and succulent. This is one way in which plants adapt to dry conditions. Succulents store water in their leaves and stems (cacti are the most effective at this), as camels do in their humps.

It is surprising to find a number of stonecrops that enjoy good garden soil and cultivation without losing their typical habit. Several of the dwarf species, such as *S. acre* and *S. anglicum,* make useful, if weedy, ground cover. *S. spurium* and others are good rock garden plants.

The big border species are extremely valuable. A good example of this is *S. spectabile* (the species name is pronounced with four

syllables), which is native to Korea and eastern China. Even its roots are fleshy—almost tuberous. Clumps overwinter with succulent leaf rosettes at ground level like tiny artichokes. From late spring to early fall they slowly extend up and out, eventually reaching about 1½ feet in height and width. The smooth, gray-green leaves make a fine foil for other plants early in the season. The leaves then provide a backdrop for the plant's own flat heads of pink, starry flowers in September. These open in time for the late summer hatch of butterflies, which find them irresistible.

Cultivars with more vivid flowers, such as 'Meteor' and 'September Glow', are worth searching out. A variegated form has attractive, bright green and cream leaves throughout summer, but it flowers

Senecio cineraria

Senecio greyi

poorly. The hybrid 'Autumn Joy' is perhaps the best of all. Two feet high, its robust clumps carry wide flower heads that open rich pink and then turn shades of bronze and copper. The effect lasts for many weeks. Even when killed by hard frost, the plant's shape and texture remain attractive throughout winter, holding snow and frost. It is best not to cut down this plant in the conventional frenzy of fall tidiness, but to leave it until spring.

S. maximum has foliage much like that of *S. spectabile,* but its star-shaped flowers are yellow. It is best in its attractive purple-leaved form 'Atropurpureum'.

All these big stonecrops need full sun and well-drained soil. They are hardy to Zone 4 and probably beyond with snow cover or mulch.

Senecio species

Senecio, dusty-miller

With between two to three thousand species throughout the world, *Senecio* is one of the biggest genera in the plant kingdom. They range from the common groundsel weed to giant plants growing on Mount Kilimanjaro. Two valuable, silver-leaved representatives are described here.

S. cineraria (the florist's potted cineraria is another species, *S.* × *hybridus*) is the dusty-miller that grows wild in rock crevices on the shores of the Mediterranean. It has become naturalized in similar spots on the West Coast. One of the most valuable gray-leaved plants, it grows from a woody base to 1 to 2 feet high. The divided, feltlike leaves are intensely silver-gray and a marvelous foil for white flowers

or the brilliant blooms of scarlet sage (*Salvia splendens*).

Dusty-miller is reliably hardy only to Zone 8. In colder areas it is usually grown as an annual for its foliage and planted outside in full sun and well-drained soil when all frosts are over. Its sprays of yellow daisies resembling those of a large groundsel are best removed.

S. greyi is a 3-foot-high shrub from New Zealand. It has silver-gray leaves, gray stems, and undistinguished yellow flowers. A fine foliage plant, it contrasts well with brightly colored flowers. It is unlikely to survive much below Zone 8 and it needs well-drained soil in full sun and regular pruning to keep it in shape. 'Sunshine' is a good garden cultivar.

Sidalcea malviflora

Sisyrinchium striatum

Sidalcea malviflora

Checkerbloom

There are a couple dozen species of *Sidalcea,* all of them native to the western and southwestern United States. As muskmallow (*Malva* species) relatives, they all share the typical flower pattern of the family—a bowl of satiny petals and a forward-thrusting mass of stamens dusted with yellow pollen. The many cultivars are derived mainly from *S. malviflora,* which grows wild in Oregon south to Baja California.

Checkerbloom resembles a miniature hollyhock (*Alcea rosea*). A clump of roundish, pleated leaves puts up narrow spires of flowers in July and August. The flower color of the many cultivars ranges through all the pinks to dusky mauve and purple. The clear pinks are especially lovely. Height varies from 2½ to 4 feet.

As must be expected of California natives, its hardiness leaves something to be desired in colder climates. In Zone 6 checkerbloom overwinters satisfactorily if snow cover comes early enough to act as a thermal blanket. Otherwise, a loose mulch is essential. The mulch must not be removed too soon or cold spring winds may dry out any growth that is just hanging on. Good drainage is also essential, since the rather woody rootstock rots easily.

Sisyrinchium striatum

Sisyrinchium

There are about seventy species of these charming iris relatives, all of them native to the Western Hemisphere. They include blue-eyed grass and golden-eyed grass, little plants that out of bloom are almost indistinguishable from the grass in which they are growing.

The Chilean *Sisyrinchium striatum* is very different. Its clumps are made up of a number of fans of narrow leaves, rather like an evergreen flag iris (*I. pseudacorus*). From each fan grows a 2-foot-high stem with leafy bracts. Pushing out from the stem and making a gentle show in early spring are pale yellow starry flowers, faintly penciled with purple.

It is not a plant for cold-winter areas. Preferring the mild West Coast, it is miserable below Zone 8. In moist soil sisyrinchium reseeds

Solidago 'Goldstrohl'

itself, although it never becomes a pest. Encourage young plants to replace clumps that have flowered, fallen open, and become untidy. Any good garden soil in full sun is suitable.

An elegant variegated form, 'Variegatum' ('Aunt May'), is worth searching out. Its leaves and bracts are vertically striped with gold. Divide sisyrinchium to get new plants; seedlings revert to the typical green.

Solidago species

Goldenrod

One of the great jokes for North Americans visiting the English gardens that they have read so much about is to see wonderful clumps of yellow flowers that turn out to be goldenrod, the dreaded weed so often mistakenly blamed for causing hay fever.

Even in England some goldenrods are aggressive and not plants for the garden. Some—*Solidago canadensis,* for example—look splendid on railway embankments, where they have gone wild, and although fine plants in a moist meadow they are not suitable for the garden. But with a total of some one hundred and thirty species, most of them North American natives, there are several good choices.

The delicate wreath-goldenrod, *S. caesia,* and *S. nemoralis* are both excellent for shady spots in which little else grows during September and into the fall. There are more sophisticated hybrids such as 'Goldenmosa', which is only 3 feet high and flowers in July and August. None of these plants are particular about soil, and all are hardy to Zone 3 and possibly beyond.

Stachys byzantina

Stokesia laevis

Stachys byzantina

Lamb's-ears, flannel-feet

Sometimes still listed as *Stachys olympica,* this is one of the most valuable of all herbaceous plants. One of three hundred or so species of *Stachys,* lamb's-ears is from Turkey and other parts of south-western Asia. It is hardy, under snow, to Zone 4 and perhaps beyond with protection.

Long cultivated in Europe, it is as-sociated with the traditional En-glish cottage garden. Both common names refer to the long, oval leaves with their silvery, soft, densely woolly covering. In the warm Med-iterranean climate of California the leaves are present throughout the year. In colder areas they die back in response to hard frost—leaving a sort of felt of dried leaves over the horizontal rhizomes (underground stems) by which the plant later extends its clumps.

When spring arrives, new growth pushes through and soon covers the ground. In June, 2-foot-high furry stems arise with tiny purple hooded flowers peering out. 'Silver Carpet', a nonflowering form, misses this attractive stage but is a better ground cover.

A plant for full sun in most soils, lamb's-ears also takes deciduous tree shade if the branches are not too low. In such a location, it pairs wonderfully with a permanent planting of the early tulips *Tulipa kaufmanniana* or *T. fosterana.* The bulb display is almost over when the lamb's-ears starts to grow. By the time the silver leaves have matured, the yellowing tulip foliage can be pulled out and a quiet, weed-free summer scene is in place.

Stokesia laevis

Stokes'-aster

This sole representative of its genus is native to the southeastern United States from South Carolina into Florida. It is hardy enough in Zone 5 with the usual winter mulch, if snow does not do the job naturally.

A useful front-of-the-border plant, Stokes'-aster forms a 1½-foot clump of narrow, semi-evergreen leaves. Beginning in early July, flowers up to 4 inches across bloom for many weeks. They resemble huge, flat cornflowers (*Centaurea* species) or, more exactly, big dan-delions. (This may sound uncompli-mentary, but it is dandelion's weediness, not its flowers, that is despised.)

The typical color is blue, shading to cream in the center. There are also lavender cultivars darkening to purple, and a white cultivar. A batch raised from a packet of seeds

Tagetes patula 'Cinnabar'

Tagetes erecta

will probably produce quite a range, but the seedlings can be grouped by color. Blue Stokes'-aster looks particularly good with pale yellow or cream flowers such as yarrow (*Achillea* 'Moonshine') and evening-primrose (*Oenothera missouriensis*). Apart from excellent drainage, Stokes'-aster needs rich soil to build up decent plants. If starved, the plant looks miserable but refuses to die.

This daisy, like most others, requires full sun. Give it plenty of room, because it does poorly when crowded by other robust plants in the border.

Tagetes species

Marigold

Summer gardens would be vastly different and dull places without the brilliance of marigolds. There are about thirty species of *Tagetes,* most of them Mexican, and innumerable cultivars.

T. erecta (erroneously called African marigold) is the tallest and has the biggest flowers. With the typically scented and divided marigold foliage, the plants reach 3 feet or more in height. Their great pompom flowers provide a season-long display. Although glow-in-the-dark oranges are offered, the pale citron and cream shades are much easier to use. They are invaluable for filling unexpected gaps in the perennial border.

T. patula is the base for the so-called French marigolds, which vary in height from 6 inches to a foot or so. They are covered with

single or double flowers in shades of yellow, orange, or bronze. Don't plant them within sight of scarlet sage (*Salvia splendens*), because the colors clash miserably.

As tender annuals, marigolds should be sown indoors and planted outside only after all danger of a late frost has passed. Good garden soil and full sun are required.

Tanacetum vulgare var. *crispum*

Thalictrum aquilegifolium

Tanacetum vulgare

Tansy

The old herb-garden tansy, native to Europe and Asia, is widely naturalized across North America. Unneeded clumps thrown out over the garden fence continue to grow as if nothing had occurred. It is obviously not a plant for a choice spot, in spite of aromatic foliage on 3-foot-high stems and pleasant heads of golden, buttonlike flowers.

Much more desirable, if only marginally less aggressive, is *Tanacetum vulgare* var. *crispum* (fern-leaf tansy). Its rich green leaves are luxuriant, divided, and wonderfully waved. Just as aromatic as the species, its leaves are ideal for drying and adding to potpourri. The flowers contribute little. A finer effect is obtained if fern-leaf tansy is considered a foliage plant and the flower heads pinched off as they appear. As a foliage plant it associates well with other herbs with decorative leaves, creating a living bed of potpourri. Such plants include green and purple fennel (*Foeniculum vulgare*); variegated apple-mint (*Mentha suaveolens*) and ginger-mint (*Mentha × gentilis*), both grown in large plastic flowerpots with the bottoms removed and sunk to the rim; golden lemon balm (*Melissa officinalis*); and golden marjoram (*Origanum* species).

Almost any soil will do, but provide a plentiful supply of moisture to ensure summer lushness. This is easier to arrange in half or even three-quarters shade, which tansy accepts. It is hardy to Zone 3 and perhaps beyond.

Thalictrum species

Meadowrue

The lovely, native North American meadowrues found in moist meadows are representative of one hundred or so species of *Thalictrum,* strewn mainly around the north temperate world. They are just as worthy of cultivation as the exotics, but the foreign species always seem to be the ones offered in the nursery catalogs.

Meadowrue is a buttercup relative, but it is wind-pollinated and thus never needed to develop spectacular petals to attract insects. Its beauty comes from the mass of stamens and the airy grace of the flower heads. Its foliage, which resembles that of columbines (*Aquilegia* species), is delightful and makes a fine base for the flower spikes. Most

Thalictrum speciosissimum

Thunbergia alata

species sold in North America are hardy to Zone 4. They enjoy sun or up to half shade in good, moist garden soil.

T. aquilegifolium is typical of the group. Native to Europe and Asia, it is about 3 feet high, slowly building up its clump of smooth, pale green, lacy foliage, above which bloom dense, fluffy flower heads. The typical color is rich lilac, but paler and darker and even white variations occur. Since the seedheads are attractive, do not deadhead the plant after it flowers.

T. dipterocarpum, from western China, deserves a winter mulch in areas on the edge of its hardiness range. Its elegant foliage is the foundation of 5-foot-high stems with a wide branching pattern, each twig ending in a mass of delicately poised flowers. These have purple sepals and a hanging cluster of cream stamens. There is a white

cultivar, 'Album', and the charming 'Hewitt's Double', which has tiny double flowers with an abundance of sepals and no stamens. This plant enjoys woodland-edge conditions: moist, leafy soil, half shade, and wind protection.

T. rochebrunianum, from Japan, is similar and under ideal conditions can grow even taller. Both of these species may need a few low stakes to keep the towering stems in place. Almost as tall is *T. speciosissimum,* a Mediterranean with wonderful blue-green foliage and fluffy heads of cool lemon yellow. Easy to grow, it looks particularly good with true-blue delphinium (*Delphinium* cultivars).

Thunbergia alata

Black-eyed-susan-vine

Plant-conscious visitors to the African tropics become well aware of this genus: There are about one hundred species—mainly spectacular climbers—with trumpet flowers in a range of colors. *Thunbergia alata,* although a perennial, is so easy to grow as an annual that it has become a common addition to summer gardens.

From early spring-sown seeds started indoors and planted outside after all danger of frost has passed, it twines rapidly up whatever support it finds. Black-eyed-susan-vine soon reaches 6 feet or more. The plant is especially attractive climbing up and through a thin shrub such as mockorange (*Philadelphus* species), giving the shrub a second season of unexpected interest. This is the same sort of effect created by morning glory (*Ipomoea* species),

Tithonia rotundifolia

another climber with which black-eyed-susan-vine looks splendid.

The trumpet-shaped flowers are clear orange with a jet black center—hence the common name black-eyed-susan-vine. A twig or pencil pushed gently into the flower's throat triggers the pollination mechanism: a hinged stigma suddenly appears.

The plant produces flowers for many weeks if given full sun, ample moisture, and a leafy soil. Because of its rapid growth and the speed with which it comes to flower, black-eyed-susan-vine is also useful when sown late and allowed to climb up the supports left over from sweet peas (*Lathyrus* species), which seldom last beyond mid-July. This sequential planting extends the color show in a garden wonderfully.

Tithonia rotundifolia

Mexican sunflower

This is among the most robust of summer annuals. One of a dozen or so fine daisies from Mexico and Central America, it is an annual species that can reach 6 feet high in a season.

Sow seed indoors a couple of months before the expected date of the last frost, and plant the seedlings outside as soon as the soil is warm enough. If the season is late and the plants are ready to go outdoors, it is wise to move them into pots two sizes larger to maintain growth. Lost momentum is difficult to recover, and the plants flower miserably at half their normal size.

A group of five seedlings planted 18 inches apart soon makes a huge clump with 3-inch, brilliant orange-red daisies. Despite the strong color, Mexican sunflower never looks brash. It associates exceptionally well with purple-leaved cannas (*Canna* × *generalis*). Together they create height and bulk. This is invaluable in new gardens and those depending too much on conventional, dwarf summer annuals.

Mexican sunflower enjoys full sun and good garden soil with ample summer moisture. Sadly, it turns to mush at the first breath of fall frost. This limits its use in the Northeast, where early September frosts may occur.

Tradescantia × andersoniana

Torenia fournieri

Torenia fournieri

Wishbone-flower, blue-wings

This charming foxglove (*Digitalis* species) relative is native to southeast Asia. For years it has been a useful container plant for spring displays indoors. Now it often appears on seed lists for outdoor color in hot-summer climates. It is also recommended for Florida gardens to replace pansies, which cannot take southern heat.

Wishbone-flower is generally sown indoors with the usual range of annuals, transplanted into individual pots, and then planted outside only after the soil has warmed up. It needs loose, moist soil in at least half shade. Liberally fed, the foot-high domes of foliage become covered with strange flowers shaped like the helmets of ancient Greek warriors. The blossoms are various shades of blue and each has a yellow throat. A white form with a yellow blotch is not an improvement and neither is the selection labeled 'Compacta', since wishbone-flower is dwarf enough already.

Tradescantia × andersoniana

Spiderwort, Moses-in-the-bullrushes

It is unlikely that the spiderwort offered in nursery catalogs as *Tradescantia virginiana* is really spiderwort. Those grown in gardens are cultivars of a complicated hybrid group better called *T. × andersoniana*. It does not much matter, since the plants referred to are useful perennials with a highly distinctive pattern of foliage and flower. Derived from species native to the eastern United States, the cultivars enjoy moist soil and are hardy to Zone 4 or beyond.

Spiderwort makes tight clumps of vertical, fleshy stems covered with wide-angled, narrow leaves that are purplish underneath. Clustered

Tricyrtis hirta

Tricyrtis hirta

among the upper leaves are three-petaled flowers, each with a bright gleam of golden stamens, which open in a long succession from July until September.

Flower color varies from white through all the blues to deep burgundy. The first couple of months of tidy growth looks splendid against the contrasting leaves of winter-begonia (*Bergenia* species), but plants are apt to flop forward unless some support is given. Division of the clumps every three years counteracts this tendency, as does the choice of the dwarfer forms.

Tricyrtis species

Toadlily

The dozen or so species of these rather strange lily relatives from the Himalayan foothills to Japan and Taiwan give valuable late-season flower interest to a shady garden area that otherwise would only have color in spring. Toadlily is perfect for a moist, leafy soil where wakerobin (*Trillium* species) has long since passed its season.

Initial growth starts early, with the formation of low rosettes of broad, shining, pointed leaves. Each year it seems as if the plant is stuck at this stage, but eventually wiry stems with wide-spaced oval leaves reach a height of 2 feet, or even more in moist weather. The terminal spray of flowers begins to open in mid-September and continues

until frost. The flowers are like small, upward-facing lilies (*Lilium* species) with a distinctive triple stigma standing above the petals.

Tricyrtis hirta is the species most likely to be available. Its white flowers are heavily marbled with lilac. Presumably, the spots brought about the toadlily name, which belies the plant's elegance. Despite the usually pessimistic recommendations, it is hardy to Zone 5 with a mulch.

Other species should be tried when found; all are elegant and unusual. They look especially good with the smaller, variegated plantain-lilies (*Hosta* species). The bigger versions may crowd out the toadlily.

Trillium grandiflorum

Trollius europaeus

Trillium species

Wakerobin

There is probably no North American plant of such wide distribution (it is native from Quebec to South Carolina) that is so universally admired. One of the supreme wild beauties of the plant world, wakerobin has no vices in cultivation.

There are about thirty species of *Trillium,* mainly North American woodlanders, although some occur in Japan and the Himalayas. All share the fascinating pattern that the genus name implies: The leaves and flower parts occur in an invariable sequence of threes.

The flower of *T. grandiflorum* can be 4 inches across. It opens pure white, and as it ages turns palest

rose. A lovely double form with flowers like a formal camellia is sometimes available.

In addition to the white wakerobin, other North American species with yellow, greenish, or blood red flowers are also very desirable garden plants. All require moist, leafy soil. Like most other spring-flowering woodlanders, they also need dappled shade at the start of the growing season and any amount of shade afterward. Plants grow to Zone 3 and probably beyond.

Trollius species

Globeflower

There are a couple dozen species of *Trollius* found around the northern temperate world. They are rather grand buttercups with basal clumps of deeply divided leaves and usually tall stems of cup-shaped flowers in shades of rich yellow and orange. Since most are plants of marshy areas, in the garden they depend on moist soil in summer. Some midday shade helps prevent plants from drying out and prolongs the flower display.

T. europaeus is widely distributed in the higher elevations of Europe, and it also occurs wild in England's Lake District. In spring its 2-foot-high stems carry lemon yellow flowers that curve inward. Worthy cultivars include 'Superbus' and 'Grandiflorus'. It is also

Trollius ledebourii

Tropaeolum majus

a parent, along with *T. chinensis* (itself worth growing) of some useful hybrids.

T. ledebourii, an Asian species, is a 3-foot-tall plant. In June it produces orange, bowl-shaped flowers with dark centers. Not all plants sold under this name actually belong to this species.

Any named forms of *Trollius* are well worth snapping up. They are safe under mulch to Zone 4.

Tropaeolum species

Nasturtium

Adding nasturtium flowers and leaves to dishes at fashionable restaurants may seem novel, but these plants have long been used as edibles. In fact, *nasturtium* is the Latin name for watercress—and that's what these plants taste like.

Aside from its culinary use, nasturtium is a splendid garden plant. *Tropaeolum majus* is a rapidly growing scrambler that climbs by its twisting leafstalks, in the same way that virgin's-bower (*Clematis* species) does. Its leaves are fleshy, smooth, and almost circular. From the leaf joints, long-spurred flowers bloom in a dazzling array of hot colors. Dwarf, nonclimbing forms and those with fully double flowers are also available. Seeds can be started indoors or sown directly in the ground, although the plant is as sensitive to frost as balsam (*Impatiens* species).

Gardeners in warm-winter areas should consider the perennial nasturtiums, including *T. polyphyllum* and *T. tuberosum. T. speciosum,* the Chilean flameflower, is particularly suited to the Northwest. Acid-loving, it is ideal for scrambling unchecked through evergreen shrubs.

Tulipa greigii

Tulipa tarda

Tulipa species

Tulip

Along with daffodils, tulips provide the major display in the spring garden. The flowers are available in every conceivable color and combination of colors from white to almost black. Only true-blue is lacking. The hundred or so species of *Tulipa* are native from Western Europe to the Himalayas with heavy concentration in the bulb-rich areas of Asia Minor to Iran. There, the arid hillsides are brilliant with tulips during a short and sudden spring.

Species vary from tiny plants no bigger than a crocus (*Crocus* species) to enormous flowers—for example, *T. fosterana,* whose flaunting scarlet petals open to blooms almost a foot across. With such diversity it is obvious that there is a tulip for almost every garden.

A major misconception is that tulips have to be lifted each year after blooming. Only in formal bedding schemes, where rigidly straight stems of identical height are required, is it necessary to consider tulips as annual plants. Elsewhere they should be treated as the perennials they are.

Tulips are remarkably tolerant of poor soil but cannot abide soil that remains wet. Although sun is essential at flowering time, the subsequent shade of a deciduous tree or shrub is perfectly acceptable. By then the tulip bulbs will have stored enough energy for next year's flowers.

As a perennial, tulip needs deep planting. Smaller species should be planted so that the top of the bulb is 4 inches deep, and big species and hybrids so that the top is at least 6 inches down. (In the wild, bulbs are often twice as deep as is recommended for garden planting.) Because the bulbs lie at such depths, summer annuals can be planted above them as the tulip foliage declines. This does not damage the tulips and the annuals are not slowed down noticeably.

In cold-winter areas, plant tulip bulbs by early October so that root growth can begin before the ground freezes. A loose compost mulch applied after planting may help extend the rooting time. However, mulch also keeps rodents warm and they are only too delighted to dine

Tulipa 'Demeter'

Tulipa 'Apricot'

on the bulbs while they hide. In mild-winter climates bulbs can be planted until November.

The bulb catalogs show the range of tulips that will bloom from as early as February to as late as June. The first to flower are the *T. kaufmanniana* hybrids. These are the waterlily tulips that bloom cream yellow with red markings outside and yellow in the center. Soon the scarlet-flowering *T. fosterana* and *T. greigii* follow, the latter with purple-striped leaves. Hybrids between these two species are now available in many colors.

Because they seldom grow above a foot high, these tulips are excellent in windy spots.

Many of the dwarf species are well worth growing. Representative of these is *T. tarda* from Turkestan. On each stalk bloom several star-shaped flowers with white tips and a yellow center. In March or April they are clustered down among the shiny leaves.

Next comes the parade of tall single and double hybrid tulips. Among them are Mendel tulips and Darwin hybrids, lily-flowered types, striped Rembrandts, peony-flowered varieties, and parrot tulips. With effective use of tulips, no garden need have a dull spring.

Tulips have a number of distinct roles. The dwarf species are excellent rock garden plants, emerging from narrow crevices as they do in their native habitats and requiring no attention once established. Dwarf hybrids with large flowers

are too flamboyant for rock gardens, but are welcome in a permanent bedding scheme when planted in combination with later-maturing ornamentals such as lamb's-ears (*Stachys byzantina*). The tall tulips are ideal planted in clusters in the herbaceous border, giving color weeks earlier than would otherwise be possible. Deep planting ensures that they last for years.

In warm Zone 9 and 10 areas, most tulips do not grow well. There are species tulips adapted to these regions that perform much better, but most tulips have a chilling requirement that is not met in mild winter climates. In these areas it is best to buy prechilled bulbs, or chill the bulbs yourself on the bottom shelf of your refrigerator for 4 to 6 weeks before planting. Prechilled bulbs planted in warm climates should be treated as annuals.

Verbascum bombyciferum

Verbena bonariensis

Verbascum species

Mullein

Of the two hundred and fifty or so of these foxglove (*Digitalis* species) relatives several are worthwhile and statuesque garden plants. Their usual combination of grayish leaves and pale yellow flowers has a cooling effect, especially in the evening when they seem to stand out dramatically from other plants in the border.

The biennial *V. phlomoides,* typical of the genus, forms a gray-green rosette of feltlike leaves during the first year. It sends up a 4-foot-high stem of yellow flowers the following year. The blossoms on the spike open erratically over a long period, and the whole plant finally dies by September. It is wise to leave it in

place to set and scatter its own seeds. You can move the seedlings that appear the following year to desired spots.

Even grander is *V. bombyciferum.* It has a similar growth pattern but is more spectacular, with a dense, white, furry covering even on the flower spike.

Mullein is easy to grow in a well-drained, sunny spot. It should overwinter well under snow, to Zone 4. Several perennial species, both dwarf and tall, are also sometimes offered and are worth trying.

Verbena species

Verbena, vervain

Although there are a number of native North American species, most of the brightest verbenas for the garden are from warm climates and so are not usually reliable perennials in all regions. Still, they are well worth trying to protect in colder climates or grow as annuals.

Verbena rigida (still often listed as *V. venosa*) has long been a valuable summer bedding plant. Native to Argentina and Brazil, it has naturalized in parts of the southern United States. From underground runners it sends up stiff, 18-inch-high stems with bristly, narrow leaves and topped with heads of tiny, royal purple flowers. The show is continuous from July on.

V. bonariensis is a rather strange, larger version of *V. rigida.* Its rough, four-sided stems with widely spaced leaf pairs can reach 5 feet

Verbena × *hybrida* 'Trinidad

Veronica spicata 'Lavender Charm'

high. Although it is a short-lived perennial in Zone 8, the plant reseeds itself. In cooler areas it should be grown as a tender annual, as should the common garden verbena, *V.* × *hybrida,* a colorful group of spreading plants derived mainly from *V. peruviana.* Their flat flower heads are available in every color of the rainbow. All of these verbenas need full sun in well-drained soil.

Veronica species

Speedwell

About two hundred and fifty species of *Veronica* are distributed throughout the Northern Hemisphere. Almost all are attractive—even some wicked weeds. (Shrubby species from Australasia, suitable only for the mild West Coast, are now included under *Hebe.*)

All of the speedwells listed here are easy-to-grow, summer-flowering plants. Hardy to Zone 3, they need full sun and good garden soil.

V. incana, native to the Soviet Union, forms a mass of narrow gray leaves from which arise narrow, 18-inch-high spikes of small, soft blue flowers. *V. spicata,* from northern Europe and Asia, makes a tussock of shining leaves and foot-high spikes of blue flowers. A hybrid group derived from these

species includes the elegant pink 'Minuet' and the violet-blue 'Sarabande'. Both deserve locations in the front of the border.

V. virginica is much larger, reaching 6 feet or so. Sometimes listed as *Veronicastrum virginicum,* it is a native of the eastern United States. A statuesque plant, its strong stems are set with whorls of horizontal leaves and narrow spikes of blue or white flowers in midsummer. Although its bloom period is short, it remains attractive throughout the growing season.

Viola pedata

Viola × *wittrockiana*

Viola species

Violet, pansy, johnny-jump-up

There are over five hundred species of *Viola,* all of them small plants (including small shrubs) from temperate regions of the world. Some have been cultivated and cherished since early times. Violet has given its name to a color and to a scent (the scent refers mainly to that of the sweet violet, *V. odorata).*

Garden species can be divided into small, perennial violets and large-flowered pansies, usually treated as annuals.

V. pedata is the native birdfoot violet that grows from little fleshy vertical rhizomes (underground stems). It puts on a splendid show of early flowers, mostly in shades of blue. An excellent ground cover in half sun or shade, it grows well in most garden soils.

V. × *wittrockiana,* the hybrid pansy, is usually around 9 inches high. Its circular, flat-faced flowers, up to 3 inches across, come in many soft colors. Pansies are popular winter bedding plants in warm areas, and they are used for a late-spring show in cooler climates. They cannot take hot, humid summers.

V. tricolor is the European wild pansy, also known as johnny-jump-up. These charming little plants seed themselves among shrubs or in the border, never becoming a serious pest.

Yucca filamentosa

Yucca species

Yucca, Adam's-needle, Spanish-bayonet

As natives of warmer-winter climates, the forty-odd species of *Yucca* can be grown in the open only in southern gardens, where some reach almost tree size. Their stiff, evergreen leaves and cruel spines seem particularly at home in arid, desert-edge locations. There the towering spikes of cream, bell-shaped flowers never cease to surprise.

In the North, a couple of species are hardy to Zone 5 and probably beyond. Native from South Carolina into Florida, they often look strangely incongruous in open woodland, where their presence indicates that, although they do best in full sun, in cultivation they can take a certain amount of shade.

Y. filamentosa makes clumps of 2-foot-long, spined leaves with distinctive curly threads along their

Zantedeschia aethiopica

Zantedeschia aethiopica

edges. Flower spikes can be 4 feet high in summer. Yellow-variegated forms, sometimes available, are very striking. *Y. smalliana,* a closely related species, has very narrow, needle-tipped leaves.

In northern climates yucca is especially valued for its vertical shape and permanent silhouette, but it needs careful placement or it can look bizarre. Well-drained soil is essential.

In the right place, the arrangement of a group of these wonderful accent plants with two or three great boulders and a stone mulch can look extremely attractive.

Zantedeschia species

Calla, calla-lily, arum-lily

The six species of *Zantedeschia* are all natives to South Africa. *Z. aethiopica,* the common florist's calla, has 3-foot-high stems, each bearing a pure white spathe, or bract, surrounding a yellow spadix, or floral spike. Cultivated worldwide in frost-free or nearly frost-free climates, it has become naturalized in many places, growing in ditches and at water edges.

Hardy to Zone 8, calla-lily needs moist soil in full sun. Its tubers can be planted in ponds up to 18 inches deep. As long as it never freezes solid, the water protects the plant during its winter rest in cool climates. In warm-winter areas growth is almost continuous, as long as moisture is available.

In early spring a flush of shining, arrow-shaped leaves appears and by Easter the first flowers begin to bloom. With heavy feeding the display lasts throughout summer.

Where calla-lily is unlikely to survive the year around, tubers can be potted and stored indoors in a cool spot for the winter. The dwarf forms of *Z. aethiopica,* as well as the yellow *Z. elliottiana* and the little pink *Z. rehmanii,* are best for this purpose.

Zauschneria californica

Zauschneria californica

Zauschneria californica

California-fuchsia

One of just four species, this is among the most beautiful plants native to California (a considerable claim in so rich a flora). Surprisingly, both this and the true fuchsia (*Fuchsia* species) are related to evening-primrose (*Oenothera* species).

California-fuchsia forms a loose shrub of gray foliage, similar to that of lavender bush (*Lavandula angustifolia*). In late summer it is covered with sprays of tubular scarlet flowers closely resembling those of *Fuchsia fulgens*.

The plant is widely distributed in the Southwest. Because of their habitats, the subspecies vary greatly in hardiness. The one to seek for northern gardens is *Zauschneria californica latifolia*. Native to high altitudes, it is hardy to Zone 6. With certain snow cover it may survive even colder climates.

California-fuchsia needs full sun and perfect drainage. For this reason it is often grown in rock gardens or behind retaining walls. The plant associates well with gray-leaved Mediterraneans, providing a bonus of late flower color from August until frost. By this time lavender and lavender-cotton (*Santolina chamaecyparissus*) will have been clipped back and will provide a good, tight frame. Catmint (*Nepeta × faassenii*), also clipped after its first flowering, will be putting on a second show of lavender-blue blossoms. Complete the grouping—and the floral progression—with an autumn-flowering crocus such as *Crocus kotschyanus* (not *Colchicum* species, whose spring leaves are too lush). Always try to plan this sort of late association to extend the gardening season as long as the climate permits.

Zinnia elegans 'Pink Ruffles'

Zinnia elegans 'Pulchino'

Zinnia elegans

Common zinnia, youth-and-old-age

One of about eighteen species of mainly Mexican daisies related to sunflowers, *Zinnia elegans* is among the most popular summer annuals. The wild plant is around 3 feet tall with coarse, bristly leaves. The flowers have a mounded central disk and wide red petals, which are actually ray florets.

Breeding selection has brought about a vast extension to the flower form, color, and size. Some of the breeding has been done with the help of other *Zinnia* species and now there are types ranging in height from 1 to 3 feet and offering single or double flowers in every color except true-blue. Petals are flat or quilled, and often the flowers resemble those of chrysanthemum (*Chrysanthemum* species) in size and shape.

Zinnia, which is frost-sensitive, can be sown indoors and planted outside after all danger of freezing has passed. Although it does well in full sun and well-drained soil, it quickly succumbs to mildew in very hot, humid climates. When well grown, the big zinnias help bulk up a thin herbaceous border and contribute a wide range of colors. They make fine cut flowers. Dwarfs such as the small-flowered 'Persian Carpet' are a good choice for low bedding schemes.

U.S. Measure and Metric Measure Conversion Chart

	Symbol	Formulas for Exact Measures When you know:	Multiply by:	To find:	Rounded Measures for Quick Reference		
Mass (Weight)	oz	ounces	28.35	grams	1 oz		= 30 g
	lb	pounds	0.45	kilograms	4 oz		= 115 g
	g	grams	0.035	ounces	8 oz		= 225 g
	kg	kilograms	2.2	pounds	16 oz	= 1 lb	= 450 g
					32 oz	= 2 lb	= 900 g
					36 oz	= 2¼ lb	= 1000g (1 kg)
Volume	pt	pints	0.47	liters	1 c	= 8 oz	= 250 ml
	qt	quarts	0.95	liters	2 c (1 pt)	= 16 oz	= 500 ml
	gal	gallons	3.785	liters	4 c (1 qt)	= 32 oz	= 1 liter
	ml	milliliters	0.034	fluid ounces	4 qt (1 gal)	= 128 oz	= 3¾ liter
Length	in.	inches	2.54	centimeters	⅜ in.		= 1 cm
	ft	feet	30.48	centimeters	1 in.		= 2.5 cm
	yd	yards	0.9144	meters	2 in.		= 5 cm
	mi	miles	1.609	kilometers	2½ in.		= 6.5 cm
	km	kilometers	0.621	miles	12 in. (1 ft)		= 30 cm
	m	meters	1.094	yards	1 yd		= 90 cm
	cm	centimeters	0.39	inches	100 ft		= 30 m
					1 mi		= 1.6 km
Temperature	°F	Fahrenheit	⅝ (after subtracting 32)	Celsius	32°F		= 0°C
	°C	Celsius	⅝ (then add 32)	Fahrenheit	212°F		= 100°C
Area	in.²	square inches	6.452	square centimeters	1 in.²		= 6.5 cm²
	ft²	square feet	929.0	square centimeters	1 ft²		= 930 cm²
	yd²	square yards	8361.0	square centimeters	1 yd²		= 8360 cm²
	a.	acres	0.4047	hectares	1 a.		= 4050 m²

Proof-of-Purchase
9721-221-5